The first 'E' Class 4-4-0 to be rebuilt to Class E1, No A179, here seen in Southern Railway colours. (Rail Archive Stephenson.)

GREAT
LOCOMOTIVES
OF THE SOUTHERN RAILWAY

O.S. Nock

PSL

Patrick Stephens
Wellingborough, Northamptonshire

First published in 1987

British Library Cataloguing in Publication Data

Nock, O.S.
    Great Locomotives of the Souther Railway.
    1. Southern Railway Company—History
    2. Locomotives—England—History—20th century
    I. Title
    625.2'61'09422   TJ603.4.G72567

ISBN 0-85059-735-8

*Patrick Stephens Limited is part of the
Thorsons Publishing Group*

Printed and bound in Great Britain.

Note
At the time the Southern Railway ceased to exist in
January 1948, and became the Southern Region of
British Railways, the art of railway photography in
colour had barely started. The colour pictures in this
book were all taken after this change and show Southern
locomotives either in their working days in post-
nationalization colours or restored to their former glory
on some of the country's many preserved railways.

Contents

Preface

In setting out to write a book about the *Great Locomotives of the Southern Railway* it needed no more than a moment's hesitation to reflect upon the bewildering choice that was presented by the classes and types that were on the very active list at the end of the Second World War. At that relatively late date in the history of the British steam locomotive the Southern still had many of the products of James Stirling, William Kirtley, Adams and Stroudley in active service, to say nothing of their successors on the South Eastern and Chatham Railway (SE&CR), on the Brighton, and on the London and South Western Railway (L & SWR) before they were incorporated in the Southern Railway itself, of 1923. So it seemed reasonable, nay essential, to take the story back to late Victorian times when the history of the locomotive itself was emerging from its formative stages, and the great men of the 1870s were beginning to make a lasting impression on the motive power scene. How effectively they did so is shown by the numerous examples of their work still in active service in 1945. At that time, of the locomotives built prior to the grouping of 1923 there were 470 ex-L&SWR, 375 ex-Brighton and 440 ex-SE&CR examples very much on the active list.

Their longevity speaks for itself. Of the earlier vintages the Adams 'Jubilees', the Stroudley 'D1' tanks, and the Billinton 'Scotchmen' immediately qualify for inclusion among the 'greats'; while some of their contemporaries, although no longer in service in 1945, should surely rank among the 'super-greats' of Southern Railway history. These include the 'Gladstones' and the Adams 4-4-0s, of which latter a distinguished technical account of their road performance graces very many pages in the *Journal of the Institution of Civil Engineers* in 1895-96. Nevertheless in this story of locomotive engineering it has inevitably been a case of rolling back the pages of history to include some of the 'not-so-greats' in order to display in bolder relief the brightest stars in their true magnitude.

On a railway such as the Southern and its pre-grouping constituents the goods engines always tended to play a minor role, at any rate so far as enthusiast interest was concerned. In fact the largest class in the Southern Railway stud, before the Bulleid 'West Countrys', were the Wainwright 'C' Class 0-6-0s of the SE&CR, with a grand total of 108. It is very pleasing that one of them has now been preserved in full working order and restored to its original gorgeous livery. The existence of so many contemporary locomotives to the 'C' Class, equally of Brighton and South Western origin, gives an interest far beyond that of the latest and largest express and mixed-traffic types.

Taking the story back to late-Victorian times gives an opportunity to touch on the personalities of the engineers themselves, in addition to the work they did. While lionizing William Adams, Stroudley, Dugald Drummond, and others scarcely less eminent who held the post of 'Locomotive Superintendent', one must also pay tribute to the chief draughtsmen, works personnel and running staff who provided the very essential back-up services. One thinks particularly in this connection of W.F. Pettigrew, Robert Surtees, B.K. Field and James Clayton.

More personally I remember the late Harold Holcroft, who was junior partner to Clayton for almost the entire span of years when R.E.L. Maunsell was Chief Mechanical Engineer, first to the South Eastern and Chatham and then to the Southern Railway. I came to value his great friendship, and his undiminished enthusiasm, when Mr Bell of *The Locomotive Magazine* asked me to write the serial article 'Locomotives of R.E.L. Maunsell', in 1949. Holcroft, who had only recently retired from his last post on the Southern Railway, of Personal Assistant to the CME for locomotives, made available to me a lifetime's memoranda on the working of all shapes and sizes of SE&CR and Southern locomotives. This serial article, which was subsequently expanded and republished as a book, forms the skeleton on which I have put a good deal of additional flesh for the Maunsell part of the present book. My indebtedness to Mr Holcroft is thereby increased.

My experience of the practical working of Southern locomotives has been immensely furthered by the very many privileges I have been granted over the years for riding on the footplate of many types of engines, and I recall the friendly relations established with successive Locomotive Superintendents, K. Cobb and T.E. Chrimes, and their drivers and firemen who always made me so welcome on their footplates. Another Southern man who I first met when he was assistant to Mr Cobb was that lifelong enthusiast for locomotives in all gauges, A.B. Macleod. In British Railways days he rose to a very high executive position, but he never lost his early love of locomotives. In the last years of the Southern Railway I was privileged to meet Mr Bulleid, to thank him for the generous foreword he contributed to my very first book, *The Locomotives of Sir Nigel Gresley* with which he had a unrivalled experience. Afterwards he was characteristically generous in the help he gave me towards my literary work, some of which has been incorporated in the appropriate parts of the present book.

The constituents of the Southern Railway, no less than the 'grouped' company of 1923, have always been popular among locomotive enthusiasts. Among Brighton followers particularly, the Stephenson Locomotive Society was born and out of it the distinguished technical offspring, in 1911, the Institution of Locomotive Engineers. Its popularity with technical and not-so-technical enthusiasts alike is reflected in the remarkable number of Southern locomotives of all vintages now preserved, both in the collection, working and otherwise, of the National Railway Museum and working steam railways like the Bluebell and Mid-Hants Railways. Alongside the ever-popular 'Terriers' of the Brighton however, one cannot but regret that there is not more than a single example of post-Stroudley engine, the Billinton 'radial' 0-6-2 *Birch Grove*, though this provides a fine example of the Earle-Marsh livery.

O.S. Nock
Bath, November 1985

Introduction

How far back could the individual locomotive histories, as connected engineering themes, be carried? The progenitors of the Southern Railway, as constituted in January 1923, certainly contained some diverse philosophies in design practice, even from the same works; yet these variations were all so essentially sound that they carried the amalgamated company forward through 25 years of most difficult history. The design practice of the London and South Western Railway, of the Brighton and of the South Eastern and Chatham all went back far in history, but not right back to the inception of those companies, because two of them in particular made what can only be called false starts. Personalities played a large part in early locomotive history, nowhere more so than south of the Thames; this was not only the case in the early pre-formative days, but equally in the latter part of the nineteenth century. The difference was that while the pioneers flew their own individual kites, often with scant regard for their works personnel and the footplate men, their successors evolved sound engineering practice and traditions of workmanship that were to last until the Second World War disrupted so many old ways of life. So while some tales of the earliest days, and of some of the characters involved, can form a colourful prelude to the main story, I have placed the origins of the Southern Railway locomotive saga at the times of Stroudley on the Brighton, James Stirling on the South Eastern, Kirtley on the Chatham and Adams on the South Western.

Two of those locomotive pioneers came to be honoured in Southern Railway days, when the Billinton 4-6-4 tanks of the Brighton, made redundant as tank engines by electrification, were converted to 4-6-0s and then named. Two of these handsome engines carried their former Brighton names, *Stephenson* and *Remembrance*, and the other five received names of eminent engineers of earlier days. Of these I suppose *Trevithick* was a 'natural' while *Hackworth*, apart from being a former Brighton engine name, recalled the engineer who built, albeit under much provocation, many engines for the Brighton Railway. Then, in Southern Railway days, came converted 4-6-0s named *Cudworth* and *Beattie*. The twentieth century septet was completed by *Stroudley*; and while a modern railway enthusiast would be readily able to point to many achievements in the career of the last-mentioned engineer, few would be able to score many points over Cudworth and Beattie. Where personalities were concerned I can well imagine why no one thought of naming an engine after Stroudley's predecessor on the Brighton

Railway, John Chester Craven!

Both Cudworth and Beattie, in their several ways, applied themselves with the utmost vigour to the task of satisfactorily burning coal in locomotive fireboxes. Until about 1850 coke was generally used, to avoid emission of smoke, but it was relatively expensive and unsuitable for the larger locomotives then coming into use in Great Britain.

Cudworth patented a form of double firebox, with separate grates parallel to each other and fed from separate firedoors. The fireboxes were divided by a longitudinal partition with a water space between. At the front end, near the tube plate, there was a deep opening in the longitudinal partition through which the gases of combustion could mix together before passing into the boiler tubes. The method of working was that coal was fired into one grate, on which the previous charge was by that time burning brightly, while on the other the coal was in process of burning through. Cudworth's double fireboxes were extensively used, not only on the South Eastern Railway, but also on the Brighton; but although the aggregate firebox volume and grate area was relatively large the engines themselves, whether of the 2-4-0 or the 2-2-2 type were small, having no larger cylinders than 16-in diameter by 22-in stroke. While Cudworth was to some extent experimenting with fireboxes he appeared to have been satisfied enough to build a standard class of 2-4-0s of which there were eventually no fewer than 126 examples. They represented nearly half the total locomotive stock of the South Eastern Railway at the time of Mr Cudworth's retirement. In the south of England in mid-Victorian times anything in the way of standardization on railways, particularly in locomotive design, was something of a phenomenon; so that Cudworth's practice stood very much on its own. The sad thing about it was it was so soon to disappear.

The South Eastern engines with double fireboxes, and their derivatives on the Brighton, and also on the Chatham, gave very good results so far as coal consumption went, at any rate when under the close observation of technical experts like Zerah Colboun and D.K. Clarke, both of whom wrote learned papers about the theory and practice of coal burning in locomotives. Apparently Cudworth's engines gave far better results than some experimental boilers that McConnell was working on at the same time at the Wolverton Works of the Southern Division of the London and North Western Railway. But of course coal consumption on individual runs did not point to the ultimate answer. Those double fireboxes were very expensive to maintain. The days of all-welded

Right *Stroudley 'Terrier' Class 0-6-0 tank engine No 82 Boxhill. (National Railway Museum.)*

Right *Charing Cross station when first opened, showing two Cudworth 2-4-0s. (Author's collection.)*

Below *South Eastern Railway Cudworth 'Mail' engine No 200 built by Vulcan Foundry in 1862. (British Railways.)*

fireboxes were still not even a dream of the future, and the rivetted joints and complicated seams inherent in ordinary firebox construction were rendered many times more so in Cudworth's design. Even so, while Cudworth's successor was making an exceedingly clean sweep of much that had gone before, on the South Eastern 2-4-0s some of the old fireboxes remained till about 1891.

Ingenious as were some of the features incorporated in these fireboxes, and encouraging as were the economics realized, the maintenance charges had to be borne in mind. While one can understand that Cudworth was anxious to continue propagating his own ideas on methods of coal burning, by the early 1860s a far simpler and more effective method had been developed on the Midland Railway—that of the brick arch built transversely across the firebox. Although other railways were quick to adopt this device—and ultimately it became universal on coal-fired locomotives—Cudworth adhered to his own complicated design of firebox until the time of his resignation in 1875. The circumstances of his going were not exactly happy. In 1866 the dour Sir Edward Watkin had become Chairman of the South Eastern Railway, and without any reference to the Locomotive Superintendent a class of twenty new 2-4-0 express locomotives was ordered, ten from Sharp, Stewart & Co and the others from the Avonside Engine Co of Bristol. It was reputed at the time that John Ramsbottom had been consulted over the design and certainly the new SER locomotives had a family likeness to his own 'Newton' Class built at Crewe for the London and North Western Railway

ten years earlier. Anyway, Cudworth was very upset at the high-handed way these new engines had been introduced and he resigned.

Similarity to Ramsbottom's engines, however, did not extend beyond 'family likeness', because the new 2-4-0s proved unreliable and soon had to be taken off the best trains. The Cudworth engines had to be re-instated, and in the meantime there was an interregnum in the locomotive department at Ashford, prior to the appointment of Mr James Stirling, from the Glasgow and South Western Railway (G&SWR). Apparently Sir Edward Watkin had learnt his lesson over the results of interfering in the work of the locomotive department and James Stirling had a clear field except, as will be told later, in respect of maximum speeds for main-line express trains. The South Eastern Railway, like its more westerly neighbour the Brighton, never showed any disposition to hurry in Victorian times, which made all the more contrasting the attitude of its arch-enemy, the London, Chatham and Dover Railway (LC&DR), which always showed a desire to 'run', at any rate so far as its principal passenger train services were concerned.

William Martley, who was appointed Locomotive Superintendent of the Chatham from the time the line was completed in 1860, was trained on the Great Western under Daniel Gooch and he had much of the fire and dash of the early broad-gauge days in his make-up. He seems to have had a strong sense of humour too, an attribute which was no bad thing to possess, to keep one going in the often chaotic state prevailing on the LC&DR at that time. On his arrival at Longhedge it would seem his first job was to

The Admiralty Pier, Dover, showing boat train preparing to leave for London hauled by an 'F' Class 4-4-0. (Courtesy Lambert Weston, Dover.)

Stroudley 'Terrier' as preserved on the Kent and East Sussex Railway at Tenterden in 1976. Sutton was then 101 years old! (Brian Morrison.)

rebuild and make something worthwhile out of the motley collection of engines that had been gathered together, while the railway itself was progressing from its origins in the East Kent project towards its London extension. Unlike his neighbour on the South Eastern Railway, Martley had no scope, or cash, to indulge in fanciful engine designs. From the available ironmongery he evolved an excellent design of 2-4-0 passenger engine, one variety of which had 5-ft 6-in coupled wheels and was used on slow and intermediate passenger work. The larger-wheeled class was reserved for the express trains, including the Dover Mails. About these latter 'prestige' jobs there is a good story to be told.

The East Kent Railway originated from a big public meeting held in Rochester in 1850, with the aim of building a line from Strood to Canterbury; but funds were very slow in coming forward and eight years from its inception the first opening took place—18½ miles of single track railway from Rochester to Faversham. Yet from this inauspicious beginning, always short of ready cash and liable to go bankrupt at any minute, the line was extended westwards into the West End of London and eastwards through Canterbury to Dover. Within two years of completing the line, and assuming the title of the London, Chatham and Dover Railway, it had

snatched the prized Post Office contract for carrying the Continental mails between London and Dover from the South Eastern Railway. Fortunately by that time Martley had got some 6-ft 6-in express locomotives rebuilt as 4-4-0s and a class of new engines of the 2-4-0 type was in course of delivery from Sharp, Stewart & Co in 1862-63. The mail contracts of those days were not things to be lightly undertaken, because the Post Office imposed a fine upon the railway for any instance of late running.

Martley seems to have entered into the spirit of the new enterprise with a light heart to judge from the names he bestowed upon his engines. In the first place he adopted Swindon practice in the days of the broad gauge by giving engines names, but not numbers. And what names! The five 4-4-0s that were rebuilt from the old Cramptons were named *Echo, Coquette, Flora, Flirt* and *Sylph*; and as if the fourth of this group were not enough one of the new 2-4-0s was named *Frolic*! Nevertheless, even Martley felt as though this engine should be occasionally restrained, so two other members of the same class were named *Alert* and *Vigilant* to keep her in order. Most of the remainder of the Sharp, Stewart & Co 2-4-0s of 1862-63 were named after spring flowers, but when a further series were supplied by Messrs Peto, Brassey & Betts of Birkenhead in 1865, there was more of a touch of 'Old

Crewe' about the names.

The full list of the 2-4-0s built by outside contractors at that time was:

Dawn	*Violet*	
Alert	*Crocus*	
Herald	*Snowdrop*	from Sharp,
Pioneer	*Verbena*	Stewart & Co
Frolic	*Bluebell*	
Vigilant	*Hyacinth*	
Reindeer	*Templar*	
Elk	*Talisman*	from Peto,
Champion	*Zephyr*	Brassey & Betts

It seemed as if Martley, in his early years at Longhedge, got together with his fellow superintendent at Ashford because all the foregoing 2-4-0s were fitted with Cudworth's patent fireboxes. In view of the 'cat and dog' attitude of the management of the two companies one is curious to know how the 'entente' between the two locomotive engineers was contrived and what arrangements, if any, were concluded over payment of royalties. One may be fairly sure that Sir Edward Watkin would have been out to extract his 'pound of flesh' from the Chatham! At any rate the Cudworth fireboxes did not last long on the LC & DR, and when the company began to build their own engines at Longhedge Works this feature was not included.

Before this time however the Chatham company had sunk into the deepest financial difficulties, and although Martley was busy developing his workshop facilities at Longhedge no funds were available at first for further new power, either contractor-built or otherwise. When, at last, authorization was granted for three additional express passenger engines of the 2-4-0 type to be built at Longhedge such indeed was the 'authorization' that work was frequently stopped for lack of money! Martley once remarked that it was an enigma to him as how they ever got the first engine finished, and when eventually this took the road he named it the *Enigma*. It was completed in March 1869 and was followed by the other two engines of the class, named *Mermaid* and *Lothair*. Although these three engines had been a long time under construction there was nothing wrong with the end product, and the three pioneer examples of Longhedge's work gave excellent service on the road. However 'dicey' were the finances of the Company itself, the 'Dover Mails' ran to time and that often involved fast running downhill to make up lost time.

All Martley's express passenger engines had double frames and outside coupling rods, and the same style was used on the very fine enlarged engines of the type that were built by Sharp, Stewart & Co, in 1873. The four engines of this class were designed particularly for the mail traffic and were named

Europe, Asia, Africa and *America*. Their leading dimensions of 17-in and 24-in cylinders, 6-ft 6-in coupled wheels and a boiler pressure of 140 psi naturally invites close comparison with certain famous contemporary designs of the same wheel arrangement, notably the 'Precedent' Class of the London and North Western Railway (L&NWR) and the Fletcher '901' Class of the North Eastern Railway (NER). Martley's engines were generally considered among the finest running in the country at that time. They were of the simplest possible form of construction, steamed freely, and had an excellent turn of speed. Above all, they were very reliable mechanically. They have been compared with the L&NWR 'Precedents' in maximum speed running; but at the time when Martley's engines were running the 'Dover Mails' the 'Precedents' were running little faster. In the 1870s rails were still made of wrought iron, so likewise were tyres of coupled wheels. Maximum speeds were not usually above 70 mph until steel rails and steel wheel tyres came into general use. Speeds run on the Chatham in Martley's day were sometimes a good deal faster than was comfortable for the rickety old coaches, not to mention the track!

While the working of the 'Dover Mails' constituted the prestige passenger train service of the LC&DR the London suburban workings were a highly competitive activity in which it was urgently needed to build up traffic to offset the high capital cost of building the new lines. Martley took up the design that had been recently introduced by the northern line that stood to gain much from the penetration of the City by the Chatham, the Great Northern Railway (GNR). Archibald Sturrock designed a class of well-tank engines of the 0-4-2 type which were of unusual proportions in that the trailing wheels were spaced far back. The Chatham variant differed in no more than superficial details, such as the placing of the dome on the forward ring of the boiler, and the elimination of the shelter over the footplate. Martley's London tanks were built by the same contractor, at the same time, as the second batch for the Great Northern. The contractor was Neilson & Co of Glasgow and the engines were built in 1866. Like all Chatham engines of the day they were named, but not numbered, and in keeping with their country of origin they carried names of Scottish islands and rivers. The titles were commendably brief, to be placed on plates just in rear of the smokeboxes. On the LC&DR they at once became nicknamed the 'Scotchmen', and no more popular local tank engines ever ran in the South of England in the nineteenth century. Their names were:

Jura	*Iona*	*Islay*	*Ulva*	*Clyde*	*Annan*	*Nith*
Arran	*Bute*	*Staffa*	*Spey*	*Kelvin*	*Tay*	*Esk*

While none of Martley's designs were perpetuated by his successor, and so came to contribute little except history to the ultimate aggregate of Southern Railway locomotive practice, his engines were immensely popular with the running staff, to such an extent as they were sometimes preferred to those that immediately succeeded them, in the years that followed.

There could not have been a greater contrast between the locomotive departments of the London, Chatham and Dover and the Brighton Railways in the mid-sixties of last century, either in the location and products of the principal works, or in the personalities of the chief engineers. For beside William Martley was the dour, implacable John Chester Craven. The excavations in the chalk, through which the Brighton Railway had made its way to its terminus on a hill at the back of the town, had left little space for any locomotive activities, and when Craven was appointed Locomotive Superintendent in 1847 he had, virtually, to excavate the site. He was the planner, architect, and builder of Brighton Works. Those were the days when great responsibilities were thrust upon young men, Craven was then no more than 34 years of age when he got the job. From the very outset he appeared to exercise a remarkable degree of autonomy, and as he got more firmly into the saddle he became very much a law unto himself. He was a prolific designer of locomotives, for whom the word standardization just did not exist. He established a high standard of workmanship at Brighton and his engines worked well, within the limits that the traffic demanded of them; but the service provided, even for those days, was not exactly brilliant.

While Craven seems to have progressed much as he pleased at Brighton, ruling his own department with a rod of iron, and always exhibiting an inflexibility of outlook that was the dismay and often the terror of fellow officers, to outward appearances, and particularly from the shareholders' point of view, the Brighton Railway in the late fifties and early sixties of last century seemed a well-established and profitable concern. From 1855-65 the dividend on the ordinary shares was never less than five per cent, and usually held at a steady six per cent. And then things suddenly seemed to go wrong. In 1867 no dividend at all was paid, following a major shake up in the top management. How this came to affect Brighton Works and the Locomotive Department generally was not disclosed, but the fact that Craven retired in 1868, at the very early age of 56 may, or may not, have been significant. Furthermore, his going seems to have left an unexpected hiatus at Brighton.

The crisis in the Company's financial affairs was marked by a sudden diminuation in the output of new locomotives from the Works, though not in the diversity of new engine designs produced by Craven himself. In 1868, for example, only two new 2-2-2 mainline express passenger locomotives were built which, although conforming to the general run of Brighton products, exhibited just those variations in detail as had become characteristic of Craven's work. Engines were turned out in two's, or even as singles. In the first pair constructed the frames were double throughout, but in the next pair they were in the 'Jenny Lind' style, with inside frames only to the driving wheels. Again there were variations in the safety valves, some mounted on the dome, and in others only on the firebox. For main-line engines the piston stroke favoured was 22-in, but the diameters varied between 16-in and 17-in—not in any ordered

Beattie 2-4-0 suburban tank engine No 314, as rebuilt by Adams. (British Railways.)

progression, but up and down, as Craven thought fit for a particular assignment. The smaller engines which were turned out individually for specific local duties were usually fitted with 15-in by 20-in cylinders; but that was about all that was alike in their make-up.

For all the wild diversity of detail Craven's engines were soundly constructed and superbly maintained. Of course they were fantastically under-utilized, even by nineteenth century standards. Although this first period in Brighton Railway history could scarcely be called a formative one, in that it did not provide any pointers towards future practice, the works at Brighton was established as a going concern and manufacturer of first class engineering. The full story of the Craven era is fascinating in its variety. It is not surprising that the enthusiasts of the turn of the century, whose interests had inspired the founding of *The Locomotive Magazine*, and subsequently The Stephenson Locomotive Society, paid particular attention to the Brighton Railway. One of the most erudite of those early enthusiasts, Mr Frank Burtt, wrote a highly detailed account of the early history of the locomotives of the London Brighton and South Coast Railway (LB&SCR). Beginning in the very first volume of *The Locomotive Magazine*, in monthly instalments, he had reached the thirtieth of these before he came to Craven's retirement. Turning through those instalments, and delighting in the numerous finely executed line drawings, whereby every design is illustrated, one may not be surprised that when Stroudley arrived from Inverness his first thoughts were towards standardization.

While Craven was ruling the locomotive department of the Brighton Railway with a rod of iron another formidable character held sway over the London and South Western Railway, in the person of Joseph Beattie. The individuality of some of these locomotive men of the mid-Victorian era takes some believing. While Craven seems to have thought up some variation for every small batch of engines he built, none of which seemed to have had a particular significance, yet all resulting in an essentially sound locomotive, Beattie, like Cudworth, fastened on to the problem of burning coal instead of coke, and evolved some highly original ways of doing it. What rivetted the attention of the contemporary connoisseurs of locomotive practice to the London and South Western, however, was the strikingly original shape of the engines, no less than their beautiful livery and superb finish. While Beattie added numerous gadgets on successive batches of his engines the predominating feature of them all was a very small boiler, a raised firebox surmounted by a tall dome, and a lofty chimney just about equal in height to the diameter of the boiler! However this

L&SWR Beattie 6 ft 6 in 2-4-0 Styx, *built in 1865. (British Railways.)*

characteristic Beattie outline did not come until a later stage in his career; though from the outset he seems to have had a fancy for ornamental dome covers. The class of six 2-2-2 express engines with 6-ft 6-in driving wheels that he built in 1855-56, sometimes called the 'Canute' Class had a tremendous erection, standing cheek by jowl with the chimney, consisting of a broad base, a Beyer-type bell-mouthed body, and a glorified Ross 'pop' valve on the top.

While Beattie's engines, both of the earlier type, and of the gadget-festooned later ones attracted widespread attention by their 'etcetaries', one must look first at their mechanical attributes, which were considerable. It is important to recall that following his appointment as Locomotive Superintendent in 1850 his earliest engines had inside cylinders, and that it was not until 1855 that he changed over to the style by which he is best remembered. In so doing he departed from the conventional completely, so far as the chassis was concerned. Until then he had used outside frames and the usual mounting of the leading wheels, and the livery was then 'Indian Red', frames and superstructure alike. The story goes, however, that Beattie's friendship with Charles Beyer led to some improvement in the outward appearance of London and South Western locomotives. One writer

complained that Beattie's engines had hitherto borne a raffish look, but for my own part, in studying many photographs of them before and since, I could not discern any difference in the general character. They all seemed to have a wild primeaval grandeur about them! A notable feature of the running gear was the leading floating axle-box. It was supported only by the underslung spring, having no horn-guides, and was intended to steady what was a rather nose-heavy type of locomotive when running at speed. The main bearings, of course, were on the inside frames. From all accounts the Beattie engines thus fitted, whether 2-2-2, 2-4-0, or of the 2-4-0 tank type ran very steadily.

The outstanding feature of all Beattie's later locomotives, both technically and in their extraordinary appearance, was the ceaseless flow of inventions calculated to facilitate burning coal instead of coke. Of course a lineside observer could not imagine the intricacies of the patent double firebox, and combustion chamber in the boiler barrel; but of externally mounted features there were enough and more to spare! Beattie was one of the first British engineers to experiment with feed-water heating, and some of his devices took 'fearful and wonderful' shapes. He built one form which was a jet condenser, fed from cold water from the tender, and a part of the exhaust steam. This took the form of a triple tube erection immediately in front of the chimney, and extending for two-thirds of the height of the chimney itself. A

Beattie 6 ft 6 in 2-4-0 Herod *at Exeter. (Loco Publishing Co.)*

later form of this condenser had only one tube. No such sophisticated apparatus as an injector for the boiler feed was used by Beattie—he used a simple donkey pump, adding to the array of ironmongery draped about the engines.

When he began his developments in feed-water heating Beattie was content with a straight-back boiler, at any rate that between the chimney and the firebox casing; but as matters progressed various additional boiler mountings appeared. The safety valves, from their conventional position on the top of the dome with spring balance levers fore and aft, were moved to the middle of the boiler barrel and housed in a picturesque affair which looked like an early version of the Great Western inverted milk-can which came to surround so many thousand safety-valve bonnets. The difference was that Beattie's version had two spring-balance arms extending outward, and the casing itself was mounted on a broad-based pedestal on the boiler barrel. By that time in the chain of development the rather stark red livery had been changed to a handsome maroon, plentifully lined out in red, black and white. At first the domes and safety-valve mountings were also maroon; then these were decked in polished brass and with copper caps to the chimneys the effect was striking in the extreme. I must be forgiven if I do not consider the ensemble beautiful in the locomotive sense, it seems to me that grotesque would be the more appropriate term. There was a magnificent colour plate of the 2-4-0

engine *Ariel* in *The Locomotive Magazine* of December 1912, from one of the beautiful oil paintings by F. Moore. Unfortunately this was one of the artist's works which was not reproduced in the famous series of postcards issued by the Locomotive Publishing Company, and consequently it is not well known.

Beattie's engines, passenger and mixed traffic alike were all named, and a rare assortment they were, in some way characteristic of the designer himself. It was said of the London and North Western Railway that its locomotive list would have been hard to beat for catholicity in the engine names, but the South Western, on a much smaller scale, could have beaten Crewe 'to a frazzle' in Beattie's day. The North Western had several generations of engines named *Vandal*, but Beattie went several stages further in the horror series with *Goth* and *Hun*! Classical names abounded, while *Fireball* and *Firebrand*, not to mention *Tartar*, were close to the designer's personality. The quaintest title, however, was that of *Canute*. One can think of several more than doubtful attributes associated with this ill-starred monarch, quite apart from his having got his feet wet on one memorable occasion. On reflection, perhaps it is just as well that the South Western did not install water troughs on any of its main lines!

Beattie '302' Class 0-6-0 No 162-A, as reboiled by Adams. (Rail Archive Stephenson.)

1. James Stirling on the South Eastern

In the spring of 1878 James Stirling was appointed Locomotive Superintendent; but he was not able to relinquish his former duties on the Glasgow and South Western Railway until the end of June that year. His work on both railways was so similar and in such a line of continuity in practice as to bespeake the same administration, though as Stirling himself found out, to his disappointment, the running conditions on the two railways were markedly different. So far as locomotive design practice was concerned it can be seen that Stirling's precepts were firmly established before he left Kilmarnock, and that the admirable work he did at Ashford was a logical continuation. He succeeded his elder brother, Patrick, on the Glasgow and South Western and although his work immediately showed strong family likenesses in many details of design any tendency towards retention of the single-wheeler for the principal main-line passenger work was at once discarded at Kilmarnock. Nevertheless James Stirling's first new engines, of the 2-4-0 type, with their tall, elegantly-shaped, polished brass safety valve covers looked very like a product of Doncaster.

It was not however until 1873, seven years after he had succeeded his brother in office, that James Stirling really blossomed forth as an outstanding forward-looking locomotive designer. In that year his epoch-making 4-4-0 express engine 'No 6' was built at Kilmarnock. It was not quite the first British example of the type— it was narrowly beaten in this respect by Bouch on the Stockton and Darlington in 1860, then on the Great North of Scotland in 1861, and by conversions from the Crampton type on the London, Chatham and Dover Railway in 1864. Then Edward Fletcher introduced his slow speed 'Whitby Bogies' in 1864, which were not bogie engines at all! In 1871 Thomas Wheatley on the North British introduced the first that looked something like an express passenger locomotive, but Stirling's 'No 6' was the first that could be regarded as any way a success, and then it was a precursor indeed. In working out the design of this big engine, with coupled wheels of 7-ft 1½-in diameter, Stirling had little in the way of previous practice to work upon, and he wisely built a single example for thorough testing before the rest of the class were put in hand.

This pioneer 4-4-0 locomotive, the progenitor of so many of the breed on the South Eastern as well as on the Glasgow and South Western, looked every inch a Stirling product, in the family tradition. The 'straight-back' boiler was characteristic of both brothers' work all through their lives, and engine 'No 6' of the G&SWR, as first built, had the beautiful polished brass cover over the safety valves that had hitherto been used at Kilmarnock. This pioneer 4-4-0 also had the Stirling cut-away cab as on all the Doncaster engines, and all brother James' until his very last design from Ashford. Still continuing on purely external features, engine 'No 6' had the picturesque slotted driving-wheel splashers, and wings to each side of the smokebox. These latter were a convenience for enginemen in the days before mechanical lubricators, when attention was frequently needed to the motion when running. The smokebox wings were a much appreciated shield from air currents when running. The valve gear itself was the Stephenson link motion, though the method of actuation was a speciality designed by James Stirling himself.

Technically, a major point of interest was the design of the leading bogie, because engine 'No 6' was only the second example of the 4-4-0 type with inside cylinders. The noted locomotive historian E.L. Ahrons, writing in 1914, went so far as to say that the British 4-4-0 design finally attained its present form in James Stirling's Kilmarnock engine of 1873. The bogie was an original design of his own and apparently entirely successfully used, although only on the Glasgow and South Western Railway. It was the progenitor of the design extensively adopted on the South Eastern Railway and so is worthy of more than a passing mention here. In 1870 Patrick Stirling had made locomotive history by building the first of the celebrated 8-ft bogie singles for the Great Northern Railway, but when his brother designed his first bogie engines for the Glasgow and South Western a notably different concept was adopted. In the Great Northern engines the pivot point of the bogie was not equidistant from the two axles, it was placed 3 ft 6 in in rear of the leading axle-centre, but only 3 ft in advance of the rearward one. It was argued that this arrangement assisted the bogie in negotiating curves. But when James Stirling brought out his bogie 4-4-0 engine not only did he position the pivot pin the reverse way round, but made the axle spacing extremely short, only 4 ft 10 in, against 6 ft 6 in on his brother's Great Northern engines. On G&SWR engine 'No 6' the axle-spacing was 2 ft 4 in ahead of the pivot, and 2 ft 6 in aft.

On applying this principle to his South Eastern engines, James Stirling made the pivot pin only 1 in in advance of the mid-point of the bogie wheelbase; but the design differed generally from that pioneered at Kilmarnock. This bogie, which is illustrated herewith, allowed only a small amount of side play, ¾ in, on each side of the centre. The plate fixed under the

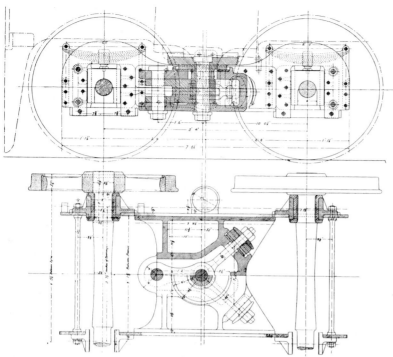

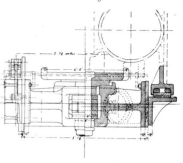

Left *The Stirling bogie used on the South Eastern Railway. (E.L. Ahrons.)*

Left *One of the celebrated 'F' Class 4-4-0s, No 201, built at Ashford in 1885. (British Railways.)*

Right *Class 'O' 0-6-0 goods on down train passing Grove Park. (L&GRP.)*

smokebox slid laterally over the bogie centre casting and had a 4-in diameter pin attached to it. This pin passed through a heavy rectangular-section double-forked link, and pivotted on another 4-in pin and placed 1 ft 2 in in front of the former. The controlling action was supplied by two smaller links of 2½ -in diameter, set at an angle towards, as shown in the drawing, and provided with India-rubber spring pads. A distinctive external feature of this bogie was the relative shortness of the wheelbase, only 5 ft 4 in, which made James Stirling's 4-4-0s recognizable above all others. From all accounts they rode well and were used on all his South Eastern 4-4-0s.

The boilers of the Scottish and the English 4-4-0 express locomotives, though so alike externally, exhibited certain technical developments, notably an increase in boiler pressure from 140 psi at Kilmarnock, to 160 psi at Ashford. The prototype of the design, the G&SWR 'No 6' was the only one to have the original Patrick Stirling lock-up type of safety valves. When the first production batch of the 4-4-0s was built at Kilmarnock James Stirling adopted instead the popular Ramsbottom type, still mounted over the firebox, although not so attractive in its appearance. There were some curious contrasts in the boilers of the large 7-ft 4-4-0s on the G&SWR and South Eastern Railways. The former, designed to provide steam for cylinders of 18-in diameter by 26-in stroke, had a combined total heating surface of 1,111.8 sq ft, though the South Eastern engines, having 19-in cylinders had a total heating surface of only 1,020 sq ft. It is true that the working pressure in the South Eastern engines was higher, but the ratio of nominal tractive effort to total heating surface was noticeably higher, as emphasized by the following table:

Stirling 7-ft 4-4-0 locomotives

Railway	SER	G&SWR
Cylinders (in)		
Diameter	19	18
Stroke	26	26
Heating surfaces (sq ft)		
Tubes	917	1027.6
Firebox	102	84.2
Total	1,020	1,111.8
Grate area	16.78	16
Working pressure (psi)	160	140
Nominal tractive		
effort (lb)	15,000	11,870

There was a considerable difference in the layout of the boiler tubes in the two designs, that of the G&SWR having 252 tubes of 1½-in diameter, while that of the South Eastern had 202 tubes of 1⅜-in diameter.

In referring to the 7-ft 1-in 4-4-0 engines however, I have stepped very much out of chronological order in dealing with James Stirling's work on the South Eastern Railway. Before leaving Kilmarnock he had introduced a powerful main-line goods engine of the 0-6-0 type, with 18-in by 26-in cylinders, 5-ft 1-in coupled wheels and carrying a boiler pressure of 130 psi. The twelve engines authorized were built at Kilmarnock works, but even before the first of them was completed Stirling had left for Ashford, and the new engines had to be completed by his successor, Hugh Smellie. Their designer evidently had full confidence in them, for he had been on the South Eastern for little more than weeks, it seemed, before he authorized construction of twenty more of almost identical design from Sharp, Stewart & Co. They were very successful, and became the standard goods locomotives of the South Eastern Railway for over twenty years. There were slight differences in the heating surfaces from that of the G&SWR and the boiler pressure was advanced to 140 psi, but the design was unchanged from that of 1878. By the year 1899 122 engines of the class had been built, 55 by Sharp, Stewart & Co and the rest at Ashford.

Although the new engines had very much the family 'look' with the straightback boiler and the cutaway cab, the Ramsbottom safety valve was moved forward from its traditional position above the firebox to the rearmost ring of the boiler barrel. Thus it remained on all South Eastern locomotives designed by James Stirling. On all the straightback boilers, and indeed all those built by his brother Patrick for the Great Northern, the regulator was in the smokebox and was actuated by a handle arranged to

18

Great Locomotives of the Southern Railway

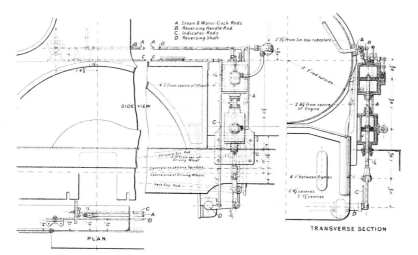

The Stirling steam reverser. (W.F. Pettigrew and A.F. Ravenshear.)

Two Class 'O' 0-6-0 goods engines on a
coal train passing Grove Park. (L&GRP.)

'A' Class 6 ft 4-4-0 on a stopping train
entering Halstead Knockholt station.
(L&GRP.)

pull out horizontally. On the footplate the controls were arranged for right-hand drive, and a novelty, so far as the South Eastern was concerned, was the steam-operated reverser. This quickly became a much-appreciated item of equipment, to be retained as standard after the merger with the London, Chatham and Dover Railway in 1898.

The Stirling steam reverser is worthy of particular attention in this account of Southern locomotives, its simplicity and reliability of operation in striking contrast to the fiddling and useless contrivances put on to certain so-called modern types to be described later in this book. In it's first form on the Glasgow and South Western Railway, and also on the South Eastern, the apparatus was mounted horizontally in the cab beside the driver's stance, and the operating rod emerging forward from the cab connected to a long vertical lever midway between the coupled wheels of the G&SWR 4-4-0s. On the South Eastern a much neater arrangement was afterwards devised, as shown in the accompanying drawing. It was arranged vertically, on the right-hand side of the engine, in this particular application just ahead of the sandbox of the leading pair of coupled wheels. The apparatus consisted of a steam cylinder and a water cylinder, or cataract. The steam cylinder was 7 in in diameter and the cataract cylinder 5 in in diameter. There were two handles, as shown in the drawing, one for supplying steam to the operating cylinder by the rod 'A'; this rod also regulated the supply of water from one side of the cataract cylinder to the other. The other handle, 'B', actuates the rod for reversing the backward or forward direction of the motion. The resulting movement of the arm on the reversing shaft, 'E', and consequently the expansion link, was indicated by a pointer in the cab, operated through the medium of the rod 'C'. In some of the footplate journeys I made on Southern locomotives of pre-grouping vintage I had the privilege of riding on some that had the Stirling steam reverser and I can testify readily to the ease of its manipulation and to its dead-beat action. Setting the cut-off on such engines was a pleasure.

Following the introduction of the 0-6-0 goods engines Stirling put in hand the design for a main-line passenger 4-4-0, but with smaller coupled wheels than had previously been used on the South Eastern Railway. Having in mind his recent association with Kilmarnock I have sometimes wondered if this small class, construction of which extended over two years, constituted something of a 'hang-over' from his previous post. A 4-4-0 with coupled wheels only 6 ft in diameter seemed much more likely for the heavily graded coastal routes of the G&SWR than for the SER. Certainly his successor at Kilmarnock was not long in bringing out a design of his own on very similar lines, though with a more conventional type

of bogie than Stirling's. Whether James Stirling had the design of the 'A' Class 4-4-0 of the South Eastern schemed out before he left Kilmarnock it is not possible to say; one thing is certain however, that the valances over the running plates, in their extension to the front buffer beam, were as near a copy of the 'No 6' Class of the G&SWR as makes no matter. At any event the dimensional comparison between Stirling's 'A' Class, and Smellie's 'Wee Bogies' on the G&SWR is striking:

6-ft 4-4-0 designs

Railway	SER	G&SWR
Designer	J. Stirling	H. Smellie
First introduced	1879	1882
Cylinders (in)		
Diameter	18	18¼
Stroke	26	26
Total heating surface (sq ft)	934.8	1,065
Grate area	15.5	16
Boiler pressure (psi)	140	140

In view of the heavy gradients on the Hastings line it could be understood if the 'A' Class engines, with their coupled wheels of no more than 6 ft in diameter, had been intended exclusively for this route, but they were rather slow in coming off the works, with only two being built in 1879, another nine in 1880, and the final one in 1881. It seemed that the immediate needs of the South Eastern Railway for locomotive power, when James Stirling took command in 1878, were not for first-line express passenger engines, for the Continental boat trains still remained in the hands of the Cudworth singles, while the Ramsgate trains were worked by the 2-4-0 'Iron Clads'. The new Stirling 4-4-0s certainly appeared on the Hastings line as they became available, but when the larger 'F' Class 4-4-0s were introduced the smaller-wheeled engines were displaced. The 6-ft 4-4-0s first came out when the SER livery for express engines was dark green, but it was soon changed to black, enlivened with an attractive and unusual scheme of lining out. The boiler bands were lined out in red, but the coupled wheel splashers had a more elaborate style in red, yellow and white, of which the combined effect was brown. The running plate valences were red-brown, lined with yellow.

An unusual feature of all Stirling passenger locomotives on the South Eastern Railway was the arrangement of the brake rigging outside of the coupled wheels. This originated on the 'A' Class 4-4-0s, which had the steam reverser inside the cab, and the rigging actuated by a vertical lever; but the outside rig arrangement was continued on the later types, with the steam reverser mounted vertically just

Above *One of the Cudworth 'Ironclad' 2-4-0s as rebuilt by James Stirling, No 75.*

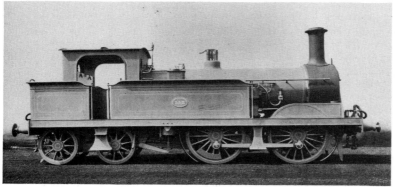

Left *One of the 'Q' Class 0-4-4 tank engines. No 352 was one of a batch built by Neilson & Co, Glasgow in 1889. (British Railways.)*

ahead of the leading coupled wheel splasher. This arrangement was once the subject of a very amusing correspondence in the 'Why and Wherefore' columns of *The Railway Magazine* in 1919. A reader using the pen-name *Luck of Edenhall* had noted what he took to be some peculiarity in a photograph of one of the Stirling 4-4-0s, and he received the following rather 'up-stage' reply from the editorial desk: 'Surely you cannot really imagine that it is possible for a locomotive to pursue the even tenor of its way with a broken crank or connecting rod? The rods to which you refer in the case of the South Eastern and Chatham Railway express engine depicted are brake rods, and this is their normal position on large numbers of the 4-4-0 locomotives of that company.'

On the eve of his departure from Kilmarnock James Stirling designed a class of 0-4-4 passenger tank engines, ostensibly for the heavy gradients of the Greenock road. But the four engines authorized were a long time in building, and when they did get into traffic, in 1879, they were unpopular from the start. It seemed that there was an age-old prejudice against any sort of tank engines on the G&SWR for anything except yard shunting duties, and the new engines

were condemned as 'unsuitable' by all the running staff. Whether these sentiments reached the ears of James Stirling it is not possible to say, but in 1881 he introduced on the South Eastern a design of 0-4-4 tank that was the living image of the G&SWR 'No 1' Class and, far from being thought unsuitable, the new SER tanks were eventually multiplied till there were no fewer than 118 in the class. They were built to a virtually unchanged design from 1881 until 1897. The variations lay in that some of them were fitted with condenser gear for working over certain London underground lines.

At the height of the rivalry between the Chatham and the South Eastern Railways the latter company entered into an arrangement with the Great Northern for a through passenger train service between Muswell Hill and Enfield, on the one hand, and Greenwich and Woolwich on the other. To make the connection the SER had to exercise running powers over the deadly-rival LC&D line via Ludgate Hill, utilizing a spur line from their own main line to Charing Cross, immediately south of the River Thames. The tunnel sections which needed the use of locomotives with condensing gear were those between Ludgate Hill and Snow Hill Junction and over the Metropolitan line between Faringdon Street and Kings Cross. This service was inaugurated in 1878, before the SER had any suitable locomotives for it, and they had to hire some Beyer, Peacock-type 4-4-0 tank engines of the same design as those used on the Metropolitan Railway. The new Stirling 0-4-4 tank engines were therefore needed in some urgency. The first twelve engines, built at Ashford in 1881-82, were all fitted for condensing, and had 3-ft diameter bogie wheels on a 4-ft 10-in wheelbase. Simultaneously a batch of twenty non-condensing engines was built by Neilson & Co in Glasgow in 1881-82.

The new tank engines had boilers and motion interchangeable with the '0' Class 0-6-0s and the 'A' 4-4-0s, but later batches of the 'Q' tanks had 3-ft 9-in diameter bogie wheels on a 5-ft 4-in wheelbase as on the 4-4-0 passenger engines. There were four exceptions to the bogie wheelbase length in respect of engines 129, 193, 237 and 239, built at Ashford in 1887. These had 3-ft diameter bogie wheels, and an even shorter wheelbase of 4 ft 5 in. The complete tally of the Stirling 'Q' Class, from 1881 to 1897, was as follows:

Year	Builders	Number
1881	Ashford	8
1881	Neilson & Co	10
1882	Ashford	4
1882	Neilson & Co	10
1885	Ashford	2
1887	Ashford	9
1888	Ashford	5
1889	Ashford	5
1889	Neilson & Co	10
1891	Ashford	6
1891	Neilson & Co	15
1892	Ashford	3
1893	Ashford	2
1893	Sharp, Stewart & Co	10
1894	Ashford	2
1895	Ashford	2
1897	Neilson & Co	15

Despite the rapid multiplication of this tank-engine class their use was confined to short distance working, almost entirely in the London area. Although my own observations were confined to the neighbour-

Right *'Q' Class 0-4-4 tank engine No 417, in SE&CR wartime livery. (British Railways.)*

Below *'F' Class 4-4-0 No 194, built Ashford 1889. This was one of the twelve not rebuilt by Wainwright, it was scrapped in original condition in 1926. (H. Gordon Tidey.)*

hood of Reading, and at a somewhat later date, one always remarked on the complete absence of tank engines on the South Eastern line, even in working the humblest of local trains. Altogether contrasting were the trains of the London & South Western that came into Reading, and always hauled in dashing style by 0-4-4 tank engines!

We turn now to the main-line express engines of Class 'F' introduced in 1883. Their salient features have already been discussed in connection with their Scottish progenitors on the Glasgow and South Western Railway. Just as these latter engines were claimed, by a noted locomotive historian the late David L. Smith of Ayr, as one of the most celebrated classes ever to run on the G&SWR so his English counterpart, Frank Burtt has described how the 'F' Class caused a sensation on the South Eastern. Like all James Stirling's engines they were built in large quantities. The prototype, No 205, was the only one built in 1883, but thereafter, to unchanged drawings, Ashford turned them out at intervals until 1898, the same year in which the larger 'B' Class 4-4-0s were introduced. The only year that did not witness new engines of the 'F' Class emerging from Ashford was 1887. The output continued unabated otherwise, indeed in 1897 there was a record, with twelve new engines, and a final four in 1898. The grand total was 88, though the principle of numbering engines as and when digits became vacant—in the Crewe style—prevailed throughout. The last four engines of the class, for example, were numbered 22, 30, 185 and 233.

Engine No 240, one of the 1889 batch of seven, was exhibited at the Paris Exhibition held in that year and was named *Onward* in honour of the occasion. Although this display of the Company's motto was appropriate to this special occasion, the name, which was out of keeping with SER locomotive policy, was removed soon after the engine's return to England. The visit to France was commemorated by applica-

tion only of the Company's coat of arms on the leading coupled-wheel splashers. After the Exhibition the engine ran a series of trials on the Paris, Lyons and Mediterranean Railway, in competition with the Brighton 0-4-2 engine *Edward Blount* of the 'Gladstone' Class. Unfortunately William Stroudley, the distinguished designer of this latter engine, caught a fatal chill during the proceedings and his sudden death cast such a cloud over all that the trials were ended therewith. No details were subsequently published, except for some references to maximum speeds run. Both Stroudley and James Stirling welcomed the chance to try for higher speeds than were permitted on their own lines. On the South Eastern there was an overall maximum of 60 mph, which, from the recordings of various enthusiasts was almost always strictly observed. In France, on the PLM line, Stirling got 78 mph out of the 4-4-0 *Onward*.

On the main South Eastern lines, to Dover and to Hastings, the train services were remarkably good considering the rigid limitation in maximum speeds, though why Stirling persisted in using coupled wheels as large as 7 ft is not clear. Over most of the main lines the ballast used was shingle, mostly from the seashore at Dungeness, and the use of this persisted until many years after the South Eastern had been absorbed into the Southern Railway. Although the prowess of locomotive engineering in the time of James Stirling ranked high in professional circles it did not attract the enthusiast fraternity in the same way as did its neighbour, the London, Brighton and South Coast Railway. Of course the Brighton had the advantage of an exceedingly colourful livery, while the South Eastern engines for all their smart turnout were basically black. This situation was clearly reflected when the Locomotive Publishing Company began to issue its famous coloured picture postcards in the 'F. Moore' series. While the majority of these were of contemporary types in their prevailing colours the series included a notable selection of Brighton celebrities of old, in the Stroudley yellow, but never anything from the South Eastern. Twenty years ago when scheming out my 'Pocket Encyclopedia of British Steam Locomotives' I had some difficulty in establishing the exact lining out of South Eastern locomotives of the Stirling period; and it was only then, when a fellow enthusiast introduced me to another friend that a treasured panel from nineteenth century Ashford was produced.

Seeing that maximum speeds were restricted to 60 mph everywhere some of the express train schedules were remarkably good; and the timekeeping was generally accurate. The following are examples of the best express runs of the 1890s. It is interesting to find that the fastest of all these runs was made to Canterbury, providing a rival service to Ramsgate to that offered by the London, Chatham and Dover Railway via Faversham and Margate. The service on the Hastings line, despite the competitive route by the Brighton Railway, reflects upon the severe gradients encountered by the South Eastern, especially south of Tonbridge.

Section	Distance (miles)	Booked time (minutes)	Average speed (mph)
New Cross–Canterbury	65.5	81	48.5
Cannon St–Dover	75.5	96	47.1
Cannon St–Folkestone	69.75	91	46.0
Sandling Junction–Cannon St	64.25	84	46.0
Cannon St–West St Leonards	59.5	88	40.6

The loads varied. On the smartly-timed Canterbury

trains they were often under 200 tons, though on the Continental boat expresses nearly 300 tons was sometimes taken punctually. On one occasion, with 'F' Class 4-4-0 No 156 and a load of 280 tons, Dover was reached in 96¼ minutes. With such a load it was hard going up to Knockholt summit, then named Halstead, taking 27¼ minutes for the 15½ miles from the start at Cannon Street; but from Dunton Green the ensuing 50¼ miles to passing Folkestone Junction took only 57 minutes including the considerable adverse stretch from Ashford to Westenhanger. On the level lengths east of Tonbridge the speeds ranged round about 55 mph. On a run with one of the Folkestone non-stops another of the 'F' Class, engine No 2, with a train of 200 tons, reached the Junction station prior to descending to the Harbour in 88½ minutes from Cannon Street, making a start-to-stop average speed of 47½ mph. The improvement in time over the previous run was entirely on the uphill section to Knockholt summit. On the Hastings line two interesting contemporary records were reproduced of speed recorder diagrams relating to the actual running of two trains booked non-stop between Cannon Street and West St Leonards. The diagrams illustrated the evident care not to exceed much over 55 mph downhill, even when the trains were running late, due to delays by signals. The loads referred on the charts as '11' and '14' vehicles represented approximately 150 and 185 tons behind the tenders. The locomotives were in both cases 4-4-0s of the 'F' Class.

Reverting to the boat-train working at Folkestone, James Stirling introduced a variant of his standard 0-6-0 goods engine in 1888 in the form of a shunting tank. In most respects it was interchangeable, having the same boiler, cylinders and motion, and indeed identical frames. The only novelty was use of a

Above left *The gold medallist 'F' 4-4-0 No 240 at Paris 1889. It was named* Onward *specially for the Exhibition. (British Railways.)*

Right *'R' Class shunting tank No 1336, built at Ashford 1888. It is shown in Southern Railway days at Folkestone Junction, and was not scrapped until 1941. (O.S. Nock.)*

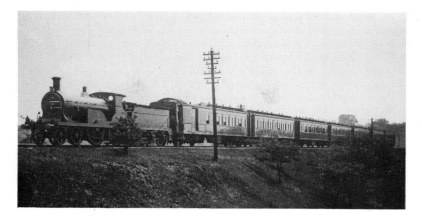

round-topped cab. A total of 25 was built, all at Ashford, between 1888 and 1898. Six of them were equipped with short chimneys to suit the restricted tunnel clearance on the Whitstable branch, while some others were used in light passenger service on the Kentish branch lines, but the most familiar tasks of these engines was in shunting the boat trains on the Admiralty Pier at Dover and working trains up the steep gradient to Folkestone Junction from which the Continental expresses started for London. With the heaviest trains usually two, and sometimes three, of these tough little engines would be needed.

Thirteen of these engines were subsequently rebuilt with domed boilers, but the others remained with the Stirling 'look' to the end of their long lives. I shall always remember engine No 336, or 1336 as she became in Southern Railway days, which remained hard at work at Folkestone until 1941. She was the last to carry the Stirling domeless boiler with the normal long chimney, and I photographed her 'simmering' at Folkestone Junction yard between trips down to the harbour and back in 1936.

In 1898, on the eve of the entente between the London, Chatham and Dover and South Eastern Railway companies, a new express passenger locomotive design was produced at Ashford which marked a notable change from the traditional 'look' of a Stirling engine. Hitherto James had been very faithful to the family tradition of cut-away cabs and domeless boilers—indeed further 'F' Class 4-4-0s had been built in that very same year. In 1897, however, a very brilliant young engineer, B.K. Field, had been appointed chief locomotive draughtsman at Ashford Works at the early age of 31 years. After a varied academic training which included a spell at Heidelberg University, he joined the South Eastern Railway as an apprentice at Ashford, and on completion of his indentures rose rapidly. It is impossible not to imagine that Field's promotion was unconnected with the evident 'new look' in Ashford's express pas-

senger locomotives, and the more modern outline of the 'B' Class. They were exceptionally attractive engines, though having no greater tractive effort than the 'F' Class. The latter were sometimes criticized as being deficient in boiler capacity, though one must admit such criticism came from theoretical grounds and from individuals who had little or no practical experience of their running. From all accounts, from those who knew them well, they steamed freely, even though the coal with which they were supplied was often very poor. Those were the days before the Kentish coalfield was opened up.

However reliable the 'F' Class 4-4-0s had proved, one can be sure the running department welcomed the enlarged engines, with their bigger boilers. The comparative dimensions were:

SER 4-4-0 locomotive boilers

Class	'F'	'B'
Diameter, outside largest ring (ft in)	4 4	4 8⅛
Length of barrel (ft in)	10 4½	10 4½
Total heating surface (sq ft)	985	1,087.5
Grate area (sq ft)	16.5	16.5
Working pressure (psi)	160	160

The first batch of the 'B' Class engines, twenty strong, was built by Neilson, Reid & Co, in Glasgow, all turned out in 1898. The remaining nine were built at Ashford, four in 1898 and the rest in 1899. Apart from their larger boilers and the handsomely-styled cabs, 'B' Class had a much more modern looking tender, in that the springs were under the footplate, and the water capacity was increased from 2,650 to 3,000 gallons. These fine engines were James Stirling's last design. With the establishment of the South Eastern and Chatham Railway Management Committee, in 1898, he retired.

2. London, Chatham and Dover

The death of William Martley in 1873 left an unexpected gap in the Chatham Railway management, particularly when his skilful and astute handling of the affairs of Longhedge Works was beginning to have a marked influence upon the mechanical engineering practice of the Company. To replace Martley a young nephew of Matthew Kirtley, of Midland Railway fame, was appointed; and it proved a very good choice. William Kirtley had himself been in the service of the Midland Railway for nearly twenty years before securing the appointment on the LC&DR. He was then only 34 years of age, though having had some years of experience as a foreman in Derby Works. Then it would seem he trod with some deference, if not to say trepidation upon the tumultous arena of the 'Chatham'. Although the fortunes of the Railway had already been taking a slightly upward turn by the year 1873 there is no doubt that all-round economy was urged upon the new Locomotive Superintendent. The celebrated 'Mail' 2-4-0 engines of Martley's design, *Europa, Asia, Africa* and *America* had scarcely been delivered from Sharp, Stewart & Co's works, in Glasgow, before their designer died; and although two further engines of the class were authorized for construction at Longhedge Works it was not until 1876 that they took the road.

These splendid little engines played a continuing part in the express train working of the Chatham, very many years after the new Kirtley 4-4-0s had entered traffic. That they remained favourites for the fast 'Continental Mail' trains was misconstrued by quite a few connoiseurs of nineteenth century locomotive practice, and inevitably perhaps, they were quoted by latter day scribes. This, however, relates to later Chatham history. Now it is the time to pay a further tribute to William Martley's 'Mail' engines. That they appealed to Kirtley was natural enough, seeing that he had been brought up on the Midland where all his uncle's express engines were of the type happily designated 'Old English' by Hamilton Ellis many years later. 'Old English' was the variety of 2-4-0 having outside frames throughout, of which the Midland '800' Class, introduced by Kirtley the elder, came out in 1870. On the Chatham the 'Europa' Class 'Mail' engines had the same basic dimensions—17-in by 24-in cylinders—but slightly smaller coupled wheels—6 ft 6 in against 6 ft 8 in. From all accounts Martley's 'Europa' class were every bit as good as the Midland '800' Class, though not engaged in such spectacular running.

When Kirtley took over at Longhedge the principal concern was for the London suburban workings, the main-line passenger requirements having been satisfied by the delivery of the four 'Europas' from Sharp, Stewart & Co in 1873. Although the two varieties of 0-4-2 tanks known as the small and large 'Scotchmen' were rendering excellent service, there was a definite need for larger engines. For his first new design Kirtley went to a type that had virtually originated on the Midland, the 0-4-4 tank. The only previous use in Great Britain had been an experimental design used by Cudworth on the South Eastern in 1866. The Midland engines, introduced in 1869, appeared to have been a largely Beyer, Peacock & Co job, with the water tank beneath the coal bunker. In those early days some engineers took the view that provision of water tanks on each side of the boiler

One of the famous 'Europa' Class 2-4-0s by W. Martley, the Asia, *before the engine had a number. (Loco Publishing Co.)*

would have an unstabilizing effect on the running and upset the balance of the engine when the tanks were getting empty. Whatever views of this were held on the Midland however none seemed to have affected the younger Kirtley, because his first engines for the Chatham were entirely in the form that became orthodox for 'side-tank' engines throughout Great Britain in the years thereafter.

The new engines, all introduced in 1875, have never been given the credit for the outstanding units they undoubtedly were. Some commentators have certainly noted that at the time that they were built they were the most powerful tank engines in the country; but they were the first examples of the design that, with no more than marginal enlargements and higher boiler pressure, saw steam traction out on the London suburban lines of what became later the South Eastern and Chatham Railway. In 1875 contracts were let for eight of the engines to Neilson & Co of Glasgow, and ten to the Vulcan Foundry. They were the first new engines on the Chatham to be distinguished only by numbers. One of the first reforms instituted by W. Kirtley at Longhedge had been the addition of numbers to all the existing locomotive stock, and the eventual removal of the names. The 0-4-4 tank engines had 17½-in by 26-in cylinders, 5-ft 3-in coupled wheels, 1,136 sq ft of heating surface and a grate area of 16.5 sq ft. The boiler pressure was originally 140 psi, but was afterwards raised to 150 psi. These engines had a tank capacity of 970 gallons and a fuel capacity of 2 tons.

The London Chatham and Dover Railway was developing an intense inner-city train service between Victoria, Brixton, Loughborough Junction, Ludgate Hill and the Metropolitan line, not only to a terminus in the City, at Moorgate Street, but also north-westwards via Kings Cross (underground) to stations on the Midland and Great Northern Railways. For working through the tunnel sections the new LC&DR engines were fitted with condensing equipment. There were appropriate balancing locomotive workings, on which Great Northern and Midland engines worked through Ludgate Hill and round to Victoria.

The introduction of the new Kirtley 0-4-4 tanks put the Chatham well ahead so far as motive power was concerned in this tripartite service, but as for coaching stock, it was the famous author E.L. Ahrons who once described the carriages as 'always poverty-stricken rabbit hutches'! When the new engines were first put on none of the trains they had to haul had any form of continuous brake. It was not until some years later that the Chatham adopted the Westinghouse as standard.

At this stage the whole family of nineteenth century 0-4-4 tanks can be considered, in their variation of coupled-wheel diameter and piston stroke.

Another of Martley's 'Europa' Class, the Africa. *(Loco Publishing Co.)*

Class	Date	Number built	Builder	Wheel diameter (ft in)	Cylinders diameter stroke (in)
A	1875	18	Vulcan & Neilson	5 3	$17\frac{1}{2} \times 26$
A1	1880	12	Kitson & Co	5 6	$17\frac{1}{2} \times 26$
A2	1883-84	6	R. Stephenson & Co	5 6	$17\frac{1}{2} \times 26$
R	1891	18	Sharp, Stewart & Co	5 6	$17\frac{1}{2} \times 24$
R1	1900*	15	Sharp, Stewart & Co	5 6	$17\frac{1}{2} \times 24$

*Class R1 had bogie wheels of 3-ft 6-in diameter. All the others had 3-ft 0-in bogie wheels.

With the exception of one Vulcan-built 'A' Class, which was scrapped in 1915, all the 'A', 'A1' and 'A2' Class lasted until 1923-26. It was a remarkable career for local tank engines engaged on work that involved constant starting and stopping. The subsequent 'R' Class, with cylinders having the shorter piston stroke of 24 in, lasted still longer and all were still in service when the Second World War broke out in 1939. In common with certain engines of the Stirling 'Q' Class of the South Eastern Railway all the 'R' Class were in due course fitted with the 'H' Class boiler, an SE&CR standard carrying a working pressure of 160 psi. This latter boiler is usually attributed to Wainwright, who was Locomotive Superintendent of the Management Committee from 1899; but, as will be discussed in a later chapter of this book, locomotive design work devolved upon Robert Surtees who had been chief draughtsman on the Chatham under Kirtley and who subsequently moved to Ashford, to hold the same post under Wainwright. There was thus a continuity in design that could be discerned in other classes in addition to the 0-4-4 tanks of Classes 'R' and 'R1'.

The next design for which Kirtley was responsible was the Class 'B' 0-6-0 goods, which had many parts interchangeable with the 'A' Class 0-4-4 tanks. The demand for a powerful main-line goods engine cannot have been very great at the time, for the first order, placed with the Vulcan Foundry in 1876, was for no more than six locomotives. Like the 0-4-4 tanks of the first batches these engines carried a working pressure of 140 psi but this was afterwards increased to 150 psi. A further order was placed for six more engines of this design in 1877, this time with Neilson & Co, and like the previous six they were not fitted with any form of continuous brake. In 1891 Kirtley introduced a modified design, having 5-ft coupled wheels, instead of 4 ft 10 in, and cylinders increased to 18-in diameter. The working pressure was advanced to 160 psi. No more than six engines were built of this variety, known as Class 'B2' on the Chatham, but they were the forerunners of a large class of standard 0-6-0s on the South Eastern and Chatham Railway. This development was to a large extent understandable with Surtees continuing as Chief Draughtsman.

What was not so clear was the evidently high prestige in which locomotive design practice on the Chatham was held in the latter years of Kirtley's time at Longhedge.

In 1899 the technical publishers Charles Griffin & Co brought out a massive compendium entitled *A Manual of Locomotive Engineering*. The author was none other than W.F. Pettigrew, Locomotive Engineer of the Furness Railway and lately chief assistant to William Adams, Locomotive Superintendent of the London and South Western Railway. One of the early chapters of this important book, described British simple locomotives and included full working drawings of four modern designs. It was natural that in view of his recent association with the L&SWR, and in particular with the testing of one of the Adams express 4-4-0s, that one of these engines should be prominently featured, but it was remarkable that a large folding plate was simply entitled 'Standard Goods Engine', and this, on further investigation, proved to be the Kirtley 'B2' Class of the London, Chatham and Dover. It is interesting that Pettigrew chose to illustrate as a standard type one of which no more than six examples had been built by the owning company. The choice however proved prophetic in view of the development of the design in SE&CR days. In any case the Chatham 'B2' 0-6-0 was an excellent and notably straightforward design, and the working drawings are reproduced herewith.

The design clearly appealed to Pettigrew himself, for he followed it closely in the 0-6-0 and 0-6-2 tanks he built subsequently for the Furness Railway. When the design was developed for general use on the South Eastern and Chatham Railway some commentators strove to draw a contrast with previous South Eastern designs pointing out particularly the inclusion of balance weights in the driving wheels. This feature had been incorporated in the Chatham 'B2' Class in 1891. The latter engines, as distinct from Kirtley's earlier 0-6-0s were equipped for mixed-traffic duties, and were fitted with the Westinghouse brake and slightly larger wheels. The boiler was only marginally larger than that of 'B' Class with a total heating surface of 1,102.4 sq ft and a grate area of 17 sq ft. The valves and motion were conventional, with the

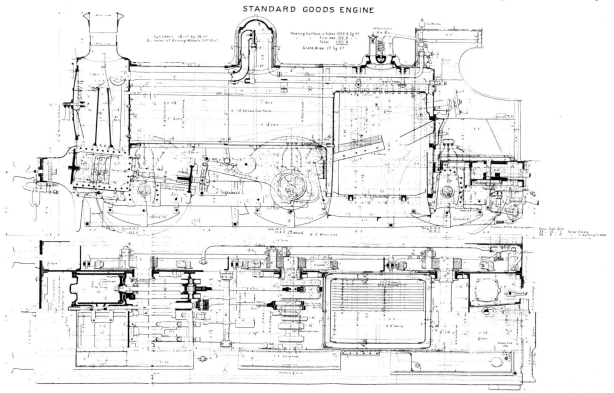

STANDARD GOODS ENGINE

slide valves mounted between the cylinders, and the blast pipe providing the direct exhaust. The valves had a lap of 1 in, with ⅛ -in lead in full gear and a maximum travel of 4¹/₁₆ in. At a first glance at the drawing it would seem that the chimney was no higher than the dome, but by a draughtsman's convention, to save space on the page, the chimney was shown truncated, whereas the top was actually 3 ft 8 in above the top of the smokebox.

Taken all round, Kirtley's 'B2' Class was a notable design. The part played in it by Robert Surtees was no small one, because it became evident from 1900 onwards how the design was relied upon for further production, of the SE&CR 'C'. The relevant dimensions of the two classes, both from the drawing boards of Surtees, were as follows:

The Kirtley 'B2' 0-6-0 goods engine. (W.F. Pettigrew and A.F. Ravenshear.)

Total heating surface		
(sq ft)	1,104.6	1,200
Grate area (sq ft)	17	17
Boiler pressure (psi)	160	160

Class	LC&DR 'B2'	SE&CR 'C'
Cylinders (in)		
Diameter	18	18½
Stroke	26	26
Wheel diameter (ft in)	5 0	5 2
Boiler (ft in)		
Diameter	4 3	4 7
Length	10 3½	10 9

After the fusion of interests the vacuum brake was preferred, though out of the large batch of 'C' Class engines built in 1900, fifteen contracted out to Sharp, Stewart & Co were dual fitted. All the 'C' Class engines, in accordance with Ashford practice, had the Stirling steam reversing gear.

The last of the new types introduced by William Kirtley was the 4-4-0 express passenger of Class 'M'. The first batch of these engines, only six in number, was built in 1877, by Neilson & Co, and it was not until three years later that any additions were made to the class. The fact that the new engines were no more than occasionally used on the 'crack' Continental Mail trains led to some misconceptions of the original purpose of the design, some of which were perpetuated many years after the true position had been made clear by Surtees himself. But I am discussing the criticisms before the salient features of the design itself. The 4-4-0 type was then coming into vogue on a number of British railways, having 17½-in diameter cylinders and boilers with around 1,100 sq ft of heating surface. In contrast to many contemporary designs on the continent of Europe and in the USA the boilers were relatively small, and this was undoubtably due to the good quality of British coal. Kirtley's first design of 4-4-0 for the LC&DR could be described as a conventional one, though excellent in all its details. It had the usual 17½-in by 26-in cylinders, 6-ft 6-in coupled wheels, 1,069 sq ft of heating surface, 16.5 sq ft of grate area and a working pressure of 140 psi. In appearance the new engines,

designated Class 'M', were non-descript, rather than possessing any marked characteristics of outline.

These engines arrived from Neilson's works in Glasgow only a year later than the last two of the 'Europa' Class of Martley's design of 2-4-0 were completed at Longhedge Works. The latter had proved immensely popular with the running staff, and although Kirtley's new locomotives of the 0-4-4 tank and the 0-6-0 goods had been readily accepted, from all accounts it was not quite the case with the new 4-4-0s, particularly when it came to occasional use of some of them on the boat trains. Use of the 'Europa' Class 2-4-0s continued on these 'crack' services for some years. This situation, which gave rise to the impression that the 'M' Class locomotives were not entirely satisfactory, may have originated in the minds of students of locomotive practice in the concluding instalments of a long series of articles in *The Locomotive Magazine*, which ended in 1905. The authorship of those articles was anonymous, but as with so many serials of that kind the treatment of the subject became progressively more sketchy as more modern history was neared, presumably with the

Below *Kirtley 'M3' Class 4-4-0 No 647 (ex-LC&DR No 188) in SE&CR wartime livery. (British Railways.)*

Bottom *'Europa' Class 2-4-0 No 54, after her name was withdrawn, on Continental boat express near Bickley. (L&GRP.)*

Below right *The Kirtley 'M3' 4-4-0 express passenger engine. (W.F. Pettigrew and A.F. Ravenshear.)*

view that readers knew enough to make detailed references unnecessary. So far as the LC&DR this might have applied in 1905, but not in 1985! In the penultimate article of this series it was stated that 'in 1877 Messrs Neilson & Co of Glasgow, received an order to build six four-wheel-coupled bogie engines which Mr Kirtley had specially designed to work the boat trains between London and Dover, which work they performed very creditably'.

In the correspondence column of the magazine a month later, hidden away on the pages dealing with carriage and wagon affairs, was a most important letter from Mr Surtees, from his current appointment as Chief Draughtsman of the SE&CR at Ashford. He wrote: 'Respecting the locomotive history of the LC&DR appearing in your June issue, I note it is there stated that the bogie engines built by Neilson & Co in 1877 were designed by Mr Kirtley for working the boat trains between London and Dover. This is not correct. These engines were originally designed for working the Kent Coast cheap fast trains to Margate, Ramsgate. These trains were timed very fast and the loads were very heavy.' Surtees also pointed out that the illustration of the 4-4-0 in the article in question was not one of the first batch built by Neilsons, but one of the second batch, built at Longhedge Works in 1880-81, and incorporating some detail alterations which will be described later. So far as the first batch of 'M' Class engines were concerned, contemporary accounts of the LC&DR gave no details of the actual loads conveyed on these 'cheap fast' trains, nor of the speeds at which they run. At the time the first six of the 4-4-0s were introduced these seaside trains were made up of four-wheeled stock, and without any form of continuous brake!

The engines built between 1877 and 1885 can be divided into three groups, all having 17½-in by 26-in

cylinders, 6-ft 6-in coupled wheels and the same-sized boiler and grate as the first series. The variations in detail are covered by the class distinctions as follows:

Class	Date	Number built	Builder	Boiler pressure (psi)	Cylinders
M	1877	6	Neilson	140	Inclined
M1	1881	4	LC&D	140	Horizontal
M2	1885	2	LC&D	150	Horizontal
M2	1884	6	Dübs	150	Horizontal

The running numbers, in LC&D days, were Class 'M' 157-162; Class 'M1' 175-178; Class 'M2' 179-186.

The final design of 4-4-0 express passenger engine was introduced in 1891, and represented no more than a modest development upon Class 'M2', with cylinders enlarged to 18-in diameter, and a slightly enlarged boiler. The first batch of Class 'M3' was built by the Vulcan Foundry, all six engines, Nos 187-192, being completed in 1891. After that it became a standard class and sixteen more built at Longhedge Works at intervals between 1892 and 1899 and replaced rebuilt engines of the 'G' Class 2-4-0s having the same numbers. These replacements were not necessarily made in the same numerical order, and as the rebuilding continued after the union of the LC&D with the South Eastern Railway, the last four of Class 'M3' did receive LC&D numbers. The first sixteen Longhedge replacements with LC&D numbers were:

Date	Engine	Date	Engine
1892	14	1896	23
1892	25	1897	3
1893	16	1897	5
1894	17	1897	19

1894	20	1898	6
1895	12	1898	7
1895	15	1898	24
1896	13	1899	4

The remaining four were built in 1899, 1900 and 1901.

Class 'M3' was distinguished by having a fully-detailed drawing in W.F. Pettigrew's book, which is reproduced herewith. The simple, straightforward design will be well appreciated from a study of the drawing, which is all the more important in being the stepping stone to the notable South Eastern and Chatham 4-4-0 designs of the twentieth century, which also came from the drawing boards of Robert Surtees.

The new SE&CR Class 'D' 4-4-0, which is described in detail in a later chapter of this book, featured in a beautiful colour plate in *The Locomotive Magazine* as early as July 1901 after the first introduction of the class. What was more unusual, in the same volume of that periodical was a fully detailed drawing of an LC&DR 'M2' Class 4-4-0, strangely enough without any accompanying description. The remarkable thing about this illustration is that it so nearly paralleled in date of publication that of the 'M3' 4-4-0, in Pettigrew's book. One can be sure that some confusion was caused at the time, particularly by the absence of any explanatory notes in *The Locomotive Magazine*. Other than the cylinder diameter, the only difference between Classes 'M2' and 'M3' to be noted on the respective drawings was in the centre line of the bogie to that of the leading coupled axle—9 ft 10 in on 'M2' to 10 ft on 'M3'. All the Kirtley 4-4-0s on the LC&DR were notably free running, despite having valve dimensions that later became to be considered inhibiting in this respect. The travel in full gear was only $3^{15}/_{16}$ in; the lap of the valves was 1 in and the lead in full gear was $\frac{1}{8}$ in.

The increasing numbers of the 'M3' Class, ultimately to twenty engines, led to the replacement of the 'Europa' Class 2-4-0s on the boat trains. Thanks to the scholarship of Mr J.P. Pattison, the working of the new 4-4-0 engines was very fully documented between the years 1894 and 1898. It is rather curious

FOUR WHEELS COUPLED INSIDE CYLINDER BOGIE EXPRESS ENGINE.

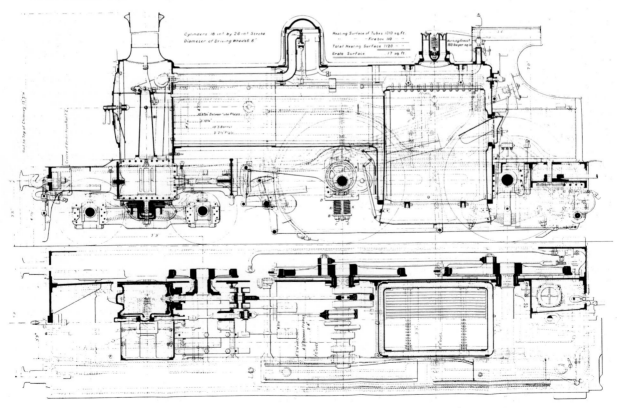

to find earlier and more recent writers alike emphasizing the difficulty of the road, not only in respect of the gradients, but also of the curves. One would not quarrel with any such statements about the gradients, but there are not any difficulties over curves. It is true that the line is severely curved from Strood, through Rochester and Chatham to Gillingham, and nowadays there is a slack through Canterbury, but the LC&DR trains used to gallop along freely enough between Beckenham and the approaches to Strood, and in the old days no slackening other than for gradients took place between Gillingham and the outskirts of Dover. Again, while the South Eastern had a line maximum of 60 mph, the Chatham trains frequently exceeded 70 mph on the down grades, and when there was particular need for hurry the drivers had no inhibitions and ran up nearly 80 mph at times.

The records made by Mr J.P. Pattinson are most comprehensive so far as the Chatham line are concerned, and while in the ordinary way comparisons between locomotive work on different railways can be invidious and unconvincing, the early chapters of his book inevitably tend to stir up, and revel in the old rivalries between the South Eastern and the Chatham, and there is no doubt that Mr Pattinson comes down heavily on the side of the Chatham. Fine though the uphill work of the Stirling 4-4-0s undoubtedly was, it is eclipsed by that of Kirtley 'M3' 4-4-0s of the Chatham. Most of the South Eastern banks could to some extent be rushed, but the Chatham had the task of starting cold up the heavy ascent from Dover to Lydden Tunnel, and Sole Street bank was commenced from the severe slack at Rochester and Strood. This restriction, like that at

Tonbridge on the South Eastern, was more often than not interpreted liberally, and so one could not put down Rochester as a serious handicap. Detailed records on Sole Street bank are practically non-existent, however, because at that time there were no mileposts west of Strood! Apparently the art of recording train speeds from the rail joints was not practised.

Locomotive work on the Chatham system is represented by four tables, the first two showing typical runs on the boat expresses, and the last two on the Kent Coast trains to and from Margate. It was a feature of LC&DR working for nearly all express trains, even including the Continental Mails, to call at Herne Hill so as to provide connections from both the City and West End of London. The exception so far as the tabulated runs are concerned is the 5.13 pm down business-men's express, which ran non-stop from St Pauls to Westgate. Taking the boat trains first, the table gives details of two runs, with the 'M3' Class 4-4-0 locomotives. The first was made on the sharply-timed down Night Mail, while the second was on the popular 11 am day service from Victoria.

From the start at Herne Hill the climbing is continuously at 1 in 101 up to Sydenham Hill, and for small 4-4-0 locomotives the attained speeds were remarkable, particularly on the second run, conveying a load of 200 tons. One would scarcely guess either, from the average speeds sustained, that the section between Shortlands and Bickley contains 1½ miles rising at 1 in 95. To Strood the honours rest with engine No 13 (making the second run) and with such a load as 200 tons the average speed of 49 mph from the start to this point was indeed excellent.

Neither of the drivers showed any trace of over-caution round the Rochester curves, and the loco-motives must have been pounded hard to produce average speeds varying between 42 mph and 50 mph between Rochester and Chatham before tackling the 1½ miles up at 1 in 132 through the tunnels to Gillingham, or New Brompton as it was then named.

Once up to the level road the running on trips was quite undistinguished to Faversham, with the more heavily loaded engine gradually falling behind, but over the hilly road from Faversham to Dover there

was some grand work. Between Faversham and Ensden Tunnel the gradient is 1 in 110-100 for 4 miles, and here engine No 25 averaged all but 50 mph. In his records Mr Pattinson does not give the milepost timings on the Night Mail, presumably because the run was made in darkness, but the average speeds shown in the table are enough to pro-vide a good assessment of the performance. Speeds were moderate down to Canterbury, and then again the climing to Shepherd's Well was extremely fine.

The return run on the 5.45 pm from Dover

LC&DR Herne Hill-Dover Pier

Run number		1		2	
Train		9.14 pm		11.14 am	
Engine Class 'M3' 4-4-0		No 25		No 13	
Load					
Coaches		'10'		'15½'	
Tons (approx)		130		200	
Distance (miles)		Time (m s)	Speed* (mph)	Time (m s)	Speed* (mph)
0.0	HERNE HILL	0 00	—	0 00	—
1.0	Dulwich	2 32	—	2 36	—
1.8	Sydenham Hill	3 52	32.7	4 12	27.3
3.2	Penge	6 02	40.5	6 33	35.0
3.8	Kent House	6 44	53.5	7 17	51.0
4.7	Beckenham	7 39	56.5	8 10	58.5
6.0	Shortlands	9 17	48.7	9 49	48.5
6.9	BROMLEY	10 14	52.1	10 46	52.1
8.0	Bickley	11 37	47.7	12 13	45.5
10.8	St Mary Cray	15 03	50.7	15 52	47.7

Distance (miles)		Time (m s)	Speed* (mph)	Time (m s)	Speed* (mph)
13.7	Swanley	18 10	54.7	19 01	54.0
16.5	Farningham Rd	20 57	61.2	21 50	60.5
19.4	Fawkham	23 56	57.3	24 51	56.9
22.0	Meopham	27 11	47.8	28 19	44.7
22.9	Sole Street	28 24	45.5	29 39	42.5
29.0	Strood	34 21	61.2	35 49	59.1
29.8	Rochester	35 29	41.7	36 59	40.4
30.4	CHATHAM	36 14	50.0	37 47	46.8
32.0	New Brompton†	38 31	41.7	40 10	39.9
35.0	Rainham	42 06	50.3	43 53	48.6
37.6	Newington	44 53	57.1	46 50	54.0
40.8	SITTINGBOURNE	48 18	54.7	50 20	53.2
44.0	Teynham	52 10	50.3	53 54	54.6
48.0	FAVERSHAM	56 42	52.9	58 48	47.9
51.3	Selling	60 42	49.7	63 53	39.1
57.9	CANTERBURY	67 57	53.8	72 20	46.0
60.7	Bekesbourne	71 30	52.3	75 52	52.4
				signal check	
63.8	Adisham	75 10	50.0	80 45	37.4
67.7	Shepherd's Well	80 21	45.1	90 21	24.1
71.1	Kearsney	83 56	57.6	94 05	55.3
73.3	Dover Priory	86 25	53.6	96 21	59.5
74.5	DOVER PIER	88 25	—	98 22	—
Schedule time		91 00		00 96	
Net time		87 45		00 93	

*Average speed from exact chainages   †Now Gillingham

Harbour to Herne Hill with a load of 215 tons included some hill climbing that was again beyond praise. One has only to mention the gradients: 1 in 100-132 continuously from the start to Shepherd's Well; 1 in 132 for 4 miles up to Ensden Tunnel; and the 5 miles of Sole Street bank, which was pratially continuous at 1 in 100. In face of such obstacles the speeds are really rather amazing from small 4-4-0 locomotives having cylinders 18 in by 26 in, a grate area of no more than 17 sq ft and a boiler pressure of 150 psi. It is evident also that there was no shortage of steam after these climbs, as witness the fast running of No 20 down to Canterbury. This train was allowed 96 minutes from Dover Harbour to Herne Hill, and with such loads it is not surprising to find there was very little time in hand.

Next comes the 5.13 pm from St Paul's, in later years known as 'The City Fast Train'. The loads conveyed on this were much less, but the logs shown have an added interest in that they feature the work of the earlier Kirtley 4-4-0s of the 'M2' Class and one example from the 'Enigma' Class of 2-4-0. The line is level to Camberwell, after which it rises sharply at 1 in 150-102 to join the main line at Herne Hill. On all

LC&DR: Dover Harbour-Herne Hill

Train 5.45 pm
Engine Class 'M3' 4-4-0 No 20
Load
  Coaches '16½'
  Tons (approx) 215

Distance (miles)		Time (m s)	Average speed (mph)
0.0	DOVER HARBOUR	0 00	—
0.7	Dover Priory	1 46	—
2.9	Kearsney	6 39	27.0
6.3	Shepherd's Well	12 38	34.1
10.2	Adisham	17 35	47.3
13.3	Bekesbourne	20 36	61.7
16.1	CANTERBURY	23 39	55.1
22.7	Selling	33 06	41.9
26.0	FAVERSHAM	36 16	60.7
30.0	Teynham	40 41	54.4
33.2	SITTINGBOURNE	44 16	53.7
		permanent way slack	

Distance miles		Time (m s)	Average speed (mph)
36.4	Newington	49 24	37.4
39.0	Rainham	52 42	47.3
42.0	New Brompton	56 09	52.3
43.6	CHATHAM	57 53	55.2
44.2	Rochester	58 32	57.7
45.0	Strood	59 31	48.2
51.1	Sole Street	68 59	38.7
52.0	Meopham	70 25	38.4
54.6	Fawkham	73 22	52.9
57.5	Farningham Road	76 17	59.7
60.3	Swanley	79 38	50.2
63.2	St Mary Cray	82 48	54.9
66.0	Bickley	86 14	49.2
67.1	BROMLEY	87 22	58.3
68.0	Shortlands	88 12	59.5
69.3	Beckenham	89 45	51.1
70.2	Kent House	90 53	46.1
70.8	Penge	91 48	40.9
72.2	Sydenham Hill	94 04	38.7
73.0	Dulwich	94 59	47.1
74.0	HERNE HILL	96 21	
Net time		95 00	

three runs the starts were extremely smart, after which all three trains were involved in a succession of signal checks. The cessation of these checks after Sydenham Hill suggests that the slower train ahead was switched on to the slow road over the quadruple-tracked section between Penge and Beckenham Junction, for after that the City express was able to get away in good style. The uphill speeds run from Shortlands to St Mary Cray were excellent, but as on the boat trains very moderate work was done after New Brompton.

There is a heavy slack at Faversham for trains taking the Margate line, and some good running followed over the level stretch to Herne Bay. The 1½ miles of 1 in 110 climbing immediately after the latter station is followed by a corresponding descent, and all three engines sustained a good pace thereafter. Schedule time for the 72½ mile run from St Paul's to Westgate was 90 minutes, so that although the little 2-4-0 did not keep strict time her lateness was due entirely to the signal checks. In passing I should add that the 'M2' Class 4-4-0s had 17½-in by 26-in cylinders, a grate area of 16½ sq ft and 140 psi boiler pressure. The 'Enigma' Class engine No 52, as rebuilt by Kirtley, had 17-in by 24-in cylinders, 6-ft 6-in coupled wheels, a grate area of 16¼ sq ft and 150-psi boiler pressure. *Enigma* herself differed from

LC&DR: St Paul's-Westgate

Run		1		2	
Train		5.13 pm		5.13 pm	
Engine number		180		52	
Engine type		4-4-0 'M2'		2-4-0 'L'	
Load					
Coaches		'10'		'10'	
Tons (approx)		130		130	
Distance (miles)		Actual time (m s)	Speed* (mph)	Actual time (m s)	Speed* (mph)
0.0	ST PAULS	0 00	—	0 00	—
0.8	Borough Road	2 02	—	1 58	—
1.2	Elephant & Castle	2 41	39.2	2 39	37.4
1.9	Walworth Road	3 41	39.8	3 41	38.7
2.7	Camberwell	4 42	47.5	4 42	47.5
3.2	Loughborough Junction	5 25	46.0	5 21	50.8
4.1	HERNE HILL	6 40	43.2	6 33	45.8
				signal check	
5.1	Dulwich	8 21	36.0	8 37	28.3
		signal stop		signal check	
5.9	Sydenham Hill	11 06	15.8	12 01	12.8
7.3	Penge	14 00	30.2	15 00	29.3
7.9	Kent House	14 45	50.0	15 48	46.9
8.8	Beckenham	15 38	58.4	16 50	50.4
10.1	Shortlands	17 17	48.0	18 39	43.6
11.0	BROMLEY	18 11	55.0	19 35	53.2

Distance (miles)		Actual time (m s)	Speed* (mph)	Actual time (m s)	Speed* (mph)
12.1	Bickley	19 36	46.6	20 58	47.6
14.9	St Mary Cray	23 05	48.2	24 27	47.7
17.8	Swanley	26 08	57.1	27 39	54.4
20.6	Farningham Road	28 52	61.3	30 49	53.1
23.5	Fawkham	31 46	60.0	34 03	53.6
26.1	Meopham	35 00	48.2	37 33	44.6
27.0	Sole Street	36 15	44.4	38 52	41.5
33.1	Strood	42 36	57.6	45 57	51.8
33.9	Rochester	43 57	35.5	47 13	38.0
34.5	CHATHAM	44 50	42.4	48 06	42.4
36.1	New Brompton	47 25	37.2	50 39	37.6
39.1	Rainham	51 02	49.8	54 13	50.5
41.7	Newington	53 51	55.3	57 06	54.1
44.9	SITTINGBOURNE	57 23	54.3	60 44	52.8
48.1	Teynham	61 20	48.7	64 16	54.5
52.1	FAVERSHAM	66 11	49.5	68 53	52.0
58.8	Whitstable	73 31	54.9	76 44	51.3
62.9	HERNE BAY	77 36	60.2	81 16	54.4
70.9	Birchington	85 42	59.2	90 13	53.7
72.5	WESTGATE	88 02	—	92 21	—
Net time		85 00		88 30	

Note: Bridge slack on all runs at Sittingbourne
*Average speeds from exact chainages.
'L' — 'Enigma' Class, formerly *Lothair*.

LC&DR: Margate–Herne Hill

Run number		1		2	
Train		6.15 pm Margate		10.10 am Westgate	
Engine number		191		54	
Engine type		4-4-0 'M3'		2-4-0 'E'	
Load					
Coaches		'13'		'17½'	
Tons (approx)		175		230	

Distance (miles)		Time (m s)	Speed* (mph)	Time (m s)	Speed* (mph)
0.0	MARGATE	0 00	—		
1.5	Westgate	2 54	—	0 00	—
3.1	Birchington	5 06	44.3	3 44	—
11.1	HERNE BAY	14 08	53.3	14 11	45.8
15.2	Whitstable	18 15	59.2	18 34	55.8
21.9	FAVERSHAM	25 43	53.4	26 35	—
				special stop	
25.9	Teynham	31 24	42.2	38 34	—
29.1	SITTINGBOURNE	35 01	53.9	42 18	52.2
		permanent way slack		permanent way slack	
32.3	Newington	40 25	34.9	47 21	36.0
34.9	Rainham	43 31	51.4	50 33	48.9
37.9	New Brompton	46 50	54.3	53 55	53.4
39.5	CHATHAM	48 42	51.6	55 46	51.9
40.9	Strood	50 32	45.8	57 28	49.4
47.0	Sole Street	60 33	36.7	68 47	32.4

Distance (miles)		Time (m s)	Speed* (mph)	Time (m s)	Speed* (mph)
50.5	Fawkham	64 47	35.4	73 18	33.2
53.4	Farningham Rd	67 30	64.2	75 58	65.2
56.2	Swanley	71 10	45.9	79 20	49.9
59.1	St Mary Cray	74 38	50.2	82 45	51.0
61.9	Bickley	78 04	50.2	86 05	52.3
63.9	Shortlands	80 01	58.5	87 59	60.0
65.2	Beckenham	81 38	48.3	89 27	53.3
66.7	Penge	83 29	48.7	91 12	51.5
68.1	Sydenham Hill	85 54	35.8	93 22	37.4
68.9	Dulwich	86 52	49.8	94 17	52.3
				signal stop	
69.9	HERNE HILL	88 24		97 10	
Schedule time		90 00		90 00	
Net time		86 00		89 00	

'E'—'Europa' Class 2-4-0 formerly *Asia*
*Average speeds from exact chainages

the other two engines of the class *Mermaid* and *Lothair*, in having coupled wheels only 6 ft in diameter.

The last two runs, contrast the work of an 'M3' 4-4-0 with one of the celebrated 'Europa' Class 2-4-0s hauling a tremendous load, for such a small engine, of 230 tons. On the 6.15 am Sunday train from Margate engine No 191 made an excellent run, with a net gain of 3½ minutes on schedule. On this run the driver must have taken his engine round the Rochester curves 'on one wheel' to get a good run at Sole Street bank. The minimum speed was 33½ mph, but this appears to have left the engine somewhat breathless judging from the slowness of the recovery downhill to Fawkham. The 2-4-0 *Asia*, starting from Westgate, had to make a special stop at Faversham and from Sittingbourne her times as tabulated were roughly 7 minutes behind those of No 191.

The subsequent running was astonishingly good. Despite the much heavier load, *Asia* ran neck and neck with the 'M3' as far as Strood—apparently taking the Rochester curves at little less than 50 mph! It was not surprising to see her fall behind to the tune of more than a minute on Sole Street bank, but from being 8½ minutes behind at Fawkham she gain upon the 4-4-0 engine by a full minute between there and Dulwich, and her net time of 89¾ minutes represents a most admirable piece of work.

3. Brighton—Stroudley's years

In November 1869 the Board of the London, Brighton and South Coast Railway received a letter of resignation from their Locomotive Superintendent, J.C. Craven, to take effect from the end of January 1870. He had held the job for twenty years and since his appointment it can be said that he virtually made Brighton Works; he retired from it at the early age of 57 years, not to a life of leisured ease but to an increasingly grim and premature old age. To replace him the Board chose William Stroudley, formerly Locomotive Superintendent of the Highland Railway. To describe the new chief at Brighton as the very opposite, in all respects, to Craven would be considerably wide of the mark. Craven was a very able and successful locomotive engineer as an individual designer, the trouble was that he paid little heed to production problems and any thoughts of standardization were not to be considered, so far as his philosophy went. To a man of Stroudley's neat and tidy mind, not to mention his abilities as an engineer, Brighton Works, when he first arrived there, might well have seemed the nearest thing to complete chaos it was possible to contemplate!

On receiving such an appointment, at such a relatively high salary for the year 1870, Stroudley's thoughts might well have turned to 'making a dash' with a new express passenger design, as a relief from the financial restraints that had been imposed upon him at Inverness. On the contrary, Stroudley's record at Brighton was, throughout his all too brief life, a model of careful perception of the overall needs of the railway. Craven's engines were good in themselves, but the immediate problem was the urgent need for rationalization of the works' layout, so that repair and maintenance work could be organized on a properly efficient basis. In 1870 there were far too many locomotives lying idle in the works awaiting repairs. Stroudley's first requirements for capital investment were not for new rolling stock, but for a complete rearrangement of the works. Although Brighton Railway finances were only beginning to recover from the disastrous year of 1867, the Board met Stroudley's requirements in full. It was significant that a full year passed after his appointment before a single new locomotive was added to the stock. A new design for a main-line 0-6-0 goods engine was worked out in 1870, but the two first engines authorized were held up, priority being given to reconstruction in the works itself. The first Stroudley locomotives for the Brighton Railway were put into traffic in the first weeks of December 1871.

At the time they were the largest goods engines in Great Britain, having six coupled wheels 5 ft in diameter, 17½-in by 26-in cylinders and a very large boiler with a total heating surface of 1,414 sq ft. They lacked one feature of the traditional Stroudley 'look', as it became familiar on so many Brighton engines, in that they had domeless boilers and Adams patent safety valves on the manhole cover on the rearmost ring of the boiler. These did not last long, being apt to seize up and free themselves with a loud and disconcerting bang! The cylinders were made in a single casting, including the steam chest, steam and exhaust branches, and as the valve faces were placed underneath the centres of the cylinders were able to be brought very close together, namely 2 ft 1 in. The inclination of the slide valves was 1 in 16½. The engine framing was of wrought iron, very deep, and of a thickness of 1⅛ in. The cab followed the style that Stroudley had initiated on the Highland Railway on the few locomotives he had modernized. The style was used not only on every tender engine he built subsequently for the Brighton Railway, but on every type introduced by David Jones, his distinguished successor on the Highland. The beautiful Stroudley chimney also made its appearance on this first Brighton design.

From the very outset Stroudley incorporated arrangements for feed-water heating. On these 0-6-0 goods engines part of the exhaust steam from this cylinder was sent into the tender, passing through a set of small pipes running longitudinally in the bottom of the tender and finally up a steam dome into the tank. A stop valve was provided in the blast pipe, worked from the footplate, there was also another in the main exhaust pipe, in order to shut nearly all the blast off the fire when shunting; this was to avoid waste of steam at the safety valves, and also to warm the water in the tender. By this means the feed water was usually heated to boiling point. The salient feature of this apparatus, externally, was the so-called 'steam dome', which took the form of a projection about three-quarters the diameter of the chimney extending upwards to almost the height of the cab. The brakes were of the most primitive description— nothing at all on the engine and a hand brake, with wooden brake blocks, on the tender. In emergency, of course, the driver could always put the engine into reverse and apply backward steam.

A month's running was enough to satisfy Stroudley of the effectiveness of the design and as early as 24 January he received authority to invite tenders for twelve engines of the class, which was designated 'C'. The reorganization work at Brighton was evidently not considered to be sufficiently far advanced for the construction to be undertaken in the

Company's own shops. The tender received from Kitson & Co was accepted, with the promise of delivery of the first engine in October 1872. Then there would be two per month, completing the order in April 1873. In the event, however, the contract fell very much into arrears, so much so that Stroudley received authority to build a further six engines of the class at Brighton. These were completed and in traffic before even the first engine was delivered from Kitson. The last of Kitson-built locomotives was not received until November 1874, more than a year and six months late! By that time three more new Stroudley designs had been introduced, all built in the reorganized works at Brighton.

Two of these new designs came as early as 1872. Among the many different varieties of six-wheeled passenger engines built by Craven was a batch of 2-2-2s contracted to Robert Stephenson & Co in 1864 which, unusually for the Brighton at that time, consisted of no less than twelve engines. Then, it would seem, someone realized the rashness of letting Craven have so many engines of one class; for Stephenson, faced with an urgent order from the Egyptian State Railways, arranged to buy four of these 2-2-2s back again! Not withstanding this the eight survivors on the Brighton Railway proved unusually good engines, and when Stroudley was considering new power for the crack 'stockbrokers express' leaving Brighton at 8.45 am non-stop to London Bridge he decided to rebuild one of these Craven 2-2-2s of 1864 as a 2-4-0. In addition to modifying the frames, by welding on the new rear portion including the horn-guides for the second pair of coupled wheels, the cylinders were new—17-in diameter by 24-in stroke instead of 16 in by 22 in.

There was a Stroudley boiler, domeless as on the first two 0-6-0 goods engines No 84 and No 85, and the 'Inverness' cab. The rebuild was so extensive that nothing had remained of the original engine except part of the frames, one pair of driving wheels and the leading wheels. This remarkable rebuild, No 204, was completed at Brighton in July 1872, and represented virtually Stroudley's first design for express passenger traffic.

Four months later two more 2-4-0s of identical design were built new at Brighton, to be followed a month later by the rebuilding of a further Craven single, No 198, on the same lines as No 204. By that time Stroudley had begun the practice of naming the passenger engines and the new 2-4-0s were distinguished thus:

Built	Number	Name	
July	204	*Westminster*	Rebuilt from 2-2-2
November	201	*Belgravia*	
November	202	*Goodwood*	
December	205	*Kensington*	Rebuilt from 2-2-2 No 198

These graceful engines were adorned in the new livery that Stroudley had brought south from the Highland Railway. The first Brighton engine that had carried it was No 173, one of a pair of 2-2-2s built in 1864 specially for the Hastings to London traffic which were notable as the first engines Craven ever built with cabs. When No 173 was sent up to London Bridge for the Directors to inspect the proposed new livery, however, the engine had been 'Stroudleyised' to some extent by having the open driving-wheel

Stroudley 'Terrier' 0-6-0 No 41 Piccadilly, built in June 1877. (National Railway Museum — F. Burtt.)

Left *One of the 'E1' Class goods tank engines, No 99* Bordeaux, *built in December 1874. (National Railway Museum — F. Burtt.)*

Left *Stroudley 'Terrier' 0-6-0 No 81* Beulah, *built in July 1880. (National Railway Museum — F. Burtt.)*

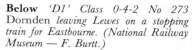

Below *'D1' Class 0-4-2 No 273* Dornden *leaving Lewes on a stopping train for Eastbourne. (National Railway Museum — F. Burtt.)*

splashers covered in, side sheets added to the cab and the functional stove-pipe chimney replaced by the designer's own shapely type, as used on the prototype 0-6-0 goods engines No 84 and No 85. Although No 173 was much admired and approved she remained unnamed, whereas her sister engine, No 172, was named *Chichester*.

By the late autumn of 1872 Brighton Works was beginning to get into its stride with new locomotive construction, and early in September the first of the celebrated 'A' Class 0-6-0 tank engines took the road. The first batch consisted of six engines, completed between 9 September and November, although the last one did not actually go into traffic until 4 December. They were named as follows, in order of completion:

Number	Name
72	*Fenchurch*
71	*Wapping*
73	*Deptford*
74	*Shadwell*
75	*Blackwall*
70	*Poplar*

One could hardly imagine a set of engine names as inappropriate as the foregoing, until some research was conducted as to how the first six examples of that famous class were first utilized. The Thames Tunnel was an ambitious though ill-starred enterprise. Engineered by Marc Isambard Brunel, work began in 1825 but financial difficulties and inrushings of water so impeded progress that it was not until March 1843 that the tunnel was finished. It was not originally a railway tunnel, but it was proved so far from a commercial success that after twenty years of operation the East London Railway bought it up at a rock-bottom price, with a view to laying a railway in its depths. The first section of this involved a connection from the Brighton Railway at New Cross, having stations at Surrey Docks and Rotherhithe, and then through the tunnel itself to a temporary terminus on the north bank at Wapping. This section was opened in 1871, and it was not until 1876 that the extension to the Great Eastern Railway, at Bishopsgate was opened.

By the time the first batch of the 'A' Class engines were in traffic the Brighton Railway was running 43 trains each way between New Cross and Wapping, in addition to eighteen each way between Wapping and Old Kent Road. Although the names chosen for the first six engines could all be readily associated with the Thames Tunnel district only Wapping itself was served by Brighton passenger trains, though Shadwell was afterwards included on the Bishopsgate extension and Deptford was a 'goods only' spur from

the New Cross purlieus with no direct connection with the East London line. Strangest of all were the three names having no association, either present or forecast; *Fenchurch, Poplar* and *Blackwall*. To see engines with these names in large gilt letters, immaculately burnished, puffing their way amid the grime of the Thames Tunnel route would have been a sight indeed in days long before smokeless zones! Technically, these splendid little engines had 13-in by 20-in cylinders, coupled wheels 4 ft in diameter, a total heating surface of 528 sq ft, a grate area 10.3 sq ft and boiler pressure 140 psi. The details can be studied from the accompanying drawing, while the diminutive proportions can be appreciated from the photographs.

At first the original six 'A' Class engines, quickly nicknamed the 'Terriers', were confined to the East London line, although the frequency of the service must have kept them busily engaged on their own particular pitch. Then another six were added to the stud in 1874 and a further ten in 1875. Their principal duties, on which they became celebrated throughout the locomotive world, were on the inner suburban runs round the South London line between Victoria and London Bridge via Peckham Rye. Contemporary accounts suggest that this line, at any rate that between Balham Junction and Old Kent Road, was not only laid with a very light section of wrought iron rail, but was in poor condition and so a tank engine weighing no more than 24 tons was very acceptable on that account. But apart from that these little engines did their work supremely well. With train loads of about 100 tons, the schedule for the 8¾ mile journey from London Bridge to Victoria, including ten intermediate station stops, was 35 minutes—very smart work, seeing that the longest station to station run was 1½ miles, and the average no more than 0.8 mile.

One of the most noteworthy features of William Stroudley's engine designing was that each new class as it emerged from Brighton Works was right 'from the word go', to use a modern colloquialism. The 'A' Class 'Terriers' set the pattern for this, with the design eventually multiplied up to fifty engines and the 'D' Class 0-4-2 tanks introduced in the following year, 1873, provided a still more striking example. In total contrast to Craven's practice the new tank engines were conceived as a general-utility passenger type for use everywhere except in the innermost London suburban areas. They reached a grand total of 125 by the year 1887. By that time there were 46 of them stationed at Battersea, 36 at New Cross and fourteen at Brighton. The remainder were distributed between eight outer suburban and country stations, of which the most, eight, were at Horsham. They had Stroudley's standard 17-in by 24-in cylinders, coupled wheels of 5-ft 6-in diameter and a working steam pressure of 140 psi. The water capacity of the tanks was 860 gallons and the coal capacity 1¾ tons. The weight in working order was 38½ tons. They were all named in the traditional Stroudley style with titles varying from *Sydenham*, the first of the class, No 1 of the LB&SCR, to some of the most remote villages on the line.

In his memorable paper read before The Institution of Civil Engineers in 1885 Stroudley emphasized the geographical difficulties of working the line, and his words may well have been used as a précis of a day's work with one of the 'D' Class tank engines, particularly of those stationed at Battersea and New Cross. He wrote: 'This railway system offers some peculiarities, when compared with its neighbours, in having no less than ninety miles within the metropolitan area, fifteen of these having three or four lines of rails. Some of the lines have very heavy gradients, and curves as small as 6½ and 7 chains radius, there are 94 junctions, and twenty terminal stations, and from some of the latter, the line rises with gradients of from 1 in 64 to 1 in 80. These features, together with a crowded passenger traffic moving at irregular intervals, over about twenty hours out of the 24, cause the working to be very difficult. Some of the engines are attached to as many as sixteen trains in one day; the loss of time in running on and off, and in standing waiting, tending to increase the cost of working, as compared with those railways having more continuous lines.'

On the outer suburban and country runs the 'D' tanks knocked up some considerable and varied mileages, particularly after the introduction of the eight-hour day when many of the engines would be triple-manned. As an example, one of the Dorking turns can be taken. The first set of men booked on shed at 6.15 am ready to take the 7 am Dorking to London Bridge. Then the day's work continued:

London Bridge to Horsham
Horsham to Brighton
Brighton to Victoria (via Horsham)
Victoria to Sutton, with Victoria portion of
    Portsmouth train
Sutton to Epsom (light engine)
Epsom to Victoria
Victoria to Dorking (10.58 pm departure)
Shunt empty train, clean fire, leave ready for men
    booking on 6.15 am next morning

Apart from shunting this represented 202 miles of main-line running, nearly as much as the top-line express engines in the early 1900s doing Brighton and London and back twice in one day.

To enthusiasts of today the 'yellow-engine' era of the Brighton Railway may well be epitomized by the 'Gladstone' type of 0-4-2 locomotive gliding in unhurried Victorian elegance down the main line towards the south coast. But so far as the locomotive works at Brighton was concerned, before Stroudley had begun anything resembling 'quantity production' of express passenger locomotives (as exemplified by the 'G' Class single wheelers) in 1880, he had all fifty of the 'A' Class 'Terrier' 0-6-0s and 66 of the 'D' Class 0-4-2 tanks at work, not to mention 56 of the larger 'E' Class mixed traffic 0-6-0 tanks which were a smaller wheeled equivalent of 'D' Class. These

latter, although named in the style of the passenger engines, were painted 'goods green', nevertheless a beautiful rich deep colour. When further 'E' Class engines were needed for duties that included some passenger workings a batch of these were painted in the full splendour of the passenger livery. Nearly all the 'E' Class engines were named after foreign destinations associated, vaguely sometimes, with the connections made via Newhaven and Dieppe, although the engines themselves seem to have spent much of their time in shunting and in short distance hauls between the London goods yards. In Stroudley's own time Class 'E' was multiplied to a total of 72, the last addition being twelve locomotives built in 1883. A further six were added after his death and these had English names.

Reverting to the 'D' Class, historians who have specialized in Stroudley's work have more than once referred to these splendid little tank engines as the 'mainstay of the line' and indeed, while the bulk of them were shedded at Battersea, New Cross and Brighton, their duties took them so far afield that at the end of the nineteenth century they might well have appeared ubiquitous. Nevertheless on the longer distance goods runs, particularly on the through workings to and from Newhaven Harbour for Continental traffic, a tender engine version was thought desirable to provide for greater coal and water capacity. Thus Class 'D2' was evolved, with wheels, cylinders and motion interchangeable with the 'D' 0-4-2 tanks, but a slightly longer firebox. At first only eight engines were built of this new class, spread out over eighteen months of construction. They were painted in the passenger livery, but owing

to the very small coupled-wheel splasher the Continental names chosen for them had to be appropriately short, namely *Lyons, Caen, Turin, Milan, Nice, Genoa, Naples, Venice.* The first two, completed in 1876-77 were shedded at Brighton while, no doubt, the general working of the new type of tender engine was being closely observed. Afterwards two were based at New Cross, three at Battersea and the rest of the eight at Brighton. They were very successful engines and did excellent work on the 'Grande Vitesse' express goods between London and Newhaven Harbour.

By the time Class 'D2' was introduced Stroudley had begun experimenting with new express passenger engines. The outside-framed 2-4-0s of 1872 were doing good work on the 'crack' Brighton business expresses, but experience with the first of the 'D' Class 0-4-2 tanks, and the layout of their machinery, had suggested that the same principles might be used on a larger engine. So, in December 1874, a prototype 2-2-2 was turned out from Brighton Works, having driving wheels of 6-ft 9-in diameter and the standard 17-in by 24-in cylinders. The boiler was large, although carrying a pressure no greater than the 140 psi used hitherto. The most obvious change was that the engine was carried on inside bearings throughout, though the tender was outside framed. The new 2-2-2 was named *Grosvenor*, and it was destined to play an unusually large part in publicising Stroudley's prowess. This engine was chosen to work the Brighton trains at the Newark brake trials in 1875 and the immaculate appearance of the locomotive and the performance of the brake itself created a profound impression. Nevertheless, it would seem

Left *Stroudley's 6 ft 9 in 2-2-2* Grosvenor *on a Portsmouth express, passing Wandsworth Common. (H. Gordon Tidey.)*

Right *'G' Class 2-2-2 No 341* Parkhurst *on a London express at Portsmouth Harbour Station. (The late W. J. Reynolds.)*

that Stroudley had not yet finished with the hitherto-conventional engine frame layout, for in November 1875 he built two more outside-framed 2-4-0s of virtually identical design to those of 1872, which were named *Carisbrooke* and *Freshwater*. The two new engines differed from the earlier 2-4-0s in having the larger boiler fitted to the *Grosvenor*.

It is significant of the way the Craven express-passenger engines fulfilled requirements in the earlier years of Stroudley's time at Brighton that so little development took place. *Grosvenor* can be seen as no more than a prototype, while the second single-wheeler, the *Abergavenny* turned out in January 1877, seemed a retrograde step in having cylinders no more than 16-in by 22-in, a smaller boiler and driving wheels of 6-ft 6-in diameter. All the same, this little engine was soon seen as a pet of the Locomotive Department, being allocated to the prestigious night Continental boat train from London Bridge to Newhaven Harbour and no other train. The inward service was tidal, and to ensure that the engine was always available the driver was paid by contract, independently of the hours worked. He paid the fireman and the cleaners, for whatever the time of day or night the up tidal boat train was required its engine, always the *Abergavenny*, had to be spotless! Her daily mileage, no more than 56.6 each way, would hardly have satisfied latter-day statisticians who are always aiming to get ever more daily mileage out of each and every engine.

By the time the *Abergavenny* was embarked upon her nightly run to Newhaven it would seem as if Stroudley felt he could no longer delay the introduction of new main-line express passenger engines, in bulk, to replace the heterogenous collection of 2-2-2s and 2-4-0s left behind by Craven. So far he had produced six new 2-4-0s and two single-wheelers, but in the event the tender-engine version of his 'D' Class 0-4-2 tanks came to point the way to his future standard. In October 1878, six months after completion of the first eight of the mixed traffic 'D2' Class 0-4-2s, the first express passenger 0-4-2, Class 'D3', was built at Brighton. This was engine No 208, named *Richmond*. It had 6-ft 6-in coupled wheels, against 5 ft 6 in on Class 'D2', cylinders 17¼ in by 26 in and as previously a boiler pressure of 140 psi. The larger engine had a total engine wheelbase of only one inch longer than Class 'D2'. Only one engine was built at first, and it was subject to some criticism in the technical press of the day over the use of such large leading wheels. *Richmond* remained the only one of its class for nine months, while exhaustive trials were carried out, but then five more were built in 1879-80 and named *Devonshire, Cornwall, Beaconsfield, Hartington* and *Norfolk*.

These engines replaced the outside-framed 2-4-0s

on the most important Brighton-London expresses, and quickly dispelled any fears that they might have been unsteady in their riding from the presence of their large leading wheels. It is certainly true that they did not have to run very fast, because the fastest trains at the time of their introduction were allowed 70 minutes non-stop between London Bridge and Brighton, 50¾ miles. But Stroudley insisted upon relatively high uphill speeds to avoid any high-speed running on the descending gradients. While the 'D3' Class were giving an excellent account of themselves on the crack Brighton expresses, the works was embarked upon the largest-yet programme of express passenger engine building with a new range of 2-2-2 singles. It could be said that the new 'G' Class was a blend of the features of the prototypes *Grosvenor* and *Abergavenny*, having the larger cylinders of the former engine and a boiler similar to the latter. The new engines formed part of a class of 23, numbered consecutively from 327 to 350, and turned out between December 1880 and April 1882. They were the first Brighton class all to be equipped with the new standard inside-framed tender, though I believe the last three of the 'D3' Class, built in 1880, also had them.

These rather ungainly-looking tenders were a further manifestation of Stroudley's drive for standardization. The wheels were interchangeable with the carrying wheels of the tank and express engines. His views was that when the tyres had worn below a certain thickness on the engine the wheels could be transferred to the tender, as they could be run with safety thus when it would not be judicious to use them under the engine. All the same it seemed a questionable argument, seeing that there were so relatively few of the inside-framed tenders in use compared to the carrying wheels of the same diameter under so many tank engines. There was also the disadvantage that the tender springs were less accessible. It was significant that the practice was immediately dropped by Stroudley's successor. Nevertheless by the time the 'G' Class were issuing from Brighton Works in ever increasing numbers, with their attractive names and their gorgeous livery, the prestige of the railway itself, and their designer, was soaring ace-high among the locomotive enthusiasts of the day, though not among the bulk of the passengers who used the railway. Taken all round, the advertised train services were slow, even by the standards of the 1880s and the punctuality, except in the case of a very few business trains, was virtually non-existent.

It is remarkable that Stroudley should have designed a single-wheeler of such modest proportions as the 'G' Class, primarily for a route involving such awkward gradients as the Portsmouth line. For

The predecessor of the 'Gladstone' Class, the 'D3' engine No 210 Cornwall *built 1879. (The late W.J. Reynolds.)*

'G' Class 2-2-2 No 336 Edinburgh. *(The late W.J. Reynolds.)*

'G' Class 2-2-2 No 334 Petworth, *a photograph showing the 'yellow' livery to perfection. (F.M. Gates.)*

Engine No 779 Sandown *of the 'Gladstone' Class. It was built in May 1890 and withdrawn in 1929. (E.J. Bedford.)*

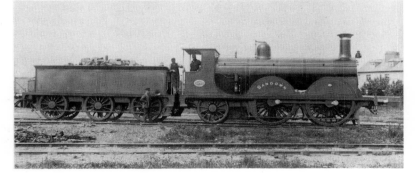

although they were originally divided between New Cross, Battersea, Brighton and Portsmouth sheds, once the 'Gladstone' Class 0-4-2s were introduced more of the singles were moved to Fratton. The best train was the 4.56 pm from London Bridge booked to run the 70.8 miles to Chichester non-stop in 94 minutes. This not very exciting average of 45 mph was made usually with a very light load, not more than nine or ten six-wheeled carriages. In such running conditions even the stiff gradients over the North Downs south of Dorking would not have been much of a handicap. It was clear from certain records of coal consumption quoted by Stroudley and other observers that these engines were mostly being run under very easy steam, indeed that was how they were designed to be driven.

Construction of the 'G' Class singles was still in progress at Brighton when Stroudley's masterpiece in engine designing appeared, the famous 0-4-2 No 214 *Gladstone*, in December 1882. It was an enlarged version of Class 'D3', with a larger boiler and cylinders 18¼ in by 26 in. They were very powerful engines for their day, and like their predecessors they were designed to be driven on a light rein and mini-

mum coal consumption. Like most of Stroudley's engines they were preceded by a single prototype. The pioneer engine entered service in mid-January 1883 and was not followed by any further examples until December of that year, and then by only three more. Another two followed in October 1885, and then, in December 1887 construction started in a relatively big way for the Brighton Railway. By the end of 1889 there were 26 of them in service. Their outstanding feature, initiated on the 'D3' Class in the large leading wheels, was explained by Stroudley personally in his paper read before the Institution of Civil Engineers in 1885, thus:

'By placing the coupled wheels forward, where the greatest weight is, the hinder part of the engine may have small wheels, the base be shortened, and the use of heavy cast-iron weights at the back of the engine be dispensed with. It is found that an engine runs much more smoothly when the centre of gravity is kept well forward. The large leading wheels pass over the points, crossings, etc very easily; causing less disturbance than small ones. They pass round curves without shock or oscillation, which is no doubt owing to the small weight upon the trailing wheels, as it is the trailing wheels that have the most influence in forcing the leading flanges up to the outside of a curve'.

None of Stroudley's contemporary engineers, however, followed his precepts, and it was probably because the speeds were so relatively slow that the 'Gladstones' ran so sweetly. These engines were certainly very popular with their drivers and the coal consumption was always notably low, even with the prestigious 8.45 am up from Brighton to London Bridge, which was accelerated to a 65 minute run. Unlike the Portsmouth trains worked by the 'G' Class single-wheelers they always loaded very heavily and were all first class too. The usual load, other than on Saturdays, was one of nineteen vehicles. With the introduction of the 'Gladstones' the Brighton Railway touched the heights of popularity with the locomotive enthusiast fraternity, though with many of that ilk the attraction, I fear, stemmed more from the colour of the engines and their usually spotless turn-out than from their performance on the line. Stroudley's engineering practice was certainly immaculate and the standards of workmanship faultless, but he was working to the rather mediocre demands of the traffic department.

The cab view of the Gladstone. *(Ivo Peters.)*

'Gladstone' Class 0-4-2 engines

Number	Name	Date built at Brighton Works
214	*Gladstone*	1882
215	*Salisbury*	1883
216	*Granville*	1883

Engine No 195 Cardew *which was reserved for exclusive use on the night boat train to and from Newhaven Harbour. (E. J. Bedford.)*

Number	Name	Date built at Brighton Works
217	*Northcote*	1883
218	*Beaconsfield*	1885
219	*Cleveland*	1885
220	*Hampden*	1887
200	*Beresford*	1887
199	*Samuel Laing*	1887
198	*Sheffield*	1887
197	*Jonas Levy*	1888
196	*Ralph L. Lopes*	1888
195	*Cardew*	1888
194	*Bickersteth*	1888
193	*Freemantle*	1888
192	*Jacomb Hood*	1888
191	*Gordon-Lennox*	1888
190	*Arthur Otway*	1888
189	*Edward Blount*	1889
188	*Allen Sarle*	1889
187	*Philip Rose*	1889
186	*De La Warr*	1889
185	*George A. Wallis*	1889
184	*Carew D. Gilbert*	1889
183	*Eastbourne*	1889
182	*Hastings*	1889
181	*Croydon*	1890
180	*Arundel*	1890
179	*Sandown*	1890
178	*Leatherhead*	1890
177	*Southsea*	1890

Number	Name	Date built at Brighton works
176	*Pevensey*	1890
175	*Hayling*	1890
174	*Fratton*	1890
173	*Cottesloe*	1891
172	*Littlehampton*	1891

His death at the tragically early age of 56, while attending trials of one of his latest express locomotives the *Edward Blount*, in France, in December 1889, poses a multitude of questions. For one thing one can be sure his work was not completed with the 'Gladstone' engines. While they were more than adequate for any main-line duty that existed at the time of his death, and indeed a further ten of the class were built by his successor in 1890-91, things were very much on the change on the Brighton Railway in the 1890s. The parochialism that had prevailed in railway travelling habits hitherto had begun to wear slightly thin after the first 'Race to the North' in 1888, and whispers of the speeds run on the north-going lines began to percolate into the precincts of London Bridge and Victoria. But until the far more exciting 'Race to Aberdeen' in 1895, when *The Times* ran a lengthy correspondence under the heading 'The Crawl to the South', did passengers by the Brighton line begin to wake up to the realization that they had been getting a very poor return for their money. But for his untimely death Stroudley would almost certainly have still been in office at the turn of the century, and it would have been intriguing to see how he would have coped. Should we have had a 'Super Gladstone'?

4. The Adams era on the South Western

Instances of sons succeeding fathers in the management of the locomotive department of British railways have not been many, and they have not been notably successful. How W.G. Beattie's career would have developed on the South Western, had his health not given way, we are not to know. He succeeded to the job on the death of his father in 1871 and he had to retire only six years later. The appointment of a successor created something of a surprise in railway circles. Although it was a common enough practice for engineers to move from one railway to another in search of promotion, William Adams came from the Great Eastern which was a larger concern than the London and South Western, albeit not then so profitable. Furthermore the railways south of the Thames were then not famed for the generosity of the salaries they paid to their engineering staff. However be that as it may, the South Western got Adams, and ultimately some very fine locomotives.

In taking over from Beattie however he was saddled with a score of newly-built 'lame-ducks'. In 1876 an order was placed with Sharp, Stewart & Co for twenty large outside-cylinder 4-4-0s, which would have been elegantly proportioned had they not had the ugly rectangular splasher over the coupled wheels that had marked, perhaps disfigured, locomotives of earlier L&SWR designs built since he had succeeded his father. If he had done nothing more than leave his imprint on the splashers all would have been well, but in working out a design for a much more powerful express passenger locomotive a number of fundamental mistakes were made which rendered the engines sadly unreliable in service. To crown all, in contrast to Stroudley's careful work on the Brighton, the contractors were passed a first order for twenty of the new and untried engines. The first problem was that they would not steam. While the customary measures, uneconomic as they had to be, and tinkering with the draughting made some slight improvement, the faulty design of the pistons crippled their performance as a whole, and gave Adams much anxiety in the first months on taking over his new command.

There was another new class introduced during W.G. Beattie's brief stay as chief at Nine Elms, and that was an equal curiosity. In 1875 an order was placed with Beyer, Peacock & Co for six of their Metropolitan-type 4-4-0 tank engines, as supplied to the Metropolitan and District Railways. Whether the London and South Western Railway ever contemplated any extensions or running powers over the London underground lines is not clear, but far from use of the new tank engines on suburban workings they were not fitted with condensing equipment, and they were allocated at almost the furthest part of the line from Waterloo, the remote section circumventing the northern heights of Dartmoor between Exeter and Plymouth! While these engines had all the technical features that made their Metropolitan predecessors so reliable and long lasting, the six 'Plymouth tanks', as they became known on the South Western, were provided with cabs, no doubt with the humane idea of affording some shelter from the wind and rain of Dartmoor.

In all the many illustrated accounts of the Beyer, Peacock & Co 4-4-0 Metropolitan tank engines, whether built for their own line, for the District or for the main-line companies that adopted the design in limited numbers for their own use, I have never been able to find any reference to the coal-carrying capacity of their bunkers. They were accommodated athwart the rear-end buffer beam and looked very

One of W.G. Beattie's short-lived 4-4-0 engines of 1876, here seen numbered in the duplicate list. (British Railways.)

small. No doubt they were large enough for many journeys round the Inner Circle in London; but on the South Western they were expected to make a main-line journey of some 60 miles, half of which involved hard pulling on very steep gradients. This was not all. The humane sentiments which led to the fitting of the cabs to these engines were hardly appreciated at the running sheds when the replenishing of those coal bunkers was in progress, for the backsheets of those cabs were flush with the buffer beam and coaling up had to be done from inside the cab! The 'Plymouth tanks' were not the most popular of W. G. Beattie's engines. However, there is a silver lining to every cloud, and in his book *Four Main Lines*, published 35 years ago, Hamilton Ellis has a charming painting of one of these engines, titled *Victoria Glory*, pounding up the hardest part on the eastbound ascent from Plymouth with a six-coach train of assorted four-wheelers, while a characteristic family group watch enraptured at the lineside. But the 'Plymouth tanks' did not stay long in such idyllic surroundings, they were demoted, on to far less prestigious duties and finished their days in comparative obscurity.

The relatively short stay of William Adams on the Great Eastern Railway had not been particularly distinguished, particularly because he had previously produced engines of quite monumental quality in his 4-4-0 outside-cylinder tanks for the North London Railway. His 6-ft 1-in express goods 4-4-0s, built variously by Dübs and Hawthorn, gave little satisfaction, while a design prepared in the last year of his superintendence at Stratford and delivered from Neilson after he had left for the London and South Western, that could have been a milestone in the history of the development of British locomotive practice proved an almost complete 'flop'. These

were the fifteen engines of the 'Mogul' type, 2-6-0, numbered 527 to 541. They were dimensionally very powerful engines, having 19-in by 26-in cylinders and coupled wheels of no more than 4-ft 10-in diameter, but despite having a relatively large boiler they would not steam. The fact of their being extremely heavy on coal and oil points to something badly wrong with the valve gear, but instead of trying to correct it Adams' successor on the Great Eastern scrapped all fifteen engines after no more than eight years' work.

Adams' first design for the London and South Western was also for main-line mixed-traffic duties and they were being built by Beyer, Peacock & Co at the same time that Neilson were turning out his ill-starred 'Moguls' for the Great Eastern. The '380' Class for the South Western, of which there were twelve in all, were 4-4-0s having coupled wheels of 5-ft 7-in diameter, cylinders 18 in by 24 in and a boiler pressure of 140 psi. They had the stove-pipe chimneys initiated by Adams while on the Great Eastern, but an innovation were their solid-disc bogie wheels of no more than 2-ft 6-in diameter, which led to their being nicknamed the 'Steam rollers'. They had a design feature used by Adams on his Great Eastern engines, namely the single bar type of cross-head used on all his subsequent types of South Western engines. The 'Steam rollers' proved excellent engines. At first they worked fast goods trains between London and Southampton, and then, as the duties grew more onerous they were moved to transfer goods working between the Midland yards at Cricklewood and the South Western at Battersea. The class was due for withdrawal in 1914, but owing to the war emergency only four were scrapped then. The remaining eight lasted until 1924-25.

Contemporary with the first Adams 4-4-0s on the L&SWR were his suburban tanks, also built by Beyer, Peacock & Co, of which there were twelve. These will inevitably be contrasted with the celebrated engines of the same type that Adams built for the North London Railway at Bow Works in 1868,

One of the first Adams 4-4-2 tank engines of 1882 built by Beyer, Peacock & Co, in original condition. (British Railways.)

and which remained a standard design on that line long after its incorporation in to the LMS. The first South Western 4-4-0 tanks differed in many important details. The outside cylinders were in a more conventional place, below the running plate, and the bogie had the disc-type wheels of only 2-ft 6-in diameter as on the 4-4-0 main-line mixed traffic engines. These South Western tanks had considerably less tractive power than their North London predecessors, in having only 140 psi working pressure against 160 psi, though the same sized cylinders, 18 in by 24 in. These engines originally suffered from the same disadvantage as the Beyer, Peacock 4-4-0s of the Metropolitan type introduced by W.G. Beattie, in having insufficient coal and water capacity. What was admirable for the North London was no good for the South Western, and after no more than four years of service a start was made upon converting these engines to the 4-4-2 type, to provide for extra coal and water capacity. The conversion was completed by 1886, by which time the engines had coal bunker space for 3 tons and the water capacity was increased to 1,650 gallons.

Both tender and tank engine varieties of these first Adams' designs on the L&SWR had the distinctive type of four-wheeled bogie which he first introduced on the North London Railway. There were some variations in detail between the earliest and later standard versions, but the design as finalized and used on the most celebrated of Adams' express passenger 4-4-0s is shown in the accompanying drawing. The original bogie wheelbase used on the North London 4-4-0 tank engines was 6 ft but as

developed, and used on the Great Eastern, it was 7 ft. This latter dimension was retained on all his London and South Western bogie engines and imparted to them an elegant striding effect. So far as I can trace however, although the Adams' bogie came to be used on a number of different British railways, the South Western was the only one that used the extreme length of the 7-ft wheelbase. When the Brighton began building 4-4-0 express passenger locomotives after Stroudley died, and they adopted the Adams' bogie, the wheelbase was altered to 6 ft.

In December 1880 there was inaugurated the first series of Adams' justly celebrated express passenger 4-4-0s, with 6-ft 7-in coupled wheels, known as the '135' Class. While generally having the look of the 'Steam rollers', they had a more comely outline due to the more central position of the dome and the use of conventional-style bogie wheels, spoked, at 3-ft 4-in diameter. As in the case of the 'Steam rollers' the cylinders were 18 in by 24 in and working pressure 140 psi. The engines were very strongly built and gave excellent service. At that time nothing much was expected from them in the way of spectacular running, but their reliability was unquestioned. In this respect the contrast to W.G. Beattie's engines was extraordinary. The next development came in 1883 with the '445' Class, having 7-ft 1-in coupled wheels, the same-sized cylinders, and working at a pressure of 160 psi. They were fine-looking engines and were followed by the '460' series, very similar in having 6-ft 7-in instead of 7-ft 1-in coupled wheels. The '18-in' express passenger 4-4-0s could be summarised thus:

Class	Date	Number built	Builder	Wheel diameter (ft in)	
'135'	1880	12	Beyer, Peacock & Co	6	7
'445'	1883	12	Stephenson	7	1
'460'	1884	10	Stephenson	6	7
		10	Neilsons		

In 1887 in celebration of the Golden Jubilee of Queen Victoria's reign an engineering exhibition was organized in Newcastle, in which eminent local firms participated. Apparently Robert Stephenson & Co were so proud of their part in building the '445' and the '460' Class for the London and South Western Railway that at their own expense they built a further engine of the latter class for exhibition, in 1887, and were rewarded by its gaining a gold medal. This engine, which was allocated the L&SWR running number 526, was afterwards taken into stock and ran for forty years on the line.

While the initial batch of outside-cylinder tank engines introduced in 1879 were passing what could be called their 'teething troubles', leading to their conversion to the 4-4-2 type, Adams produced a modified design with 17½-in by 24-in cylinders, normal spoked bogie wheels and boiler pressure that was later increased to 160 psi. Beginning in 1882 with a first batch of twelve by Beyer, Peacock & Co, the design was a great success, totalling up to 71 engines by 1885. The successive batches were built by Stephenson, Dübs, Neilson, Stephenson again, and the final ten by Dübs. When new most of them were in the London or in the outer residential area, and they did consistently good work. After Adams

Above left *One of the last of the Adams 4-4-2 tanks built by Dubs & Co, as rebuilt by Dugald Drummond. (Rail Archive Stephenson.)*

Right *Adams' bogie. (W.F. Pettigrew and A.F. Ravenshear.)*

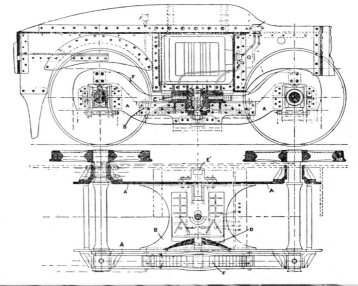

Below *Adams '445' Class 7 ft 4-4-0 express passenger engine, modified with Drummond chimney. (Rail Archive Stephenson.)*

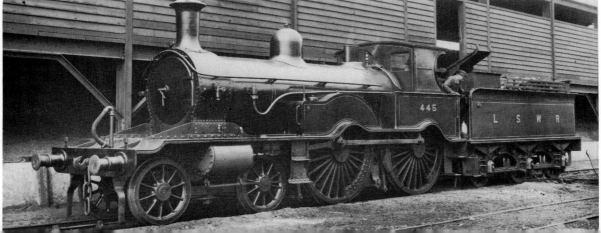

changed from the 4-4-2 to the 0-4-4 type for his local tank engines the older units gradually moved to country locations with no diminution in their usefulness. I observed engines of this class on the branch from Axminster to Lyme Regis doing good work nearly fifty years after their first construction.

The South Western was always considered to be a 'passenger line'. Although there were a number of purely freight hauls, such as locomotive coal from the Great Western to Southampton and Bournemouth, the South Western's own traffic was largely agricultural and consisted of trains that came within 'mixed' categories and required handling more expeditiously than the slow pick-up goods. In the London area there was, in Victorian times, a great amount of exchange traffic to and from the South Western, particularly with the Midland Railway in locomotive coal from the Cricklewood yards, and the joint lines running through West London to the junctions south of Battersea were teeming with goods traffic at night. In 1887 Adams introduced a sturdy straightforward 0-6-0 goods tender engine for this traffic with 17½-in by 26-in cylinders and 5-ft 1-in wheels. The first twelve were built by Neilson and after they had proved themselves another 58 were added to the stock between March 1883 and February 1886. Until that time they were the only inside-cylinder engines that Adams had built. The entire class of seventy engines all came from Neilson. These engines came to have a notable war record from 1916 onwards which is mentioned in a later chapter of this book, but that was not all—eighteen of them survived not one, but *two* world wars, and from 1948 for a few years onwards bore the name 'British Railways' on their tenders.

Having provided power for the slower and heavier categories of goods traffic in the seventy 0-6-0 tender engines of the '395' Class, Adams next turned his attention to mixed traffic, in a manner notably different from his previous practice, in 1887. Whereas on the Great Eastern he had used a medium-wheeled 4-4-0, then his unsuccessful essay into the 'Mogul' type, and followed with his initial South Western design of 4-4-0, the 'Steam rollers', for his next and highly successful venture one could say that he might have looked over his shoulder and studied what his neighbour on the Brighton was doing. By the year 1887 Stroudley had far advanced from his initial adaptation of the 'D' Class 0-4-2 tank engine into a main-line 0-4-2 tender engine for mixed traffic; but while it could well be understood that Adams had no intention of abandoning the 4-4-0 type, guided by his beautifully-designed leading bogie, for the fastest express work, it was another matter for mixed traffic. At the same time a new and powerful influence was coming upon the scene at Nine Elms. In 1886 the

Board of the L&SWR had appointed W.F. Pettigrew, from the Great Eastern Railway, as Works Manager. At Stratford he had served under Adams himself, Bromley, and T.W. Worsdell, while attaining a high degree of professional eminence by his contributions to learned societies.

The presence of Pettigrew at Nine Elms from 1886 onwards can, therefore, be roughly indicative of the change of policy of the locomotive department, as witness the abandonment of outside cylinders for all except the high-speed express passenger locomotives, and the resumption of new construction at the works. The building of the first 0-4-2 mixed traffic engine, No 527, at Nine Elms in May 1887 was thus something of an event on the London and South Western Railway. Although the wheel arrangement was the same the new Adams engine had nothing of Stroudley in its external appearance. Engine No 527 remained a prototype for five months and then she was followed by nine more engines that were identical except that the trailing wheels had springs inside the frames. The 'A12' Class of 0-4-2s, popularly known as the 'Jubilees', differed in the important respect of their rear framing from their Brighton counterparts. Adams used outside frames to provide maximum space between the trailing wheels for the firebox. Except in this one detail of the positioning of the trailing axle springs the 'Jubilees' were accepted at once, and 29 more engines of the class were built at Nine Elms from October 1887 till December 1889.

While on the subject of the springing of Adams engines, throughout his time at Nine Elms he used the compensated principle, almost universal in America and elsewhere, where the track is not so even as with the highest class of British main lines. Whether he felt that South Western track left something to be desired was not likely to be disclosed, but it is certain that little restraint was placed on fast downhill running in contrast to that currently enforced on the South Eastern and on the Brighton. With the compensated arrangement the principle was to distribute the weight equally on the coupled wheels, the weight of the engine being supported at the centre of the beam on each side. When he was on Great Eastern T.W. Worsdell introduced a radial axlebox to ease the passage of axles supported in fixed framings. Adams adopted it for the rear carrying wheels of his 4-4-2 tanks, though whether he did also for the carrying wheels of the 'Jubilees' I cannot say.

In 1892 a contract was awarded to Neilson & Co for forty more 'Jubilees', and this was made the occasion for some modest changes in design. Originally the steam chests were placed beneath the cylinders, as on the Brighton 'Gladstones', while on the new engines, and on those subsequently built at Nine Elms, they were accommodated between the cylinders. A signifi-

Right *An Adams rebuild of W. G. Beattie's 4-4-0 of 1876, No 0357, with considerable improvement. (Real Photographs Co Ltd.)*

Right *One of the 'A12' Jubilee 0-4-2s of 1887 at Waterloo. No 556 was fitted with both vacuum and Westinghouse brakes. (British Railways.)*

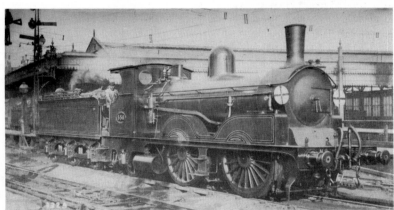

Below *One of the Jubilees, No 530 on a Waterloo to Guildford train approaching Surbiton in 1925. (Rail Archive Stephenson — F.R. Hebron.)*

cant operational change was the substitution of lever for screw reverse. While the latter provides for finer adjustment of the point of cut-off in the cylinders when making main-line running, a lever provides a ready means when starting, stopping and reversing which was all part of the 'stock-in-trade' of a mixed traffic engine. Duties apart, the new engines from Neilson were more ornately finished than the previous batch from Nine Elms, with brass beading adorning the splashers and a high degree of excellence in their general appearance. With a further multiplication of this class to ninety locomotives, by the addition of the final twenty built at Nine Elms from December 1893 to May 1895, the standardization of South Western motive power would seem to have been well under way, coupled with the collateral development of the 0-4-4 tank type from 1888 onwards.

In view of the earlier large scale introduction of outside-cylindered engines for all duties other than the 0-6-0 goods type, it is impossible not to associate the change as having some connection with Mr Pettigrew's arrival from Stratford. The new Works Manager at Nine Elms, in his previous work with T.W. Worsdell and James Holden, had become an inside cylinder man and this was further manifested in his later activities on the Furness Railway which, in 1901, included a close copy of Adams's express passenger L&SWR 4-4-0s with *inside cylinders*. The new 0-4-4 tank engines of 1888 have been referred to as a tank engine version of the 'Jubilees', though having coupled wheels of 5-ft 7-in diameter instead of 6-ft. Again a single prototype was built first, engine No 61 in June 1888, and quantity production, entirely at Nine Elms, started in December of that year. The first twenty, construction of which was spread over the period between that time and September 1890, had the steam chests below the cylinders as on the earlier batches of the 'Jubilees'. The new tank engines took up fast suburban duties alongside the 4-4-2 tanks, and quickly proved very popular through their general handiness and considerably increased tractive power, from 18 in by 26 in cylinders. In 1890, also, the smaller 0-4-4 tank, known as Class 04, came out. They were designed for branch line and other short distance work and had 17½-in by 24-in cylinders and coupled wheels of 4-ft 10-in diameter. They were an equally popular class. During the Adams regime they were multiplied up to a total of sixty, and it was not until 1933 that the first of

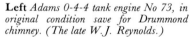

Left *Adams 0-4-4 tank engine No 73, in original condition save for Drummond chimney. (The late W.J. Reynolds.)*

Left *Adams 0-4-4 tank engine No 19 E in Southern livery, retaining the original chimney. (British Railways.)*

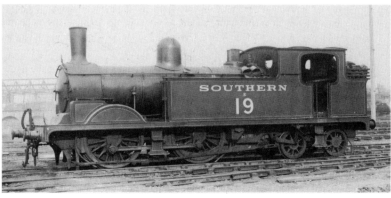

Above right *Adams small 0-4-4 tank, Class 'O2'. (W.F. Pettigrew and A.F. Ravenshear.)*

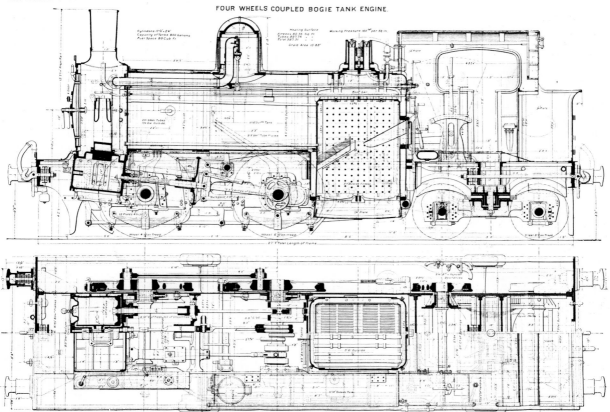

FOUR WHEELS COUPLED BOGIE TANK ENGINE.

them were scrapped. Before that time distinction had come upon certain members of the class by their being chosen to reinforce, and ultimately replace entirely, the motive power stud of the Isle of Wight. for that duty they were all eventually named. This phase in their existence is covered in a later chapter of this book.

The earliest form of these notable engines is shown in full detail in the accompanying working drawing, reproduced from Pettigrew's book *A Manual of Locomotive Engineering.*

Last and most notable of all of Adams' locomotives of the London and South Western Railway was the range of high-powered 4-4-0 express locomotives which eventually numbered sixty. At the time they were considered by some expert judges to be among the most powerful and economical locomotives in the world. In appearance alone these new engines far surpassed anything that had been built previously on the South Western. The straight running plates, the elegant curving of the splashers instead of the rectangular supports for the cab, not to mention the polished brass edgings, provided a splendid finish in which all who had care of the engines could take justi-

fiable pride. Technically, with cylinders 19 in by 26 in and a higher boiler pressure, 175 psi, they were certainly among the most powerful British passenger engines at the time of their construction. The first batch, twenty engines built at Nine Elms in 1890-92, had coupled wheels of 7-ft 1-in diameter, and a succeeding lot, intended for the more heavily-graded Salisbury-Exeter line had 6-ft 7-in coupled wheels. There were also twenty of this batch, turned out in 1892-93. Those who believed that at the time of their construction, in 1890, the 7-ft engines were among the most economical in the world had some solid facts to support their opinion when Adams and Pettigrew read their monumental paper 'Trials of an Express Locomotive' before the Institution of Civil Engineers in 1895.

The design of these beautiful engines included certain features requiring special notice, particularly the smokebox, which included the Adams Vortex-type spark arrester and blastpipe. A diagram of this appliance is shown herewith, as fitted to an inside-cylinder engine. This arrangement allowed the exhaust steam to be emitted at a lower velocity than in the ordinary blastpipe, and the area for its escape was

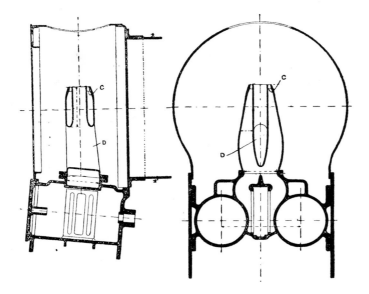

Adams' vortex blastpipe. (W.F. Pettigrew and A.F. Ravenshear.)

Adams 7 ft 4-4-0 No 579 of 1890 outside Waterloo. (Loco Publishing Co.)

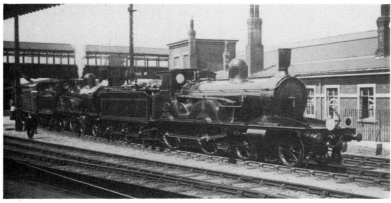

Two Adams 7 ft 4-4-0s heading an up express ready to leave Salisbury for Waterloo. (British Railways.)

so proportioned as to reduce the back pressure on the piston to a minimum. The reduction in the velocity of the blast, accompanied by an equable action on the tubes, causes a more uniform flow of air through the fire. No holes were formed, even with a thin fire, and no large cinders were thrown through the chimney. Adams always held the view that the smokebox should be made as small as possible and his largest express locomotives were certainly outstanding examples of this practice. The use of the Vortex blast-pipe, and the very soft beat in consequence, made economical working of the engines a regular feature. The results of the tests of the latest 4-4-0 amply bore out with what moderate coal consumption the fastest express running was made.

The trials were actually made with the first of the new 7-ft engines, No 577, and the meticulous detail recorded on the five test runs was due to the very careful planning conducted previously by Pettigrew. By the time arrangements were in hand for these trials, and still more so when the results had been accumulated and the data scientifically analysed, Adams himself was sadly beginning to lose his grip on day to day affairs. He was then approaching seventy years of age, and although he was still in a fine physical state of health there were signs that his mind was beginning to give way. So far as the trials themselves were concerned, no dynamometer car was then available but very careful arrangements were made to have a virtually continuous record of the speed by means of an apparatus known as the Boyer speed indicator, fitted to and driven off one of the bogie wheels. Besides showing on a dial the speed in miles per hour, a continuous record was made on a metallic strip with the 'miles' on the paper agreeing exactly with the mileposts along the line. The engine was fitted up for a comprehensive series of indicator diagrams to be taken, a robust wooden shelter being erected round the front of the engine to protect the men engaged on this work. Diagrams were taken about every three miles on each of the tests, and with the speeds ranging up to 80 mph at times the men in that shelter on the front of the locomotive had a busy time of it!

The principal table of results of the five trials carried out in July 1891 confirms the excellent character of the overall performance, as evidenced by the consistent values of the figures for the coal consumption per indicated horsepower hour, varying only from 2.31 to 2.61 lbs. Even so in relation to the running average speeds and the loads hauled, the actual coal consumption per train mile does not seem particularly moderate. The second table includes details of the running conditions obtained when the maximum speeds and maximum horsepower values

L&SWR Trials on 7-ft 4-4-0 engine No 577, July 1891

Run number	1	2	3	4	5
Route	Waterloo to Bournemouth	Bournemouth to Waterloo	Waterloo to Exeter	Exeter to Woking	Waterloo to Salisbury
Train	5.50 am	1.55 pm	11 am	12.45 pm	2.40 pm
Average load (tons tare)	179.75	136	168.25	198.75	137.5
Train miles	111	111	171.5	147.25	83.63
Actual running time (h m s)	2 59 30	2 27 15	3 43 15	3 18 15	1 47 15
Actual journey time (h m s)	3 29	2 41	4 4	3 47	2 4
Speed exclusive of stops (mph)	37.0	45.2	46.1	44.4	46.7
Coal per train mile (lbs)	30.5	28.1	28.4	32.98	28.16
Coal per indicated horsepower hour (lbs)	2.31	2.61	2.34	2.52	2.45
Indicated horsepower maximum	684.1	610.1	803.6	804.3	626.1
Indicated horsepower mean, from indicator card	490.6	485.1	558.1	582.0	536.7
Maximum speed (mph)	68.5	67.1	78.0	81.0	75.0
Overall efficiency of locomotive	7.7	6.88	7.6	7.34	7.25

	Maximum speed				Maximum indicated horsepower			
Run number	Location milepost	Speed (mph)	Cut-off (per cent)	Indicated horsepower	Location milepost	Speed (mph)	Cut-off (per cent)	Indicated horsepower
1	65	68.5	17	480	28	40	29.5	684.1
2	24	67.1	17	571.6	60	43	26	610.1
3	58	78	17	517.2	152	31	44	803.6
4	148	81	17	636.2	115.5	27.5	48	804.3
5	65	75	17	601.9	69	50	20	626.1

were recorded. This table contains some very significant, and certainly some surprising figures. It will be seen that all the instances of maximum speed occurred when the engine was being worked at the short cut-off of no more than seventeen per cent, and yet steaming hard enough to produce indicated horsepowers in some cases approaching the maximum values attained over the whole run, as in the second and fifth tests. Equally the circumstances in the maximum speeds recorded during the third and fourth tests are remarkable—the third test occurred near the 58th milepost, at 78 mph, while the fourth, in the descent of Seaton bank at 81 mph, registered an indicated horsepower of no less than 636.2.

Having regard to the fact that the train was descending a gradient of 1 in 80, the combined weight of engine and train, 292 tons, at such a speed as 81 mph, would provide a gravitational assistance of no less than 1,700 horsepower to the effort of the locomotive. The frictional resistance of a train of around 210 tons would have been much the same figure, leaving the indicated horsepower developed by the engine just about enough to propel itself along at 81 mph. Confirmation of this came indirectly in the discusson on a paper read before the Institution of Mechanical Engineers on 'Compound Locomotives in France', in April 1904. In that discussion Vaughan Pendred, then editor-in-chief of *The Engineer,* asked how far the external characteristics of a locomotive affected the power of pulling at high speeds. Following that, after some correspondence with Dugald Drummond, he reported to a resumed discussion at the Institution of Mechanical Engineers that he had received some figures relating to two London and South Western 4-4-0 express locomotives on which Drummond had taken indicator diagrams when running light engine, and on level track. One of these was a 'T9' Class No 706, and the other was an Adams seven-footer, No 582.

The results from the Adams engine, with full regulator working in all cases, were as follows:

Speed (mph)	Cut-off (per cent)	Indicated horsepower
52	15	487
60	18	563
71	20	710
72	30	803

The first three results were from normal working, but the last instance was abnormal, when the engine was driven hard against a gale of wind and rain in an attempt to get a high maximum speed. Despite the use of thirty per cent cut-off, instead of twenty per cent as in the third case, the attained speed was no more than 72 mph. The details submitted to the Institution of Mechanical Engineers by Dugald Drummond however were interesting in that at speeds below 60 mph the resistance absorbed by the 'T9' Class inside-cylinder engine was markedly less than that of the Adams, whereas at over 60 mph the 'T9' went soaring ahead, to 780 ihp at 67 mph and to no less than 912 ihp at 70 mph!

Dugald Drummond's assistant G.R. Sisterson, speaking later in the discussion, admitted that the extenuating circumstances prevailing at the time the tests were made may have affected the reliability of the results, and Vaughan Pendred comparing the London and South Western locomotive figures with some dynamometer trials on the then-new LNWR 4-4-0 engine *Precursor*, was surprised to observe 'that the resistance of the engine was enormously greater per ton than the resistance of the train. Why was that? He did not know and he had never met with anybody who could tell him.' In 1904 the days were far ahead when engine trials would be carried out with the certainty and the exactitude to which we became accustomed in the 1950s. Be that as it may, Adams's successors one and all, Drummond, Urie and Maunsell, realized that they had a winner in those beautiful outside-cylinder 4-4-0s, and although the first withdrawals of them began in 1930 the last were not taken out of traffic until 1946.

Adams 6 ft 7 in 4-4-0 No 571 of 1892 at Nine Elms shed. (Loco Publishing Co.)

5. Brighton—years of evolution

The death of William Stroudley at the relatively early age of 56 inevitably provokes questions as to how his locomotive practice might have developed had he lived to enjoy the normal span of years vouchsafed to many of his contemporaries in Victorian England. Would, for example, his front-coupled design of express passenger locomotive been enlarged to a 'super-Gladstone'? There is no doubt that among engineers nurtured on the railways south of the Thames the mystique of Stroudley lingered long after the man himself, indeed, until the Brighton Railway was becoming little more than a memory. I shall always remember an occasion in 1955 when the British Transport Commission invited me to write a booklet to be published to accompany an exhibition as a farewell to the steam locomotive. My own theme was to take, as typical, a retrospect of the work of eight great engineers. Much was discussed as to who those eight men should be and eventually the choice fell upon Robert Stephenson, John Ramsbottom, Edward Fletcher, Patrick Stirling, S.W. Johnson, Dugald Drummond, G.J. Churchward and Sir Nigel Gresley. Not long after the choice had been made, and preparations begun for collection of material for the exhibition at Euston, I met an old friend who had been in the locomotive department of the Brighton Railway and then on the Southern, but who was, in 1955, a very senior executive officer on the Railway's Board. I told him of the difficulties we had had in choosing who the eight men should be, and he looked extremely blank and said: 'What about Mr Stroudley?'

His death, in December 1889, certainly took the Brighton management by surprise, and they turned to an old assistant of Stroudley's as a successor. R.J. Billinton had been in general engineering practice before joining the Brighton Railway as an assistant in the locomotive works in 1870, not long after Stroudley himself had taken over from J.C. Craven.

But Billinton went to the Midland Railway in 1874, just as S.W. Johnson was succeeding Matthew Kirtley as Locomotive Superintendent at Derby. It would have been surprising if the fifteen years he spent as assistant to such a master engine designer as Johnson had not had a profound influence on his subsequent work at Brighton. It was evident in his very first new design, prepared in 1891 though not put into production until 1893. Johnson had already introduced the 0-4-4 type of passenger tank engine even before he took charge at Derby, but the Midland version built by Neilsons, in 1875-76, became one of the most popular sights in the West Riding. Billinton produced a much more powerful version of the same general design for the Brighton.

It was not merely a new wheel arrangement for the LB&SCR; the entire styling was new, except for the painting and the naming. Gone was the Stroudley copper-capped chimney, in its place came the shapely Midland type of the Johnson era. While the safety valves were still mounted on the dome the latter was placed further forward on the boiler, and the new Brighton tank engines revived an old Kirtley practice on the Midland by having a manhole cover over the top of the firebox, on which was mounted the whistle. Apart from outward styling the new 0-4-4 tanks were powerful engines, having 18-in by 26-in cylinders and coupled wheels of 5-ft 6-in diameter. They were intended more for country branch lines, rather than suburban work.

This class was followed by one of a series of 0-6-2 tanks for goods working, with radial axles on the trailing pair of wheels. The new 0-4-4 tank engines, of which there were 36, broke with Brighton precedents in having bogies. Mr Billinton soon gave evidence of further following Midland practice, rather than traditional Stroudley style, in designing a class of 4-4-0 express passenger locomotives. How far Stroudley would have persisted, had he lived, in

Billinton 0-4-4 tank engine No 364 Truscott, *the second of a class of 36 built at Brighton from 1892 to 1896. (National Railway Museum — F. Burtt.)*

Billinton Class 'B2' 4-4-0 No 171 Nevill *in Brighton station. (The late W.J. Reynolds.)*

building locomotives without bogies, either leading or trailing, is a matter for conjecture. What is certain is that within a dozen years of his death Brighton engines were occasionally being called on for speeds of around 80 mph.

The first Brighton 4-4-0s, somewhat naturally, bore a strong resemblance to those of the Midland. They had the same-sized cylinders, 18 in by 26 in, and boilers with a tube heating surface of 1,227.3 sq ft. The firebox heating surface was 114.74 sq ft, the grate area was 18.73 sq ft and the working pressure was 160 psi. It was said at that time that the new engines were built for replacement of the 'G' Class 2-2-2 on the London and Portsmouth service, but connoisseurs of Brighton locomotive practice criticized the design as having inadequate heating surface as compared to the 'Gladstone' Class. The Billinton 4-4-0s had the same-sized boiler as the Stroudleys, but a less crowded tube layout, and tubes of 1⅝-in diameter against 1½ in on the 'Gladstones'. In any case one could hardly imagine that a man who had the important post of Chief Locomotive Draughtsman of the Midland Railway at Derby, and had designed more than one hundred 4-4-0s of closely similar proportions, would be likely to err in the vital matter of boiler details. In the more superficial matters of external styling, the high raised running plates and the artistically-curved splashers over the bogie wheels were to be noted.

The Brighton practice of naming every engine in the stable, except the main-line goods units, was carried a stage further than in the 'Gladstones'. In the latter, while the traditional style of naming engines by stations on the line had been to some extent followed, with titles like *Fratton, Hayling* and *Sandown*, others were named after directors, public figures and even politicians of both major parties. While the class leader had been named for the Liberals, the Tories were not forgotten in the name of engine No 218, *Beaconsfield*. The names of the first Billinton 4-4-0s were all of personalities, some of Brighton directors,

but the majority those of eminent engineers in railway history.

Ten of the first eleven of the class to be built, outshopped at Brighton in 1895-96, were stationed at Fratton, the remaining one of this lot was allocated to St Leonards. When the next batch were turned out they likewise were shedded away from Brighton apart from two isolated ones. It would seem that Billinton was content to leave the 'Gladstones' at first in possession of the heaviest main-line work and to reinforce the lesser routes on which the 'G' Class 2-2-2s had hitherto been used. The new Billinton 4-4-0s were named and stationed as follows:

Number	Name	Shed
314	*Charles C. Macrae*	Portsmouth (Fratton)
315	*Duncannon*	Portsmouth (Fratton)
316	*Goldsmid*	Portsmouth (Fratton)
317	*Gerald Loder*	Portsmouth (Fratton)
318	*Rothschild*	Portsmouth (Fratton)
319	*John Fowler*	Portsmouth (Fratton)
320	*Rastrick*	Portsmouth (Fratton)
321	*John Rennie*	Portsmouth (Fratton)
322	*G. P. Bidder*	Portsmouth (Fratton)
323	*William Cubitt*	St Leonards
324	*John Hawkshaw*	Portsmouth (Fratton)
201	*Rosebery*	Portsmouth (Fratton)
202	*Trevithick*	Battersea
203	*Henry Fletcher*	New Cross
204	*Telford*	New Cross
205	*Hackworth*	Brighton
206	*Smeaton*	Battersea
207	*Brunel*	St Leonards
171	*Nevill*	Brighton
208	*Abercorn*	St Leonards
209	*Wolfe Barry*	St Leonards
210	*Fairbairn*	St Leonards
211	*Whitworth*	Eastbourne
212	*Armstrong*	New Cross

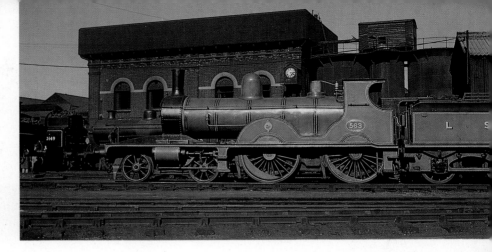

Right *An Adams 4-4-0, No 563, outside Brighton Shed in 1958 after being restored to her original L&SWR colours. She is now in the National Railway Museum at York. (R.C. Riley.)*

Below *Stroudley 'Gladstone' No 214 shows off the LB&SCR livery at the Sheffield Park Station on the Bluebell Railway when on loan from the National Railway Museum in 1982 (R.C. Riley.)*

A Urie 'H15' Class 4-6-0, No 30473, at Southampton Terminus, June 1957. The distinctive three funnels of the Queen Mary can be seen to the left of the background. (R.C. Riley.)

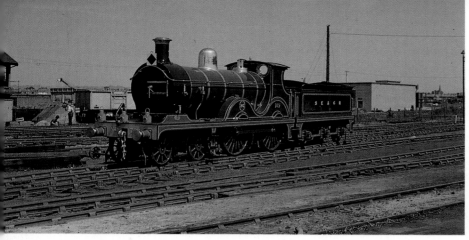

Left *Restored Wainwright 'D' Class locomotive No 737 in SE&CR colours at Ashford, Kent in June 1960. This engine is currently in the National Railway Museum. (R.C. Riley.)*

Below *Drummond 'T9' Class 4-4-0, No 30289, one of the greyhounds of the LSWR express service when built in 1900 and for many years after, but reduced to working local freight in its last years. (R.C. Riley.)*

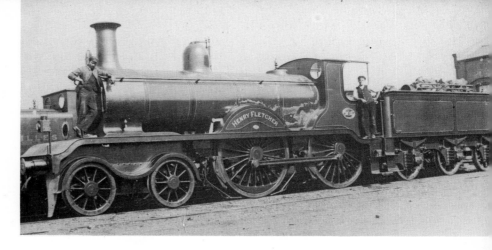

Class 'B2' 4-4-0 No 203 Henry
Fletcher, *one of the only three engines of the
class stationed at New Cross. (H. Gordon
Tidey.)*

These engines, nicknamed for some reason the
'Grasshoppers', never seemed to show up to any
great advantage over the Portsmouth line, possibly
because the train running schedules were so easy that
they had no opportunity of showing any superiority
over the 'G' Class 2-2-2s. However, when the special
Sunday Pullman was put on in October 1898, running from Victoria to Brighton in the even hour, one
of the Battersea-based 4-4-0s, No 206 *Smeaton,* was
put on and with a good load of 190 tons tare made a
fine run, both out and home. The detailed log of the
down run is of considerable interest in that it provides
one of the very few instances of the recorded work of
the 'Grasshoppers' on real express duty. On the
Portsmouth line the schedules were so slow that the
'G' Class 2-2-2s could keep time easily, if they were
not too delayed by signal checks.

Victoria-Brighton

Train 11.00 am Sunday Pullman
Engine 4-4-0 No 206 *Smeaton*
Load 190 tons tare

Distance (miles)		Time (m s)	Average speed (mph)
0.0	Victoria	0 00	—
2.7	Clapham Junction	5 04	32.0
4.7	Balham	7 59	41.1
8.7	Thornton Heath	13 17	45.0
10.5	Croydon	15 44	46.1
13.6	Purley	19 39	47.5
15.4	Coulsdon	22 03	45.1
20.9	Redhill	28 36	51.0
25.8	Horley	32 56	67.8
29.5	Three Bridges	36 41	60.0
34.1	Balcombe	41 58	52.1
38.0	Hayward's Heath	45 31	65.6
41.7	Burgess Hill	48 54	71.7
43.8	Hassocks	50 58	60.5
49.5	Preston Park	57 14	54.5
50.9	Brighton	59 09	—

This run was made over the original line via
Merstham Tunnel and Redhill, on somewhat easier
gradients. The engine did very good work on the continuous ascent of 1 in 264 from Croydon to the summit point at the north end of the tunnel and, despite a
very substantial load for this class of engine, the working times subsequently scheduled for the 'Southern
Belle' were comfortably maintained, both uphill and
down. On the return journey equally good work was
done, passing Haywards Heath in 16 minutes 9
seconds, Redhill in 34 minutes 34 seconds and Croydon in 45 minutes 15 seconds. After an easy run
through the suburban area Victoria was reached in 58
minutes 30 seconds.

While the small boiler currently being used by
Johnson on the Midland Railway, and copied by Billinton when he first got to Brighton might have been
adequate enough for the 'Grasshoppers' on the Portsmouth Line something considerably larger was soon
to be needed for the ever-growing traffic of the
Brighton main line, and in 1898 the last engine of the
new 4-4-0s was built with a larger boiler, having a
total heating surface of 1,464.8 sq ft and a grate area
of 20.6 sq ft. This was No 213 *Bessemer*, and as a unit
naturally under special observation it was stationed at
Brighton and worked daily on the 'Stockbrokers
Express', at 8.45 am to London Bridge. *Bessemer* was
by way of a 'trial heat' however, for in the following
year Billinton brought out the first of his celebrated
'B4' Class with 19-in by 26-in cylinders, still larger
boilers than *Bessemer* and a notable increase in working pressure from 160 to 180 psi. The first three
engines of this series, No 52 *Siemens*, No 53 *Sirdar* and
No 54 *Empress* were built at Brighton in 1899-1900
and were among the most powerful engines in the
country at that time.

Engine No 54 had the melancholy task of hauling
Queen Victoria's funeral train from Fareham, where
the Brighton took over from the London and South
Western after the short run up from Gosport. The
Royal Train was then run non-stop to Victoria. The

Left *One of the first three of the engines of Class 'B4', originally named* Siemens, *here seen in Earle-Marsh livery. (National Railway Museum — F. Burtt.)*

Left *One of the 'Scotchmen' batch of 'B4' 4-4-0s, No 65* Sandringham, *built by Sharp Stewart & Co in 1901 and shown in the yellow livery. (National Railway Museum — F. Burtt.)*

Below *The 'Sunny South Special' near Purley, hauled by an unidentified 'B4' Class 4-4-0. (British Railways.)*

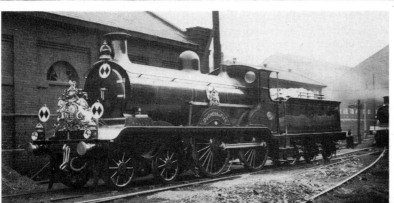

Left *One of the last Brighton built 'B4's, No 48* Duchess of Fife, *decorated for a Royal Train. (National Railway Museum — F. Burtt.)*

schedule time for the 87.7-mile run was 122 minutes, but because of earlier delays the train was ten minutes late in leaving Fareham, and then was required to reduce to dead slow speed to set down the L&SWR pilotman at Farlington Junction. The driver had been instructed to make up as much time as he could. It was known, of course, that King Edward would be meeting the train at Victoria, and in view of his well-known dislike of unpunctuality something had to be done about it. The result was that the dead Queen's mortal remains were hustled up to London far faster than she would ever have permitted in her lifetime! From setting down the pilot, the train ran the 71 miles to passing Clapham Junction at an average speed of 47 mph, inclusive of the severe speed restrictions at Ford, Horsham, Dorking, Leatherhead, Epsom, Mitcham, Streatham and Clapham Junction. A maximum of 80 mph was attained on the level between Chichester and Barnham, and 75 mph descending towards Dorking from the North Downs. The result was the train reached Victoria two minutes early, a run that earned the commendation of the German Kaiser, who sent an equery to the driver to convey his congratulations on the engine performance!

In the year 1901 a contract was placed with Sharp, Stewart & Co for 25 further engines of the 'B4' Class, and these new engines were all delivered between July and October of that year. At first they were known in the railway press as the 'Canada' Class, from the name given to the first one built, but among the Brighton enginemen they quickly became known as the 'Scotchmen' and this persisted long after their original, official titles had been removed. Their original names and numbers were:

47	Canada	62	Mafeking
48	Australia	63	Pretoria
49	Queensland	64	Windsor
50	Tasmania	65	Sandringham
51	Wolferton	66	Balmoral
55	Emperor	67	Osborne
56	Roberts	68	Marlborough
57	Buller	69	Bagshott
58	Kitchener	70	Holyrood
59	Baden-Powell	71	Sussex
60	Kimberley	72	Goodwood
61	Ladysmith	73	Westminster
	74	Cornwall	

The 'Scotchmen' differed from the three original engines of the class built at Brighton works in having the dome over the centre of the driving wheels, there being only one lagging belt on the boiler barrel. The engines were finished in the beautiful style that Billinton inherited from Stroudley, and their handsome appearance was matched by their excellent performance on the road. Five further engines of the class were built at Brighton Works in the summer of 1902. They were named thus:

42	His Majesty	44	Cecil Rhodes
43	Duchess of Fife	45	Bessborough
	46	Prince of Wales	

Engine No 45 was built with a trial of Dugald Drummond's cross water tubes in the firebox, the function of which is explained in Chapter 6 of this book. Mr Billinton was honoured, in April 1903, by an 'Illustrated Interview' in *The Railway Magazine*, in which he described the latest production practices in his works at Brighton, and the issue was adorned with a colour plate of the *Duchess of Fife* locomotive. In addition to references to new classes, which, like the 18-in 0-6-0 goods, were a direct development of Stroudley's work, he described and illustrated his new 0-6-2 radial tank engine with 5-ft 6-in coupled wheels, 18-in by 26-in cylinders and an altogether modern look. These new engines, Class 'E5', were undoubtedly intended to be a twentieth century development of the Class 'D' 0-4-2 tank, and to be multiplied accordingly. The first ten were turned out between November 1902 and April 1903, and then a further twenty between November 1903 and November 1904. Before that time however Billinton himself was in failing health and he died on 7 November, just as the last two 'E5' engines were being completed.

One can be sure that the locomotive department at Brighton was hard put to find new names for all these additional engines, seeing that the majority were of little more than 'one-horse' villages. These titles deserve to be set on record seeing that they were almost Brighton's last fling in extensive engine naming. The 4-ft 6-in Class 'E6' goods tanks of the series 407-418, introduced in December 1904, had names selected for them, but engine No 414 was the last to be so distinguished. The new Locomotive Superintendent did not agree with naming. For the record, the names alloted to the thirty 5-ft 6-in fast mixed traffic tanks of the 'E5' Class were as follows:

November 1902 to April 1903

567	Freshwater
568	Carisbrook
569	Kensington
570	Armington
571	Hickstead
572	Farncombe
573	Nutbourne
574	Copthorne
575	Westergate
576	Brenchley

November 1903–November 1904

583	*Hardcombe*	593	*Hollington*
584	*Lordington*	594	*Shortbridge*
585	*Crowborough*	399	*Middleton*
586	*Maplehurst*	400	*Winchelsea*
587	*Brighton*	401	*Woldingham*
588	*Hawkenbury*	402	*Wanborough*
589	*Ambersham*	403	*Fordcombe*
590	*Lodsworth*	404	*Hardham*
591	*Tillington*	405	*Fernhurst*
592	*Eastergate*	406	*Colworth*

The new Locomotive Superintendent was Douglas Earle-Marsh. He had been a pupil of William Dean, at Swindon, and rose rapidly to become Assistant Manager of the Locomotive Works in 1889. On the death of Patrick Stirling in 1895, and the appointment of H.A. Ivatt as Locomotive Superintendent of the Great Northern Railway, Earle-Marsh was appointed assistant and manager at the famous 'plant' at Doncaster, from which he transferred to Brighton at the end of 1904. In a very short time the works personnel, and many lineside enthusiasts of the LB&SCR, realized that they had an out-and-out reformer in their midst! In a short time the air was thick with rumours of new painting styles, engines newly repaired emerged from the works minus their former names and as early as May 1905 the railway press contained news that the first locomotives of Mr Earle-Marsh's design would be five 'Atlantic' express engines of very similar dimensions to the '251' Class of the Great Northern Railway. When they did appear, at the end of 1905, apart from superficial details one could well imagine a casual observer having difficulty in telling the two classes apart. Unlike Stroudley and Billinton it seemed that Earle-Marsh was intent upon beginning his time at Brighton with a major new express passenger design, with more regard for publicity than the traffic needs for such a great machine.

The new 'Atlantic' attracted much attention from their similarity to Ivatt's '251' Class on the Great Northern. The boilers were virtually identical, except for the pressure being 200 psi instead of 180 psi, and the cylinders had 26-in stroke, instead of 24 in. So far as nominal tractive effort was concerned the huge new engines were not all that more powerful than the 'B4' Class 4-4-0s, which were then doing admirable work on the fastest trains. These large 4-4-0s had a total heating surface of 1,650 sq ft and a grate area of 23 sq ft, whereas the 'Atlantics' had an enormous boiler with a total heating surface of 2,473 sq ft and a grate area of 31 sq ft. Yet, when the 'Southern Belle' was first put on, the Brighton's star train, even the 11.00 am down train from Victoria frequently loaded to no more than four Pullman cars.

Furthermore, the 8.45 am crack express to London Bridge, even after the introduction of the 'Atlantics', was frequently worked by one of the 'Scotchmen'. Lovers of the individuality of Brighton locomotives deplored the lack of names on Earle-Marsh's great new engines, but still more so the edict that had gone forth towards the end of the year 1905 that the cherished yellow livery was to go, for all passenger engines, and be replaced by sepia, albeit smartly lined out. In the event the superseding of the old Stroudley colours took a long time to complete. Apparently the paintwork on the older engines had been so beautifully and efficiently done that it lasted through several visits to the shops for machinery overhaul.

The lack of originality in new engine design on Earle-Marsh's part was shown in still greater extent than in the 'Atlantics' in the next new class he introduced, the 'I1' 4-4-2 tanks. The first of these was completed at Brighton in September 1906, and the rest of the batch of ten turned out between November 1906 and June 1907. Once again a Great Northern design, with which Earle-Marsh had been closely copied at Doncaster, had been closely copied—moreover it was one nearly ten years old and well on the way to being obsolete! In 1906 Ivatt was planning a powerful new suburban tank engine of the 0-6-2 type, and the Brighton had already commissioned thirty of the type in the shape of the excellent Billinton 'E5' Class; and yet Earle-Marsh built the feeble and outdated 'I1' Class, with boilers even smaller than Ivatt's 4-4-2s of 1898. The new Brighton engines had 17½-in by 26-in cylinders, 5-ft 6-in coupled wheels and 170 psi boiler pressure, as on the Ivatt 4-4-2, but only a total heating surface of 1,040.9 sq ft and a grate area 17.48 sq ft against 1,123.8 sq ft and 17.8 sq ft on the Great Northern engines. The new Brighton engines quickly gained the reputation of being poor steamers, despite which one of them, No 600, was allocated to the Royal Train to convey King Edward VII to Epsom Downs station for the 'Derby'. Even though Earle-Marsh himself rode on the footplate there were some palpitating moments before the sumptuous five-car train was hauled up the steep gradient to the racecourse terminus. Despite their indifferent reputation ten more of the class were built in June-December 1907.

In 1907 B.K. Field was appointed Chief Locomotive Draughtsman at Brighton, and from that time the works began to regain some of its old prestige. Field was little more than forty years of age at the time of his appointment, yet he had enjoyed a classical education at Dulwich College and Heidelberg, and technical training at the City and Guilds of London Technical Institute, before apprenticeship under James Stirling on the South Eastern Railway at Ash-

Right *Class 'E5' 0-6-2 tank engine No 573* Nutbourne, *one of the first batch of these engines. (National Railway Museum — F. Burtt.)*

Right *First of the Earle-Marsh 'Atlantics', No 37, on the turntable at Victoria. (Loco Publishing Co.)*

Below *The up 'Sunny South Special' leaving Brighton hauled by Class 'B4' 4-4-0 No 63. (Author's collection.)*

Left '*B2*' *4-4-0 No 317, rebuilt with larger boiler on indicator tests, climbing Forest Hill bank with a Brighton express. (H. Gordon Tidey.)*

Right '*I3*' *Class 4-4-2 tank engine.*

ford. He rose rapidly, becoming Chief Locomotive Draughtsman in 1897, at the age of 31. At the time of the fusion of the staffs of the South Eastern and London Chatham and Dover Railways, Surtees, of the LC&DR was far senior in status to Field, and was naturally preferred as the chief of the amalgamated staff, and Field was fortunate in securing another chief draughtsmanship, that of the North Staffordshire Railway, which he held until his appointment at Brighton. His work for the North Staffordshire Railway included carriages as well as locomotives.

Before Field was appointed, Earle-Marsh had embarked upon a programme of boiler standardization on certain older classes, though it had not proceeded further than the alteration of isolated engines until the autumn of 1907. Then one of the 'Grasshoppers' was so treated, engine No 321 formerly *John Rennie*, and this was the signal for the whole class to be rebuilt. The new boilers had a tube heating surface of 1,183.41 sq ft, firebox 101.27 sq ft and grate area 18.64 sq ft. The rebuilds had a smart and attractive appearance in the new sepia brown livery, with the initials LB&SCR on the tender, and a monogram incorporating all the initials on the leading coupled-wheel splasher. Although having a larger boiler, the rebuilt engine, classed on 'B2X', had the same tractive effort as the original 'Grasshopper's' and was thus a lower power classification to the 'Scotchmen', having 18-in as against 19-in cylinders. An isolated development of this latter class had come in the autumn of 1907 in a tank engine version, No 21, having the same basic dimensions as Class 'B4', but as a 4-4-2 carrying 3 tons of coal in the bunker and 2,110 gallons of water in the tanks. What the purpose of this isolated engine originally was I do not know, but its development, largely due to the influence of Field, was startling.

The immediate utilization of engine No 21 was interesting, as it was put on to the up 'Stockbrokers'

Express' leaving Brighton at 8.45 am and returning from Victoria at 11 am before that train became 'The Southern Belle'. The northbound working was a very heavy train, for those days, weighing 360 tons behind the locomotive, but it was then allowed 70 minutes non-stop from Brighton to London Bridge. On one recorded occasion the run was made exactly to time in spite of two severe permanent way slowings and several signal checks. On the return journey, despite three checks, Brighton was reached five minutes early, in 55 minutes from Victoria. The load however was much lighter, totalling no more than 242 tons. The engine was an 'odd man out' in the Brighton express locomotive fleet, having been built with coupled wheels of 6-ft 9-in diameter, instead of the usual 6 ft 7 in. When a second engine of the 'I3' Class was completed at Brighton in March 1908 it had the usual standard wheels.

The construction of this engine No 22, was passed over in a curiously casual manner in the railway press of the day. Accompanying an illustration in *The Locomotive Magazine* of 15 July, the only comment was 'the new engine differed from No 21 in having an extended smokebox fitted with the Schmidt superheater, and minor alterations to detail; but the general dimensions are practically identical with those of the large 4-4-0 passenger tender engines. Far from it, however! When the full details were published, with a beautifully executed drawing, one year and six months later, it was revealed that the cylinders of the superheater engine were no less than 21-in diameter, with piston valves above, and working pressure reduced to 160 psi. The boiler details as used on the first superheater 'I3' were; small tubes 850 sq ft, superheater 305 sq ft and firebox 126 sq ft. These proportions gave a very high degree of superheat. One engine was thus equipped at first, and No 22 ran in competition with No 21 through the summer and autumn of 1908. From December of that year four

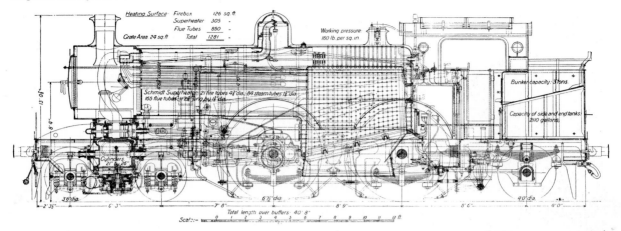

more superheated engines were built, No 23 - No 26, then curiously one more 'saturator' with 19-in cylinders, No 27.

Indicator tests made between engines No 21 and No 22 revealed the marked superiority of the superheater engine, not only in coal and water consumption but in free running. This could be attributed to the use of piston valves. Nevertheless it seemed that Earle-Marsh himself was not entirely convinced of their all-round advantages, having regard to the additional costs of superheaters and the royalties to be paid to the German owners of the patents. Three more non-superheated 'I3' 4-4-2 tank engines were built at Brighton between October 1909 and January 1910, numbered 28-30. However, events far afield from the LB&SCR came to settle the future of superheating so far as Brighton Works was concerned. In 1909 C.J. Bowen Cooke had succeeded George Whale as Chief Mechanical Engineer of the London and North Western Railway, and the ensuing summer was enlivened by some locomotive interchange trials between North Western engines and certain of those of the Great Northern and Caledonian Railways. Then when the summer was gone, and the exchange trials seemed to be passing into history, Bowen Cooke initiated another set of trials that proved of infinitely greater significance.

Ever since his early education in Germany he had been interested in their railway practice, and particularly in the development of the Schmidt superheater. In Great Britain at that time however, superheating was generally regarded as an expensive luxury which was not really necessary, because our railways had ample supplies of coal of a far higher quality than that generally available on the Continent of Europe. On the London and North Western however train loading was considerably higher than on most other British railways, and it was a year-round loading in contrast to some others which experienced peaks in the summer holiday season only. On the L&NWR the Whale locomotives were coping with heavy loads adequately enough, albeit often on a very heavy coal consumption, and Bowen Cooke was anxious to try superheating as a possible means of reducing the coal bill. Unfortunately for him the Company's finances were in a very healthy state, and the top management saw no reason to increase the cost of locomotives by addition of superheaters. Then Bowen Cooke sought the aid of Earle-Marsh in furthering his programme of locomotive exchanges, by running one of the 'I3' superheated tank engines on the L&NWR.

After some preliminary running, regular exchange working was organized with the 'Sunny South Special' between Rugby and Brighton on alternate days, the 'I3' working north one day and an L&NWR 'Precursor' working south. Then the two competitors lodged overnight and worked the corresponding duties to their respective home bases. With the tests made in the late autumn the train loads were relatively light, for the North Western, at around 235 tons and Earle-Marsh stipulated that so far as his engine was concerned the round trip must be made on a single heaped-up bunkerful of coal, 3½ tons. Although the train loads were relatively light this was no mean assignment for a total mileage of 264, with the 77.2 miles between Willesden Junction and Rugby to be run non-stop in each direction, at an average speed of 53 mph. While this schedule would have been nothing to the North Western, on which the 'Precursors' were rostered to take 420 tons without a pilot, an average of 53 mph on the Brighton line was faster than its crack train, 'The Southern Belle'. I have not seen any detailed logs of the running of either competitor during the period of the exchange. There were many stories going around at the time, of very hard running on both sides; but these can be regarded as pure fiction. Even if the Brighton engine had no coal left at all when she got home she would have burned no more than 27 lb a mile, and that presumably would have meant re-kindling the fire while on shed at Rugby. The performance of the 'I3' created a most favourable impression on the L&NWR, and though it was followed eventually by the building of a large batch of new 'I3s' at Brighton, oddly enough the first three turned out in January and February 1910, No 30, No 75 and No 76, were non-superheated with 19-in cylinders.

Although a biographical account of Brighton locomotives published about forty years ago averred that Earle-Marsh had reached his zenith, I quote: 'his ''I3s'' firmly established in triumphant vindication of a new practice and the prestige of ''Brighton'' locomotive engineering greater than at any time since Stroudley's', I find it hard to echo such enthusiasm. While the performance of engine No 23 in the exchange trials with the London and North Western at the latter end of 1909 gave very good results so far

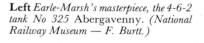

Left *Earle-Marsh's masterpiece, the 4-6-2 tank No 325* Abergavenny. *(National Railway Museum — F. Burtt.)*

Left *The first superheater 'Atlantic', No 421. (British Railways.)*

Above right *Billinton's 4-6-4 tank engine. The first of the post-war batch, No 329* Stephenson, *at Brighton. (Lord Monkswell.)*

as coal consumption was concerned only four super-heater 'I3s' were built in 1908-9 after the first one, No 22 in March 1908, and continuation of the class, until February 1910, were all non-superheated. Then as if to emphasize the mood of uncertainty in Brighton locomotive practice at that time, in late summer of that year the news got around that a large new express tank engine of the 4-6-2 type was under construction, at the same time that a batch of six more 'I3s' were in hand, this time with superheaters and 21-in cylinders. The enlarged tank engine was clearly meant as the prototype of a new design, having outside cylinders and a much enlarged boiler; but events did not finally turn out that way.

Individually, the 4-6-2 No 325 completed in December 1910 could well be regarded as Earle-Marsh's finest engine. Certainly he spent a great amount of time and trouble on its detail. He went to the extent of altering its running number twice, from 36 its first allocation, next to 100, and finally to the historic 325, which had been left vacant by the scrap-ping of the Stroudley 'single' *Abergavenny*. By some high-level prompting Earle-Marsh was persuaded to break his rule about no engine naming by reviving the old title of No 325, and as flamboyantly ever as Stroudley decked his local tank engines. The new *Abergavenny*, with the same-sized cylinders as the superheater 'I3s', but with a larger boiler, provided a fine engine in traffic. It was intended that it should be followed by a companion engine with Walschaert's valve gear, as tests were to be made prior to the authorization of twenty more 4-6-2 tanks with which-

ever valve gear was favoured. Early in 1911 however it became known that Earle-Marsh's health was beginning to give cause for anxiety, and that he was not in any fit state to follow up his programme of big engine development. More express engines were needed and instead of building more superheated 'I3s' an order to design a superheated version of the Doncaster-style 'Atlantics' was given. Field did the drawing office work, and as always he made an excellent job of it.

The new 'Atlantics' numbered 421-426, had 21-in by 26-in cylinders and much larger boilers than those fitted on to *Abergavenny*. Although the latter engine had the advantage of six coupled wheels, and thus an ability to get away more rapidly, the tender engines would be better on the run. The comparative dimensions were thus:

Class	'Abergavenny'	421-426
Heating surfaces (sq ft)		
Tubes	1,462	1,895
Firebox	124	135.6
Superheater	357	460
Total	1,943	2,490.6
Grate area (sq ft)	25.2	30.5
Boiler pressure (psi)	160	170
Tractive effort (lb)	20,800	22,100

By the autumn of 1911 it was clear that Earle-Marsh's health was not improving and before the end of the year he resigned. He was succeeded by L.B. Billinton, the son of the former chief at Brighton.

6. Dugald Drummond

It was about the year 1893 that the decline of William Adams began, and the management of the locomotive department of the L&SWR devolved more and more upon his Works Manager at Nine Elms, W.F. Pettigrew. Indeed such was the extent that Adams had come to rely upon him, particularly over the running of the trials of one of the 7-ft 1-in 4-4-0 express locomotives, that Pettigrew could well have looked forward one day to succeeding his chief at Nine Elms. On the other hand, in the railway world in Scotland it was generally well known that Dugald Drummond was far from happy in his unaccustomed role as a commercial engineering manufacturer. The 'grape vine' would no doubt have told him of Adams' failing health, and it is more than likely that he made some tentative enquiries as to whether the post of Locomotive Superintendent was likely to fall vacant in the near future. Be that as it may, when Adams retired, early in 1895, it is generally understood that Dugald Drummond was offered the job, albeit at a considerably lower salary than he had relinquished when he gave up the top job on the Caledonian in 1890.

In the intervening years it soon appeared that Drummond had lost nothing of his style in locomotive designing. In 1897 an order was placed with Dübs & Co for thirty 0-6-0 goods tender engines, which, except for the safety valves on the dome, looked the 'spitting image' of the Caledonian '340' Class, which he had built at St Rollox in 1887, or equally the North British engines of 1876. All of these showed their parentage to Stroudley's Brighton 0-6-0s of 1873 except in the conspicuous feature of their safety valves. On the North British and on the Caledonian Drummond used the familiar Ramsbottom type, but when mounted on the dome cover and surmounted by the spring balance lever its prominent elevated position gave it the look of a fierce moustachio! In Drummond's brief absence from the railway scene his successor on the North British, Matthew Holmes, replaced these picturesque mountings by a pair of lock-up valves, also on the dome-top, and when Drummond began designing locomotives once more, for the London and South Western Railway he adopted Holmes' type of safety valve. Although his new 0-6-0 goods engines, apart from colour, might have been mistaken for either of their Scottish predecessors, the South Western's were considerably more powerful, not only having cylinders of 18½-in diameter instead of 18 in, but carrying a boiler pressure of 175 psi instead of 150 psi. Beginning in 1920 all thirty of the class were superheated, all survived to enter National ownership in 1948.

While Dübs & Co were busy with construction of the '700' Class goods engine, Nine Elms was engaged upon a modified design of 0-4-4 tank engine to do the same work as the larger class of the same wheel arrangement designed by Adams. It is interesting to study two such designs of roughly the same tractive power exhibiting so many differences, and apparently so equally successful in traffic. Withdrawal of the Adams engines did not begin until 1931, 43 years after the first of them were introduced, and nine of them were still in service at the end of 1948! The Drummond 'M7' Class had cylinders 18½ in by 26½ in and carried a boiler pressure of 175

Left *One of the '700' Class 0-6-0s of 1897 built by Dübs & Co. Shown in Southern Railway colours at Raynes Park in 1926 (Rail Archive Stephenson — F.R. Hebron.)*

Right *'M7' Class 0-4-4 tank engine No 669 on a Woking to Waterloo train near Walton-on-Thames. (Rail Archive Stephenson — F.R. Hebron.)*

psi. Apart from the style of boiler mountings, the principal differences in design lay in the firebox. While Adams had used a horizontal grate, and a relatively deep box, Drummond used a longer box, with the forward end 6 in lower than the footplate end. A Stroudley feature was retained in that the firebox back was lagged to keep the cab cool, while another important characteristic which Drummond took to Scotland with him, and brought back to introduce on the South Western, was the moving of the driver's position from the right to the left hand side of the cab. So far as longevity of service was concerned, there were eventually 105 of the 'M7' tank engines and all except one were still in service at the end of 1948. The exception was engine No 672 which fell down the lift shaft of the 'Waterloo and City' tube in April 1948 and had to be scrapped.

There was an intention, early in the life of these engines, to use some of them on express passenger service west of Exeter, where their front-coupled driving wheels seemed to make them suitable for the curvatious nature of many of the sections of the line. But it appeared that the 0-4-4 wheel arrangement did not take so kindly to the curves as the 0-4-2 of the 'Gladstones' or the Adams 'Jubilee', or even the Billinton radial 0-6-2 tanks, to judge from a Board of Trade report after the derailment of one of these engines on a curve near Tavistock. The Inspecting Officer went so far as to suggest that engines of this type—0-4-4 tanks in general—should be prohibited from running at more than 40 mph, regardless of what they were doing elsewhere in the country, notably on the Chatham, on the Midland and, not least, elsewhere on the South Western. It would seem however that the Inspecting Officer panicked over the type of locomotive when the true villain of the piece was the faulty track. Be that as it may, the South Western had to take the new tank engines off the Plymouth road until the furore had died down. In the meantime they skated merrily along with the London outer suburban residential trains at speeds often exceeding 55 mph; but nobody told the Board of Trade at that time! Many years later, admittedly when the track was quite first class, I had some footplate runs on those engines down in the West Country, at speeds of around 55 mph, and found the riding was quite immaculate, even though the particular engine was then 49 years old! They were delightful little engines.

After turning out the first fifteen of his 'M7' tank engines in March-August 1897, Dugald Drummond sprang a surprise on the British locomotive world by building a large eight-wheeled express passenger engine with four cylinders, non-compound, in which the two pairs of driving wheels were not coupled—it was, thus, a 4-2-2-0. Engines with uncoupled driving wheels had been familiar enough since the advent of the Webb three-cylinder compounds on the London and North Western, but Drummond's 4-2-2-0, No 720, had originally four cylinders of the exceptional size of 16½-in diameter by 26-in stroke. These were lined up to 15 in before the engine was released to traffic. The reason for the non-coupling of the driving wheels and for the size of the cylinders themselves is rather obscure. The engine was the first on which Drummond tried out his firebox water tubes, though not in their later familiar form. The total heating surface was very large, 1,700 sq ft, and the provisions for the cross water tubes low down in the firebox apparently necessitated spacing the independent pairs of driving wheels no less than 11 ft apart, while the grate area was 27 sq ft. It was this physical condi-

Left *One of the double-singles, No 372, on West of England restaurant car express passing Maldon. (British Railways.)*

Left *One of the first batch of 'T9' 4-4-0s without cross water tubes, No 282. (The late W.J. Reynolds.)*

Below right *Up Bournemouth express near Earlsfield hauled by one of the later 'T9' Class 4-4-0s with cross water tubes, No 716. (British Railways.)*

tion, and the inadvisability of having coupling rods 11 ft long that probably led to the decision to have uncoupled driving axles. Further unusual features of this engine were the splashers over the bogie wheels, in the Brighton style, and an enormous double bogie tender with inside frames and a height level with the top of the boiler. As first turned out No 720 was painted in Brighton yellow, but one can gather that this was not approved by 'higher authority', and it was quickly changed to the standard L&SWR green.

While the experimental '720' was running its trials and the Adams 4-4-0s of both 6-ft 7-in and 7-ft 1-in varieties were carrying on the express traffic of the line Drummond, in 1898, fell back on his standard express passenger design of Scottish days though with slightly larger cylinders and higher boiler pressure of 175 psi, against 150 psi. Apart from the lock-up safety valves on the dome the South Western engines of the '290' Class, designated 'C8', looked just like the Caledonian '60' Class. They had slightly larger boilers with a grate area of 20.4 sq ft against 19 sq ft. The new South Western engines had large six-wheeled tenders carrying 3,500 gallons of water and 4 tons of coal. The big bogie tender attached to the experimental No 720 carried 4,300 gallons. The 'C8' Class had Drummonds standard arrangement of the Stephenson link motion. This had also been used for the inside cylinders of No 720, but on this latter

engine the outside cylinders were controlled by the Joy valve gear. Both inside and outside valve gears were controlled simultaneously by one steam reverser, on the left hand side of the cab. This form, which was similar to that used by James Stirling, was used on all Drummond's 4-4-0s. So far as No 720 was concerned, and equally the uncoupled four-cylinder engines built in 1901, the dissimilar form of valve gear for the inside and the outside cylinders did not seem to affect the speedworthiness of the engines, which lived up to the Drummond tradition in every respect.

Some years ago I was amused to see one writer suggest that the 'C8' Class could not be really considered as express passenger engines. Seeing that they were directly developed from such Scottish flyers as the Caledonian '60' Class this seems a strange assertion. It is well known that Drummond kept in close touch with development on his former railway, and there were more signs of competition between the engine designing activities of Nine Elms and St Rollox in addition to the classic story of Drummond's visit to the seat of his former labours around the year 1904, as will be told later in this chapter. So far as 4-4-0s were concerned, the relative proportions of successive batches of the 'Dunalastairs' and the South Western 4-4-0s are revealing.

On the South Western Drummond went in for large

Class	Date	Cylinder diameter	Fixed wheelbase (ft in)		Tube heating surface (sq ft)	Firebox heating surface (sq ft)	Cross water tubes heating surface (sq ft)	Grate area (sq ft)	Boiler pressure (psi)
Caledonian 'Dunalastairs'									
I	1896	18¼	9	0	1284.4	118.78	—	20.6	160
II	1897	19	9	0	1381.2	118.78	—	20.6	175
III	1899	19	9	0	1402	130.0	—	22	180
London and South Western 4-4-0s									
'C8'	1898	18½	9	0	1067.7	123.9	—	20.4	175
T9-I	1899	18½	10	0	1187.0	148.0	—	24.0	175
T9-II	1901	18½	10	0	1187.2	148.0	165	24.0	175

fireboxes, with the aim of an economical rate of fuel consumption, whereas McIntosh provided a larger tube heating surface for high sustained power output. Caledonian locomotive performance at the turn of the century was second to none the world over in respect of weight haulage at high speed, but the 'Dunalastairs' of the non-superheated classes were notoriously heavy coal burners, whereas the 'T9s' were not so.

The 'T9' series of 4-4-0s could well have been judged as Dugald Drummond's finest-ever locomotives, with a magnificent steaming boiler, ample firegrate, and a beautifully-designed layout of the Stephenson link motion which gave an astonishingly free-running engine. The first variety, twenty engines with running numbers 113 to 122 and 280 to 289, had ordinary fireboxes and were built at Nine Elms between June 1899 and February 1900. At the same time a contract was placed with Dübs & Co for thirty more engines, 702 to 719 and 721 to 732, with cross water tubes in the firebox. These differed from the experimental arrangement on the 4-2-2-0 engine No 720 in having the outer casings higher up on the firebox. This became the standard arrangement on all future Drummond passenger engines and is illustrated in the accompanying drawing. The cross water tubes increased the heating surface by 165 sq ft. The Dübs contract was completed by February 1900. The third variety consisted of fifteen engines built at Nine Elms between December 1900 and October 1901. They were distinguished by having a wider cab and coupling rod splashers, to enclose the throw of the coupling rods and avoid the need for separate coupling rod splashers. These fifteen engines were fitted with large bogie tenders of a much more elegant appearance than the enormous 'water cart' originally attached to the 4-2-2-0 engine No 720.

Following the 'T9' express passenger engines Drummond built two separate series of mixed traffic 4-4-0s with 5-ft 7-in coupled wheels, forty of each

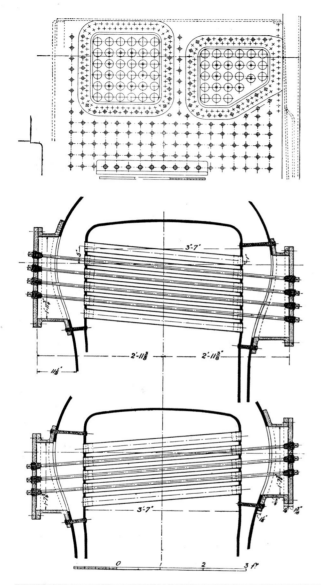

series. The first had the smaller boiler as used on the 'C8' Class, but fitted with the firebox water tubes, and the second forty had the larger boiler and the firebox of the 'T9' Class. Both classes, designated 'K10' and 'L11' respectively, were used in express passenger service on certain routes where there were severe gradients, as for example between Exeter and Plymouth and on the Portsmouth main line. Both classes had the same cylinder and valve design as the 'T9s' and were correspondingly speedy, though on a slightly lower level. The 'T9s' were among the fastest-running engines in Great Britain at that time, frequently attaining speeds of well over 85 mph, and it was not surprising that the 'K10s' and 'L11s' touched the high seventies on occasions. Class 'K10' were all built at Nine Elms in 1901-2 and the first five of 'L11' followed in May/June 1903. Then there was a pause while the first batch of a new class, 'S11', was turned out, following which another five 'L11s' and five more 'S11s' completed the output from Nine Elms for the year 1903. Subsequent batches of Class 'L11' followed up till 1907, by which time there were forty of these excellent engines in service.

Class 'S11' was a new design. It was based on the 'T9' chassis, with a larger boiler and cylinders 19-in diameter by 26-in stroke. To suit the severe gradients west of Salisbury the coupled wheels were of 6-ft diameter, and this dimension was used by Drummond in his later developments of the 4-6-0 type. Class 'S11' had an important part to play in the exciting year 1904, but before coming to these events there are certain features of the design itself that need special mention. The boiler was the largest that had so far been built at Nine Elms. The barrel was the same length as that of the 'T9', but of 4-ft 9-in diameter against 4 ft 5in and of greater heating surface. On these engines Drummond incorporated a built-up steel crank axle in which the crank webs were

Left *Cross water tubes in the firebox. (E.L. Ahrons.)*

Below *'K10' Class 5 ft 7 in 4-4-0 No 391, built in 1902. (British Railways.)*

Right *'S11' Class 5 ft 7 in 4-4-0 No 403, built in 1903. (Real Photographs Co Ltd.)*

Below *Class 'L11' 4-4-0 No 167 (with firebox water tubes removed) passing Raynes Park on an up express in 1926. (Rail Archive Stephenson — F. R. Hebron.)*

extended in a direction contrary to the crank pins, and the extensions thus formed acted as a counter-balance and obviated the need for balance weights in the driving wheel. Drummond patented this arrangement, and Class 'S11' were the first British locomotives to be so equipped. Although designated 'mixed traffic' these engines were cast for a momentous role within the very first year of their lives, that of working the Ocean Mail specials up from Plymouth in the fierce competition that developed with the Great Western Railway early in 1904. The only understanding that was reached between the two companies was that the London and South Western should take the passengers from each incoming liner and that the Great Western should take the mails.

From the passenger viewpoint each special was booked non-stop from Plymouth to Waterloo, but the working arrangements provided for one intermediate stop to change engines and there was a brief stop in the Great Western station at Exeter St David's. I have always been puzzled by the location of the South Western stop for engine changing. While Templecombe roughly halved the distance (117.8 miles from Devonport, leaving 112.2 miles to go to Waterloo) there was no comparison between the relative gradients and numerous speed restrictions, permitting no higher average speed than 47 mph from Devonport to Templecombe, whereas on the second stage average speeds of more than 65 mph were

made. In the latter case engines of the 'T9' Class, with double-bogie tenders were used; but while the 'S11' Class also had these tenders, even with no more than the four-coach load to which these 'Ocean Specials' were made up it was no mean task to make a 2½-hour journey, non-stop. On other assignments the 'S11' engines were required to run the 88 miles from Salisbury to Exeter non-stop in 96 minutes with loads of about 200 tons. While this section was relatively free from speed restrictions there were many heavy gradients, and the making of such an overall average as 55 mph with an engine having coupled wheels of no more than 6-ft diameter was no light task.

The building of an express passenger version of the 'S11' Class, from June 1904 onwards, was a natural sequel. This was designated as Class 'L12'. Except in the use of 6-ft 7-in coupled wheels instead of 6 ft, the two designs were virtually identical and I have always held the view that the 'L12s', as originally turned out, were the most handsome engines Drummond ever built. But while they had larger boilers than the 'T9s' and larger cylinders they did not seem to justify their larger dimensions, and in the really high ranges of speed they were not so fast. When the two-hour Bournemouth trains were put on, making the non-stop run at an average speed of 54 mph, the drivers seemed to have difficulty in making their water supply last out when the loads much exceeded 240

Up West of England express near Earlsfield, hauled by 'L12' Class 4-4-0 engine No 730. (Author's collection.)

The original double-single No 720, built in 1897, as rebuilt in 1905 with large boiler. (Author's collection.)

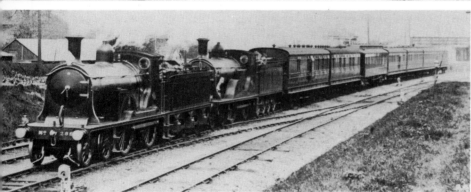

Two 'T9' Class 4-4-0s, of the first and third batches, on a Bournemouth express near Swaything. (Loco Publishing Co.)

Drummond four-cylinder 4-6-0 No 335, as originally built in 1907. (British Railways.)

tons. On the Bournemouth trains making one or more stops, when one had the chance of taking water intermediately it was very different. On the West of England road, to Salisbury and to Exeter, the 'L12' Class did very good work. In the heavy summer traffic, even after the introduction of the Drummond four-cylinder 4-6-0s, the 'L12s' were still regularly used on some of the fastest trains. On the downhill stretches they ran freely at 75 mph to 77 mph. The twenty engines were all built at Nine Elms between June 1904 and March 1905.

The introduction of Class 'L12' in 1904 was coincidental with that of the 'Dunalastair IV' Class on the Caledonian, and the two designs were similar in many ways. When they were being built at St Rollox Dugald Drummond paid a visit to McIntosh and was duly shown the latest Scottish pride and joy, the huge '49' Class 4-6-0, the two examples of which had been built in the previous year, and which had the prime task of climbing the Beattock Bank unaided with maximum load West Coast expresses. Drummond was not impressed, or he said he was not, and he went so far as to upbraid McIntosh for building such unnecessarily large engines. They were then, certainly, the largest and most powerful engines in the country. Drummond, however, returned south and set the Nine Elms drawing office on to designing something considerably larger! He was then 65 years of age and had reached a time of life when many men were thinking of retirement, or of attaining some degree of leisure in their daily work, but for Drummond there was never the slightest hint of any let-up. For one thing, he was actively planning the transfer of his main works from Nine Elms to Eastleigh, a move that was eventually carried out with the utmost prescience and skill.

The building of the large 4-6-0s always seems like an auxiliary exercise in Drummond's engine designing programme. By the beginning of the year 1905 he had ten Class 'C8' 4-4-0s, 66 'T9s', ten 'S11s' and twenty 'L12' 4-4-0s to say nothing of the later Adams 4-4-0s with 19-in cylinders, sixty of them. There were also the six 4-2-2-0s, always regarded as top ranking express units by the running department. There were, in addition, the eighty mixed traffic 4-4-0s of the 'K10' and 'L11' Classes, of which latter the number had been built up to its total of forty in 1907. There were thus 256 modern and efficient 4-4-0 locomotives to form the backbone of main-line motive power. The fact that Drummond kept a keen eye over the entire locomotive department, and not only the sheds concerned with the top line express workings, is shown not only by his book *Lectures on the Locomotive*, but also in that he delivered the lectures personally in London, Exeter, Guildford, Portsmouth, Salisbury, Southampton and Yeovil. The railway itself was consistently prosperous througout his time of chieftainship as it had, indeed, been during the time of William Adams. In Drummond's years the dividend on the ordinary shares never dropped below 5⅜ per cent, and for most of the time it was six per cent, or slightly over, despite the heavy capital expenditure in building the new works at Eastleigh.

It was no more than natural, however, that intense interest should have been aroused throughout the locomotive world when Drummond, in the autumn of 1905, not only built a class of five 4-6-0s, but built them of such colossal proportions as to leave the railway littérateurs of the day bereft of superlatives! Among locomotive engineers, privately, it was questioned whether 'DD' really knew what he was doing. With engines of such mammoth size, immeasurably larger than anything that had been previously built at Nine Elms, it would have seemed natural to have a single prototype; but instead five of these were built in the one quarter of the year. That there was something unusual about them could be sensed when it was reported that all five of them would be withdrawn from traffic for the winter months. Subsequently, when they were recommisioned for the summer service of 1906, it was revealed that the six 4-2-2-0 four-cylinder engines had also been withdrawn for the same winter season. So far as No 330 and her four sisters were concerned, the huge boiler of 5-ft 6-in diameter, the total heating surface of 2,727 sq ft and the grate area of 31.5 sq ft, was enough to cause surprise, but no less the pitch of the centre line of the boiler, 9 ft above rail level, which reduced the height of the boiler mountings to what one contemporary account described as 'mere buttons'. The general effect was tremendous.

To locomotive engineers, rather than enthusiastic members of the general public, it was the machinery below the running plate that created the most attention, and while the outside valve gear was Walschaerts', for the inside cylinders, driving the leading pair of coupled wheels, the Stephenson link motion was used. It was generally understood that the '330' Class were to be used for the Salisbury-Exeter section, and like the 'S11' Class they had 6-ft diameter coupled wheels—perhaps it was hoped that they would also prove as speedy. While the 'S11' 4-4-0s were always very restrained in running downhill in making the long non-stop runs between Devonport and Templecombe with the American Specials it was very much the reverse sometimes between Salisbury and Exeter, where Charles Rous-Marten clocked them up to 88 mph! But while he, and other devotees of the train-timing art like R.E. Charlewood, went hot-foot after each new engine-design as it became available for traffic, complete silence reigned over the comings and goings of the gigantic '330s', other than a brief note in *The Locomotive Magazine* of July 1906 to the effect that the 4-6-0s that had been in cold storage during the winter months were again at work. There was not a word about a run behind one of them.

At the end of the following year a still more powerful version was built at Nine Elms, engine No 335, with the same-sized boiler but still larger cylinders—16½ in by 26 in instead of 16 in by 24 in. This impressive looking giant, which had a nominal tractive effort of no less than 29,000 lb—larger even than *The Great Bear* which came out of Swindon a few months later—did once appear in Charlewood's notebooks in a not very distinguished non-stop run from Salisbury to Exeter, with a 295-ton load, on which 2½ minutes were lost on a schedule of 98 minutes. The dissimilar valve gear which this engine shared with the five '330' Class was sometimes mentioned as a likely cause of the reputed sluggishness of these engines and for their subsequent withdrawal from express traffic, but this log of Charlewood's shows plenty of downhill running at speeds of 75 mph to 78 mph. The deficiency seems to have lain in the hillclimbing, though when the ultimate 'crunch' came in the formidable ascent to Honiton Tunnel the engine climbed magnificently, at a minimum speed of 30 mph, though not well enough to regain the 2½ minutes lost earlier in the run.

No more than four months after the supermammoth was out-shopped from Nine Elms a third design of four-cylinder 4-6-0 was produced, as in the case of the '330' Class, restricted at first to five engines. Class 'G14', as they were designated, had considerably smaller boilers than the '330s', and as previously intended for the Salisbury-Exeter route, were fitted with 6-ft coupled wheels. The new engines, numbered 453 to 457, went straight into service from Salisbury shed and with considerably greater success than their large forebears. Moreover,

from the outset they seemed to work regularly east as well as west of Salisbury, and had a good turn of speed. With only five of them available for the first two and a half years of their existence, the various 4-4-0s on the West of England road still had to do most of the work. In examining the proportions of these engine in relation to their 'mammoth' predecessors, one notes that although the tube heating surface had been reduced from 2,210 to 1,580 sq ft and that of the firebox from 160 to 140 sq ft the grate area remained at 31.5 sq ft. Although the cylinders of Class 'G14' were reduced to 15-in diameter, the nominal tractive effort was still no less than 23,000 lb.

The very large grate area provided on these engines, and equally on all Dugald Drummond's four-cylinder 4-6-0s raises doubts about their effectiveness in traffic. Their scarcity in numbers meant that the train loads had to be fixed so that a 4-4-0 could be used if a 4-6-0 was not available; indeed in the height of the summer traffic, when the morning express to the West of England was regularly scheduled to run in three portions daily from Waterloo throughout to Exeter, there was rarely more than one 4-6-0 ready for any of these trains, even in the last Drummond days when there were twenty 4-6-0s on the strength. Reverting to that very large firegrate, in studying the details of many runs with the 'G14' engines, and equally with the larger-wheeled 'T14' Class which were introduced in 1911, it seemed that the overall results in terms of load haulage and maintenance of scheduled speed were very little better than those yielded by the 4-4-0 engines; in fact some of the finest runs on record in the years 1908 to 1913 were made by the 'T9' Class 4-4-0s.

It is very unfortunate in view of the facilities for observation from the footplate accorded to him by Dugald Drummond that the late Cecil J. Allen, then the author of the 'British Locomotive Practice and

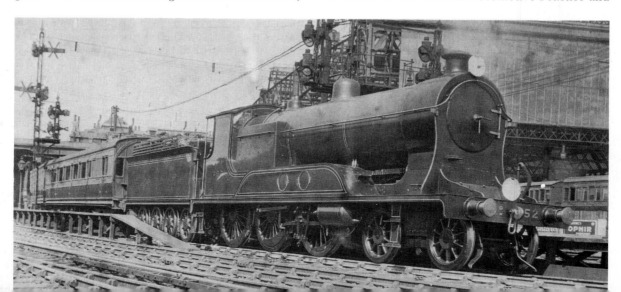

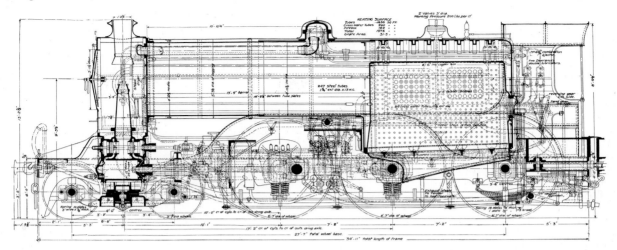

Performance' feature in *The Railway Magazine,* did not take any details of the engine working, such as regulator openings and setting of the reversing lever, with its indication of the point of cut-off. More significant perhaps would have been the details of the firing, on those longer non-stop runs like those to and from Bournemouth on which there were signs, in the detailed logs subsequently published, of shortage of steam. More particularly in respect of the 4-6-0 engines, that 31.5 sq ft of grate area could be a distinct liability, in that the floor of the grate was nearly level, as can be seen from the accompanying cross-sectional drawing, and the restricted headroom between the grate and the underside of the brick-arch. Physical conditions alone would make it difficult to maintain a bright even fire over such an area as 31.5 sq ft, when firing well-nigh level through the door all the time. In his booklet on the management of locomotives, even in the later editions, Drummond did not illustrate the form of firebox used on all the 4-6-0s. It would have

been interesting to have had an exposition from him personally as to the best method of firing those boxes in heavy steaming conditions.

The second batch of 'G14' Class engines, numbered 448 to 452, were the first express passenger engines to be built at the new Eastleigh Works. The first three came out one per month at the end of 1910, and the remaining two early in 1911. By that time preparations were well advanced for production of Drummond's fourth 4-6-0, the 'T14', having the same boiler and firebox as Class 'G14', but 6-ft 7-in coupled wheels and a rearrangement of the front end in which all four cylinders were in line. This involved much longer connecting rods to the outside cylinders, but having the cylinders compactly arranged beneath the smoke box made a much neater steam circuit. The single wide splasher with its circular inspection cover led to the engines of Class 'T14' receiving their celebrated nickname. In recent years however this name has become distorted from its original use, and

Left *Drummond 6 ft four-cylinder Class 'G14' 4-6-0 No 452 on a West of England express at Waterloo. (Author's collection.)*

Above *The 'T4' 4-6-0.*

Right *A 'paddleboat' four-cylinder 4-6-0 No 443 on a down West of England express in Earlsfield cutting. (Author's collection.)*

is sometimes rendered 'Paddlebox'; but from an old L&SWR man who was firing when the 'T14s' were new I heard the true name, the 'Paddleboats'. These engines, although having the same boiler as the 'G14s' had a higher working pressure of 200 psi. The first five followed in the erecting shop immediately after the last of the 'G14' Class, and were numbered 443 to 447. They were ready for the summer traffic, on which they marked the first introduction of 4-6-0 locomotives on to the Bournemouth trains. They quickly estalished themselves as easily the fastest running 4-6-0s that the L&SWR had, attaining maximum speeds of well over 80 mph on the well-

'D15' 4-4-0 showing, through the open smokebox door, the Drummond steam dryer. (National Railway Museum.)

aligned racing stretch from Litchfield Tunnel down to Eastleigh.

Unlike his neighbour on the Brighton, Drummond made no advances towards superheating, but on a second batch of the 'T14' 4-6-0s he installed his steam-dryer. This device provided for a moderate degree of superheat, no more than 20°F above the temperature of formation of the steam at 200 psi. This was considered adequate, and no special arrangement of dampers or forced lubrication was necessary. The device consisted of a number of 2-in diameter tubes which were in line with the flue tubes of the boiler, in such a way that the hot gases of combustion were drawn through both sets of tubes. The steam entered the chamber containing these tubes through a tee-pipe and was directed by three baffle plates to the bottom, and thence upward to the cylinder steam pipe connection at the top. The device required no alteration to the design of the boiler, and it could be readily removed for cleaning. No outward evidence of the presence of the steam-dryer was to be seen on any of the engines so fitted.

The first of the 'T14s' with the steam-dryer was completed at Eastleigh in December 1911, but by then there was another new engine in the erecting shop alongside the next of the new 'T14s'. This was the first of a new and enlarged design of 4-4-0, to be known as the 'D15' Class, with 19½-in by 26-in cylinders, a boiler with no less than 1,724 sq ft of total heating surface and 27 sq ft of grate area. The boiler pressure was 200 psi and the steam-dryer was fitted in the smokebox. When the first of the new class, engine 463, came out of Eastleigh Works in February 1912 there was some surprise that Drummond had reverted to the 4-4-0 type. At that time however, with the advent of superheating there was a marked trend in British locomotive practice to introduce super-heated versions of favourite four-coupled types, notably the 'Dunalastair IV' Class on the Caledonian, and the 'George the Fifth' Class on the London and North Western. The 'D15' as it happened, was Drummond's last design, and it was one of his best. It was notable as he used the Walschaerts' valve gear instead of Stephenson's, and this class as a whole were very free-running engines. The first of them, No 463, was a 'loner' at the time while two more 'T14' 4-6-0s were being completed. Then followed No 464, in May 1912, and the last of the 'T14s'. The rest of the 'D15s' were built at intervals between June and December 1912. The last three of the class were completed after Drummond's death. In excellent health, and active as ever at the age of 72, on the footplate he suffered so severe a scald that his leg had to be amputated. The shock was more than a man of his age could sustain and he died the very next day, 8 November 1912.

7. The intervening years

The resignation of Earle-Marsh, through ill-health, and then the sudden death of Dugald Drummond, might well have led to eras of new and original engine design on both the Brighton and South Western railways had these events not been so closely followed by the outbreak of the First World War in August 1914. Although there was at first a pretence that railway business was being carried on as usual, at any rate as far as ordinary passengers were concerned, to the bulk of professional railwaymen, and particularly those concerned with engineering and operation, the door was slammed, forever, upon much that had gone previously. The new locomotive chiefs on both the Brighton and the South Western began to mark their individuality with certain new designs before the storm broke in 1914, but any continuance of building in the former style was precluded, by the gradual transference of works' capacity to arms production in various forms.

The South Eastern and Chatham Railway had reached a crossroads of its own even before the national emergency. This, like those of the Brighton and the South Western, was one of personalities though of a more serious and deep-seated nature. In the manner of its resolution, the South Eastern crisis had repercussions extending eventually over the whole of the South of England, so that developments in what I have termed 'the intervening years' can be considered more towards the Southern Railway as it was constituted in 1923, rather than of its pre-grouping fractions.

The situation that had been reached by the locomotive department of the South Eastern and Chatham Railway had its origins in the 'working union' of the South Eastern Railway and London, Chatham and Dover Railway which was set up in 1898, in which the engineering and operating departments of the two railways were amalgamated. With James Stirling and William Kirtley both on the point of retirement the post of Locomotive, Carriage and Wagon Superintendent of the combined railways was awarded to H.S. Wainwright formerly Carriage Superintendent of the South Eastern Railway while Robert Surtees, Chief Draughtsman of the Chatham, and formerly based at Longhedge, was appointed Chief Draughtsman of the SE&CR, in the combined headquarters offices at Ashford. At first all went well. Surtees was a first class locomotive man, and Wainwright was content to leave all matters of detail design to him. The combination of robust construction traditional at Ashford, and the finer points of design practice developed at Longhedge by Kirtley and Surtees quickly bore fruit in some remarkably handsome new locomotives to which Wainwright's artistry provided the finishing touches in decorative elegance. The new engines were among the most beautiful in England at the time.

But before any new locomotives from the amalgamated drawing office at Ashford could come forth, five 4-4-0 engines of an alien design were delivered from Neilson, Reid & Co at New Year 1900. The first news of them was in an illustrated article in *The Locomotive Magazine* of March 1900, and the description included a note that they were for 'mixed traffic'. The coupled wheels were 6-ft 1-in diameter, the cylinders 18 in by 26 in and the boiler pressure 165 psi. The 'ensemble' was generally handsome, but what aroused speculation as to the future intentions of Ashford Works was the closed-in cab, such as T.W. Worsdell had standardized on the North Eastern Railway. The Ramsbottom safety valves were closed in, and the lining and lettering was described as of the new standard style of the SE&CR. The engines were fitted with the Westinghouse brake, though the equipment included the connections and appliances for operating vacuum fitted stock as used on the former South Eastern lines. The appearance of these engines raised the question, albeit only briefly, as to what form of brake might be standardized on by the amalgamated railway. Some of the queries raised by that article in *The Locomotive Magazine,* however, were answered the very next month, though in a curiously indirect way.

Another illustrated article, containing precisely the same technical information, was published on some new 4-4-0s that Neilson, Reid & Co had delivered to the Great North of Scotland Railway, to the designs of Mr William Pickersgill. The answer to the question about the South Eastern engines, as subsequently revealed, was that the GNofS had originally ordered ten new 4-4-0 engines of Pickersgill design, and then could not pay for all of them. The newly formed SE&CR, being short of engines, bought them off Neilson, Reid & Co and had the vacuum brake fittings added before they left Glasgow. The five SE&CR 4-4-0s, as delivered, did not quite accord with the new livery, which was seen in all its new-found glory when the first of the new Wainwright Class 'C' 0-6-0 goods came out in the spring of that same year. The Scottish-built 4-4-0s, in slightly later years, were dolled up in the full Ashford style by having their safety valve casings removed, their pedestals and mounting bases in polished brass and their domes 'got-up' as magnificently as any other SE&CR express engines of the Wainwright era.

At the time of their introduction they were the most

powerful engines on the Chatham section of the line, and although at first used on the Continental mail trains they were regarded as the 'odd men out'. Because of their origin they were designed to be driven from the left-hand side of the cab, and this feature was not altered subsequently. They remained the only SE&CR engines with left-hand drive. In Wainwright's time the Westinghouse brakes were removed, and it was in this form that one of the class featured in a series of coloured picture postcards issued about 1906. These engines, or rather their counterparts on the Great North of Scotland Railway, had a good turn of speed and were sometimes clocked up to nearly 80 mph, but the Chatham engines were soon taken off the best trains when the new Wainwright 'D' Class 4-4-0s were introduced. In later years these five engines worked from Gillingham shed. They had all been scrapped by the end of 1927.

The first new SE&CR engine from Surtees' drawing board was the 'C' Class 0-6-0, destined to be a long-lived standard type. The South Eastern had 122 of the Stirling 'O' Class, but they were less powerful than the Kirtley type of the Chatham and the new engines were based on the 'B2' Class of 1891, of which only six were built by the Vulcan Foundry. These had the same-sized cylinders as the SER 'O' Class but a considerably higher boiler pressure, 160 psi, instead of 140 psi. It was on the Chatham design that the new standard class was based. The similarity in dimensions will be apparent from the accompanying table:

Railway	LC&DR	SE&CR
Class	'B2'	'C'
Cylinders (in)		
Diameter	18	18½
Stroke	26	26
Wheel diameter (ft in)	5 0	5 2
Total heating surface		
(sq ft)	1,104	1,200
Grate area (sq ft)	17	17
Boiler pressure (psi)	160	160

The only Ashford feature to be included was the Stirling steam reverser. The first engine to be completed was No 255, in June 1900, and this was the 430th engine to be built at Ashford Works. Fourteen further engines of the class were turned out in that same year, together with thirty more that were contract built—fifteen by Sharp, Stewart and Co and fifteen by Neilson, Reid & Co. Steady additions were made to the class in 1901-4, all except nine being built at Ashford. The exceptions were built at Longhedge. By that time there were 98 of them at work, and they were all decked in the ornate passenger livery. They did not last long in such finery, but they, and the eleven further engines of the class built in 1908, survived to

enter national ownership in 1948, and happily one of them, No 592 has been preserved in working order and restored to what a wag once called 'glorious technicolour', for operation on the 'Bluebell' line.

The delightful new engine livery bestowed on all SE&CR locomotives, both large and small, by the beginning of the year 1901 received its crowning feature with the arrival of the first Class 'D' 4-4-0 express passenger engine from Sharp, Stewart's Works. This was the first of an order for ten, meanwhile five further engines of the class were under construction at Ashford. The veteran journalist F. Burtt, writing forty years ago, said that in appearance and in detail the engines were a radical departure from anything seen hitherto on either the Chatham or the South Eastern Railways. I disagree however for the 'D' Class could be described as an enlarged and beautified version of the Chatham 'M3' Class. In Martley's time at Longhedge, and subsequently, locomotive production was on a shoe-string basis, and although the engineering was sound the structural work was on the light side and the engines were noisy in consequence. After the amalgamation the Chatham express engines became known as the 'Clatterbangs' by South Eastern men who had to use them occasionally. It was far otherwise with the Ashford-designed types, however, and in the 'D' Class Surtees took every opportunity of building a Chatham-style 'engine' on a massive South Eastern-style frame. The result was a locomotive that was not only beautiful to look at and did an excellent job of work, but also seemed as if it would last for ever! Although 21 of them were extensively rebuilt, with superheaters, between 1921 and 1927, as will be told in a later chapter, the rest of them, thirty in all, remained as built and all but one entered national ownership in 1948.

These notable engines had 19-in by 26-in cylinders, 6-ft 8-in coupled wheels and carried a boiler pressure of 175 psi. The boilers were much larger than those of the 'M3' Class, having a total heating surface of 1,505 sq ft and a grate area of 20 sq ft against 1,110.2 sq ft and 17 sq ft. They were excellent runners, and in this respect they were more fortunate than their Stirling predecessors in that the 'line maximum' speed limit had been raised well above the '60' that had so inhibited South Eastern running in the nineteenth century. Building of 4-4-0 express engines in the first decade of the SE&CR followed a somewhat unusual course, in that a modified design with a Belpaire firebox was introduced in 1905, and production of both variations continued until the end of 1907. The Belpaire engines had slightly larger cylinders of 19¼-in and 6-ft 6-in coupled wheels, but there did not seem to be any difference in their running. All 26 of the Belpaires, Class 'E', were built at Ashford,

Right *The beautiful Wainwright 'D' Class 4-4-0. This is No 748 of the 1903 batch in original condition (Loco Publishing Co.)*

Below *Up Kent Coast train near St Mary Cray, hauled by a glittering 'E' Class 4-4-0, No 516. (H. Gordon Tidey.)*

Bottom *'E' Class 4-4-0 No 165 on up Continental boat express passing Folkestone Junction sidings. (British Railways.)*

whereas the chronology of Class 'D' was thus:

Date	Builders
1901	726-735 Sharp, Stewart & Co 736-740 Ashford
1902	57, 246, 487, 488, 490 Ashford
1903	75, 95, 145, 247, 489, 492-4, 501, 502 Dübs & Co 741-745 Robert Stephenson & Co 745-750 Vulcan Foundry
1906	470, 509, 545, 549, 577, Ashford
1907	477, 496, 505, 574, 586, 591 Ashford

The first Belpaire, No 273, was built in 1905, then in 1906 followed 273, 504, 506 and 511, and eight more in 1907. It will be seen that Ashford was building Classes 'D' and 'E' simultaneously in 1906 and 1907. In 1908 a variation of Class 'E' was introduced having an extended smokebox, and a further eleven of this type were built during that year and 1909.

Both 'D' and 'E' Class engines did superb work on the heavy Continental boat expresses. These trains were very heavy for the period, frequently loading to as much as 350 tons. In the height of the tourist season it was often necessary to run two boat trains to carry the passengers arriving on one crowded steamer, and then it was usually the practice to run one of the trains by the South Eastern route to London, and one by the Chatham. As early as 1907 Ashford prepared a design for a 4-6-0 express engine with inside cylinders that would have looked like an elongated version of Class 'E', as per the accompanying line drawing. But the proposal was not accepted by the Civil Engineer, and neither was the subsequent one for an outside-cylinder 4-6-0 put forward in 1911. Both these handsome designs were for non-superheater engines.

The intensity of the suburban traffic in south-east London, on both the Chatham and South Eastern routes, highlighted the importance of maintaining a high standard of locomotive performance throughout the area. Both railways had been well served in the past, particularly by the Stirling 0-4-4 tank engines of the 'Q' Class, which had been first introduced as long before as 1881 and unchanged in design until the final fifteen, built by Neilson & Co in Glasgow in 1897. By the early 1900s the first batches were becoming due for boiler renewal, and Surtees rebuilt one or two of them in 1903 with Chatham-style domed boilers of a slightly enlarged version of that used on the LC&DR 'R' Class 0-4-4 tanks, of which the last batch had been built by Sharp, Stewart & Co in 1900. The three engines thus dealt with in 1903, namely No 180, 319 and 362 became, virtually, the prototypes of the new Wainwright 'H' Class of 0-4-4, introduced in 1904, and eventually 66 strong. These had the same-sized cylinders as the Stirling 'Q' Class but carried a higher boiler pressure of 160 psi. They had the same chassis, and were decked in the ornate style of the new association, with highly-polished brass domes and safety-

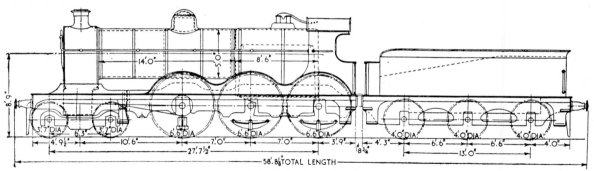

1907 design for inside-cylinder 4-6-0

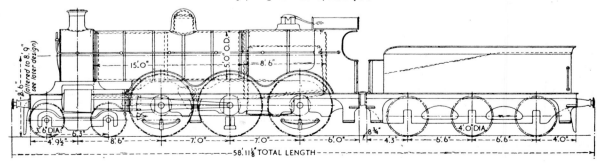

Below left *Proposals for 4-6-0 locomotives for the SE&CR.*

Right *Down Continental boat express near Orpington, hauled by 'E' Class engine No 179 in the Maunsell era just before World War 1, brass painted over. (Author's collection.)*

Right *Hastings express passing Chislehurst in 1914, hauled by rebuilt Stirling 'B' Class 4-4-0 No 452. (L&GRP.)*

valve mountings. The reboilered 'Q' Class were similarly adorned at first, but although there were eventually 55 of these rebuilds many of them were not so treated until after the year 1913, and in that year the gay livery was suppressed.

In 1912 the Locomotive Department, having had both their proposals for a 4-6-0 express engine vetoed by the Civil Engineer on the grounds of excessive axle loading, turned to superheating as a means of augmenting engine power, particularly for the heavy Continental trains, and authority was granted for two of the 'E' Class engines to be rebuilt, No 36 and No 275. Because of the increased weight involved these two engines were prohibited from running over any part of the former Chatham line. At that time however most of the boat trains were worked from Charing Cross, with certain services calling in at Cannon Street and reversing direction there while attaching post office vans. The superheater engines thus could be used with impunity on these trains.

The rebuilt engines were provided with new cylinders of 20½-in diameter, with piston valves of 8-in diameter instead of the slide valves, and in consideration of the larger diameter of the cylinders the

boiler pressure was reduced to 160 psi. One engine was fitted with the Schmidt superheater and the other with the Robinson. The maximum axle load was increased from 17½ to 18½ tons. These two superheated 'Es' were lovely engines. Although they came to be rather overshadowed by the subsequent 'L' Class, and equally by the Maunsell-rebuilt 'E1' Class, they remained as first class medium power units until after nationalization. In the last years of the Southern Railway I had some footplate runs on No 1275, as she then was, and found her as smooth and free-running a 4-4-0 as I have ever ridden upon, and responsive to my adjustments of the regulator. The Stirling steam reverser, as always, was a pleasure to use.

The last new engine design of the Wainwright era was to me something of an enigma, the Class 'J' 0-6-4 tank engine of which only five were built, all at Ashford Works in 1913. The original proposal was for a 0-6-2 radial tank on the lines of R.J. Billinton's design for the Brighton some fifteen years earlier, but the outcome was a superheated engine with coupled wheels of only 5-ft 6-in diameter and ample coal and water capacity. The cylinders were 19½ in by 26 in

Above *Rebuilt 'F' Class Stirling 4-4-0 No 94, on Reading train on Brighton line near Purley. (The late C. Laundy.)*

Left *Unrebuilt Stirling 'F' Class 4-4-0, No 198, on Oxted line train. (The late C. Laundy.)*

Below *LB&SCR 'Mogul' No 337, of 1913, by Colonel L.B. Billinton. (British Railways.)*

Below right *The first Brighton 4-6-4 tank, No 327* Charles C Macrae, *on Pullman car express near Coulsdon. (Author's collection.)*

and the boiler pressure 160 psi, as on the superheated 'E' Class 4-4-0s. According to the literature of the day the new tank engines were intended for the outer suburban service between London and Redhill, but I have never seen one photographed on such duties. My own recollection of such trains, both before and after the First World War was that they were worked by Stirling 4-4-0s, rebuilt with domed boilers, and were extended from Redhill to Reading. The 0-6-4 tank, as a type, did not have a particularly good reputation as a fast passenger engine, and it did not seem surprising that the 'J' Class of the SE&CR was limited to no more than five examples. The closing months of the Wainwright era were marked by the designing of the new superheated 'L' Class 4-4-0s, which was a development of the superheated 'E' Class. However as this was modified before going into production it will be dealt with in the account of Mr Maunsell's early work.

It is interesting that the years 1912-13 marked a climax in the locomotive history of all three railways that were merged to form the Southern Railway ten years later. On the South Eastern and Chatham, both in personnel and engineering practice, the war years formed a natural prelude to the twelve years when Maunsell reigned as Chief Mechanical Engineer of the Southern and events at Ashford require special attention, which will be given in a subsequent chapter. On the Brighton the change from Earle-Marsh to the younger Billinton was the least marked of any. There was certainly a call for larger passenger engines, for while the 4-6-2 tank engines *Abergavenny* and *Bessborough* had been acclaimed as Earle-Marsh's masterpieces they had little more tractive power than existing types. The new chief at Brighton was fortunate in having B.K. Field at the head of the drawing

office, and this ensured that progress would continue in line with established tradition. In any case Colonel Lawson Billinton was not the man to turn the place upside down for the sake of innovations. His first new design was reminiscent of one of Stroudley's in that it provided a mixed traffic type ostensibly for the fast Continental goods traffic via Newhaven. The new engines, of which the first five were built at Brighton in 1913, were of the 2-6-0 type, with outside cylinders 21 in by 26 in and 10-in diameter piston valves. While the second of the 4-6-2 passenger tank-engines, *Bessborough,* had Walschaert's valve gear, the new 2-6-0s had the Stephenson link motion. They had a neat, handsome outline and quickly established a reputation for being excellent in traffic.

For the maximum demands in express passenger duty, the 4-6-2 tank type envisaged by Earle-Marsh was not pursued. Instead an altogether larger design was worked out, of the 4-6-4 type, with 22-in by 28-in cylinders, Walschaert's valve gear, 10-in diameter piston valves and a maximum valve travel that was unusually long for those days of 5⅛ in. The first of the new engines, completed at Brighton Works in April 1914 numbered 327 and named *Charles C. Macrae,* was a remarkably handsome machine though entirely in the style developed by the elder Billinton and continued by Earle-Marsh. When engine No 327 first appeared it was announced that it was one of a class of seven engines, though because of the outbreak of war in August 1914 only two were built at first. The remaining five were not built until 1922. The second engine of the class was not named. By reason of their ample dimensions, 6-ft 9-in coupled wheels, a boiler with a total heating surface of 2,070 sq ft and a grate area of 26.7 sq ft, the new 4-6-4s were the most powerful engines in the south of England. On their intro-

duction it was emphasized that the tank capacity of 2,700 gallons and coal capacity of 3 ½ tons made possible non-stop running between Victoria and Portsmouth Harbour, 87 miles, with maximum load trains.

At that time the Brighton was still in competition with the South Western for the Isle of Wight traffic, in fact it seemed to be the most favoured route of the two, and there were some triangular engine workings from Brighton to London, then to Portsmouth and then via the coast line home to Brighton. Because of the onset of war little was known of the workings of the two giant 4-6-4 tanks until 1919, indeed, although I visited the line frequently from the autumn of 1921 onwards it was not until the post-war members of the class began to enter traffic that I saw any of them. By that time they had some rivals for the most powerful passenger engines south of the Thames in the form of the new Urie 4-6-0s of the London and South Western Railway.

In 1897, when Pettigrew had left the L&SWR to join the Furness Railway, Drummond invited his old colleague of Caledonian Railway days to join him at Nine Elms. Robert Urie had previously been Chief Draughtsman at St Rollox, indeed his initials appear on the general arrangement drawing of the first 'Dunalastair' Class 4-4-0. Later he was Works Manager, the post he vacated to take up the same job at Nine Elms. So for fifteen years he followed in the footsteps of the indomitable 'DD', playing no small part in the very smooth transfer of the works from Nine Elms to Eastleigh in 1910. After Drummond's death in 1912, and his appointment as Chief Mechanical Engineer of the London and South Western Railway, he soon showed that he disagreed with some of the most cherished Drummond pre-

cepts, namely cross water tubes in the firebox and multi-cylinder 4-6-0 engines. His first new design, the 'H15' Class 4-6-0, introduced less than a year after Drummond's death, was as different as could be imagined from anything that had gone before.

Urie was the first British locomotive engineer to adopt the design principle of what his neighbour on the SE&CR, R.E.L. Maunsell, used to call 'make everything get-at-able'. The 'H15' Class had cylinders of 21-in diameter by 28-in stroke, outside Walschaert's valve gear and outside frames on their large bogie tenders. The boilers broke clean away from Drummond's practice, with the first eight of the class having relatively high degree superheaters. The remaining two used saturated steam at first. Of the former, four, numbers 482-485, had the Schmidt apparatus and numbers 486-489 had the Robinson. At first the new engines, having 6-ft coupled wheels, were described as 'mixed traffic', though why this should have been so is not clear, seeing that the 'G14' Class of Drummond's design, also with 6-ft coupled wheels, were used exclusively in express passenger service. Moreover, when the 'H15' engines went into regular work they were used from Nine Elms shed on some of the fastest expresses, like the 11 am from Waterloo to Salisbury. They also showed that they had a fine turn of speed, frequently attaining maxima of between 75 mph and 80 mph. How they rode at those speeds is another matter, in comparison to the multi-cylindered Drummond 4-6-0s.

Proprietary brands of superheaters did not last long on the London and South Western Railway, for by the end of 1914 Urie had patented his own 'Eastleigh' type and fitted it to one of the two 'H15' Class engines previously using saturated steam. In this design the headers were connected by a system of small vertical headers, those from the saturated steam header connecting with the inlet ends of each superheater element, and those from the superheated steam header with the outlet ends thereof. In each large fire tube there were four tube lengths as usual. On the large boiler of the 'H15' Class there were 21 elements each consisting of a 5¼-in large firetube and a total of 138 small tubes of 1¾-in diameter. In addition to the 'H15' Class, one of the first of the Drummond 4-6-0s, No 335, was extensively rebuilt, bringing it in accordance with the 'H15' Class with Eastleigh superheater. The only difference between the rebuilt No 335 and the new 'H15' Class lay in the retention of the big inside-framed Drummond tender. In connection with this rebuild it will be recalled that No 335 was the only one of the second variety of the large-boilered 4-6-0s and had been built as recently as December 1907.

Despite war conditions at Eastleigh, Urie pressed on with the modernization of the passenger locomotive stock of the L&SWR, and during the year 1915 three more Drummond classes were rebuilt with superheaters, not so extensively, however, as No 335. The extent to which he disagreed with his predecessor's practice was shown by his alteration of the '463' Class 4-4-0s barely three years after they had been put on to the road, and one of the 'L12s' No 421, followed shortly afterwards. These two classes of 4-4-0s were modified by the removal of the firebox water tubes, and in the case of the '463' Class of the Drummond steam-dryer. The smokeboxes were extended and the 'Eastleigh' superheater fitted. While no doubt the efficiency of both classes was improved the appearance was not! The 'L12' and 'D15' Classes in their original form I always thought were among the

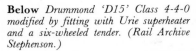

Left *The first Brighton 'Mogul', No 337, as subsequently fitted with top feed apparatus. (Rail Archive Stephenson — F.R. Hebron.)*

Right *The first Urie two cylinder 4-6-0 on the L&SWR one of those originally fitted with Robinson superheater in 1913. (British Railways.)*

Below *Drummond 'D15' Class 4-4-0 modified by fitting with Urie superheater and a six-wheeled tender. (Rail Archive Stephenson.)*

most handsome 4-4-0s ever built. As rebuilt the engines had the following dimensions:

Class	'D15'	'L12'
Small tubes		
Number	156	136
Heating surface (sq ft)	782.5	682
Large tubes		
Number	21	21
Heating surface (sq ft)	357	311
Firebox (sq ft)	144.5	161
Superheater (sq ft)	231	195
Total heating surface (sq ft)	1,515	1,349
Boiler pressure (psi)	180	175

While all ten engines of the 'D15' Class were rebuilt during the war years, and most of them allocated to Bournemouth shed, only one 'L12' was so treated up to 1919. I had a number of runs with the 'D15' Class in 1922-25, and while the performance was generally adequate it was never at any time sparkling. Drivers seemed to be holding their engines in to avoid taking water at Southampton.

During the war all ten four-cylinder 4-6-0s of the '443' Class were rebuilt with 'Eastleigh' superheaters and although the degree of superheat was not very high it seemed that the performance of these engines had been significantly improved. Wartime loads were ever on the increase before much had been done to increase the running times of the principal expresses to and from the West of England. Some of the work of the superheated four-cylinder 4-6-0s in 1915-16 was

considerably finer than that which came to be recorded with Mr Urie's own express passenger 4-6-0s in post-war years, or with much of the early running of the 'King Arthurs'. On the pre-war timing of 91 minutes for the 83¾ miles from Waterloo to Salisbury, one of the rebuilt Drummond 4-6-0s hauling a heavy wartime load of 370 tons passed Basingstoke, 47.9 miles, in 51 minutes, 3 minutes early, and had time in hand to cover the loss of time due to two subsequent delays and still arrive in Salisbury on time.

Urie's own express passenger 4-6-0 design, the 'N15' Class, came out in the autumn of 1918, but only three engines had been turned out of Eastleigh works by the end of that year. The rest of the first batch of ten came out between February and November 1919. Except for the stove pipe chimney, which became characteristic of all the later Urie engines, the 'N15' Class followed the style set by Class 'H15', in 1913, the Drummond-type cab being also retained. The cylinders were still larger, 22 in by 28 in, and it is thus interesting to compare the boiler proportions of Classes 'H15' and 'N15' alongside those of the rebuilt and superheated Drummond 4-6-0s.

Above right *Urie 'N15' Class two-cylinder express passenger 4-6-0, as originally built in 1918. (Real Photographs Co Ltd.)*

Below *Drummond 'Paddleboat' four-cylinder 4-6-0 No 443 as modified by fitting with Urie superheater. (The late W. J. Reynolds.)*

Class	T14	H15	N15
Cylinders			
Number	4	2	2
Diameter (in)	15	21	22
Stroke (in)	26	28	28
Heating surfaces (sq ft)			
Tubes	1,280	1,716	1,716
Firebox	158	167	162
Superheater	269	337	308
Total	1,707	2,220	2,186
Grate area (sq ft)	31.5	30.0	30.0
Boiler pressure (psi)	175	180	180
Nominal tractive effort at 85% working pressure (lb)	22,300	26,450	26,500

The 'N15' Class were very well received by the running department when they came out, but the timing of the principal express trains were then slow and maximum speeds were rigidly restricted to 60 mph. When schedules were smartened up some adjustments had to be made to the draughting, as is told in the chapter dealing with the development of the 'King Arthur' Class.

In 1920 a third variety of the Urie 4-6-0 was built at Nine Elms, with boilers the same as the 'N15' Class, but with coupled wheels of 5-ft 7-in diameter and cylinders of 21-in diameter. They were classed 'S15' and like the 'N15s' a total of twenty was built before the L&SWR became merged into the Southern Railway in 1923. The 'S15' Class, like the 'N15' Class, became a major feature of the Maunsell locomotive programme, for the simplicity of their machinery was in full accord with the new locomotive engineer's precepts. Before grouping took place however, the commissioning of the new hump marshalling yard at Feltham, and the traffic routed thereto, needed some very powerful new tank engines for hump shunting and some goods tank engines for working the heavy transfer goods trains between the yards on the L&NWR at Willesden, the Midland at Cricklewood and the new yard at Feltham. For this traffic Urie built four 4-8-0 humping tank engines for purely yard duties and five 4-6-2 tank engines for the transfer goods runs. They were massive jobs, entirely in the latest style, though having somewhat smaller boilers than the main-line 4-6-0 engines. Their leading dimensions were:

Type	4-8-0	4-6-2
Cylinders (in)		
Diameter	22	21
Stroke	28	28
Wheel diameter (ft in)	5 1	5 7
Heating surfaces (sq ft)		
Tubes	1,267	1,267
Firebox	139	139
Superheater	231	231
Total	1,637	1,637
Grate area (sq ft)	27	27
Total weight (tons)	95.2	96.4

8. All change at Ashford

When R.E.L. Maunsell took up the post of Chief Mechanical Engineer of the South Eastern and Chatham Railway at the end of 1913 he was faced with the design of a new superheater express passenger 4-4-0 being complete in all its details, and authorization for 22 of the new engines obtained. But as yet no steps had been taken to start on their construction. As usual Robert Surtees had supervised the design, which was a development of the superheated 'E' Class 4-4-0s No 36 and No 275. Obviously there was a need to start building them as soon as possible, but in this respect Maunsell was in some difficulty. He was in no respect an engine designer; his talents lay in workshop management, and at Ashford he had no opportunity of appraising the drawing office staff before he was called on to take responsibility for a new design. Faced with this situation he took the unusual step of referring the project to his former chief draughtsman at Inchicore on the GS&WR, W. Joynt, and on his recommendation some alterations were made to the valve setting. Of course this did not go down well in the Ashford drawing office, but Surtees was on the point of retiring anyway and the way was clear for considerable changes.

The new 4-4-0s, known as Class 'L', had the same nominal tractive effort as the superheated 'E' Class, having 20½-in by 26-in cylinders and 160-psi boiler pressure, but the boiler and firegate were larger. The comparative dimensions were as follows:

SE&CR Superheater 4-4-0s

Class	'E'	'L'
Heating surfaces (sq ft)		
Tubes	1,063	1,252
Firebox	136	160
Superheater	231	319
Total	1,430	1,731
Grate area (sq ft)	21.15	22.5

In the Ashford Works at that time a rather unsatisfactory state of affairs had been allowed to develop, much of it due to the personality of Mr Wainwright. He was more of an artist than an engineer, and certainly not a strong administrator. Maunsell found the works in no state to undertake the production of a new class of locomotive. The contract for the first ten of the 'L' Class was awarded to Borsig of Berlin, because no British firm could then meet the delivery date, June-July 1914. The order for the remaining twelve engines was given to Beyer, Peacock & Co. The delivery of the Borsig engines savours of the dramatic, because the German fitters who had come to Ashford to erect those engines, the boilers and frames

The palatial frontage of Borsig's Works, Berlin with the first of the 'L' Class 4-4-0s posed outside. (Author's collection.)

'D1' Class 4-4-0, No 31743, at Ramsgate Shed in 1960. This was a very successful rebuild of a Wainwright design. (R. C. Riley.)

Above *Adams 'Radial' 4-4-2T No 30582 at Exmouth Junction Shed in 1960. Built in 1885, she was used on the Lyme Regis branch for many years. No 30582 survives on the Bluebell Railway as LSWR No 488. (R.C. Riley.)*

Below *Wainwright 'C' Class 0-6-0, No 31575, taking milk empties to Kensington at Stewarts Lane, Battersea. (R.C. Riley.)*

Above *'H16' Class 4-6-2T, No 30517, at Wimbledon in 1962. She was mainly used on transfer freight trips or empty stock working to and from Waterloo. (R.C. Riley.)*

Below *'S15' Class, No 30501, on the 3.54 pm Waterloo-Basingstoke train at Clapham Junction on 20 June 1959. (R.C. Riley.)*

Left *'S15' Class 4-6-0 No 30824 with an up freight train from Exeter to Salisbury at Broadclyst in 1961. (R.C. Riley.)*

Below *'King Arthur' No 30770,* Sir Prianius. *By the time she was withdrawn from service in 1962 she was the last survivor of her class and had worked over 1,100,000 miles. She is seen here in Eastleigh Works in 1957. (R.C. Riley.)*

Folkestone express passing Elmstead Woods hauled by 'D' Class 4-4-0 No 477 in wartime grey livery. (H. Gordon Tidey.)

having been sent separately, were working in the shops up to within a few weeks of the declaration of war in August 1914.

With the new engines on order Maunsell turned to the far bigger problems of administration, which urgently needed resolving on a long-term basis. Wainwright's *laissez-faire* attitude had led to not merely the detailed work, but much of the direct control of the department drifting into other hands. With Surtees as Chief Draughtsman, locomotive design was sound enough and the workmanship put into the engines was evident by the longevity of the old SE&CR classes built at that time, and their continuing usefulness even into British Railways days. Ashford was always fortunate in its shop foremen, who were all sound, capable and conscientious men. But the drawing office of 1912-13 and the technical staff generally were not the controlling influences in the department's activities. With a chief of Wainwright's disposition control tends to pass naturally to the subordinate with the strongest personality, and at Ashford the power behind the throne came to be the Chief Clerk, Hugh McColl, a Scot who had come south from Kilmarnock in the wake of James Stirling. From all accounts he seems to have been a man of dour and indomitable character. In his position as Chief Clerk he was in the confidence of the chief and gradually he gathered the threads of the whole organization into his own hands. Though entirely a non-technical man he assumed virtual control of the locomotive running and the footplate staff were ruled as with a rod of iron. Being a non-technical man however he could work only to rule-of-thumb principles,

and such were hardly equal to the demands of the time.

Then, over from Inchicore, came Mr Maunsell—energetic, full of ideas, enterprise and enthusiasm, a hard worker, who expected hard work from all his staff. In his younger days he played as hard as he worked and earned a reputation as a fine cricketer, but above all Maunsell was a really strong personality. His constant solicitude for the staff and all works personnel made him a well-liked and highly respected chief. Joynt, the chief draughtsman, has recorded his own dismay on learning that Maunsell was leaving Inchicore; in that works it was widely felt that with his going the place had seen its best days, and Joynt himself added the quotation: 'There arose up a new King over Egypt which knew not Joseph'. It was the same thing in England among those who knew him best on the South Eastern and Chatham, and later on the Southern he is remembered with affection, but this is somewhat anticipating the present theme. The imagination can almost picture the clash which would inevitably have taken place at Ashford between McColl, the dour Scots Chief Clerk, who seemed to have absorbed something of the granitic personality of James Stirling, and Maunsell, still relatively young, Irish and ready to sweep tradition to the four winds.

At the time of Maunsell's appointment, however, the directors of the South Eastern and Chatham made an important change in organization which relieved the Locomotive Department of part of its previous authority. Following to some extent the Midland example, they created an independent Locomotive Running Department. A.D. Jones from the Lancashire and Yorkshire Railway was appointed as Superintendent and the headquarters of the new department was made at London Bridge.

Above *Folkestone express passing Elmstead Woods hauled by 'L' Class 4-4-0 No 770. (H. Gordon Tidey.)*

Left *'L' Class 4-4-0 No 760, one of the Beyer, Peacock & Co built batch. (The late W.J. Reynolds.)*

Below right *The first 'N' Class 2-6-0, No 810, built at Ashford in July 1917. (The late W.J. Reynolds.)*

Thus Maunsell's title of Chief Mechanical Engineer, as distinct from Wainwright's Locomotive, Carriage and Wagon Superintendent was a logical one. The position of the Locomotive Running Superintendent on the Southern Eastern and Chatham Railway, and indeed throughout Maunsell's chieftainship on the Southern, differed from that of his counterpart on the Midland, and later from those on the LMSR, in that it was partly an independent command, responsible only to the General Manager for administration, though to the Chief Mechanical Engineer for locomotive maintenance and to the Traffic Manager for operation. On the Midland, locomotive running came under the direct responsibility of the General Superintendent. The fact that the first holder of that office, Sir Cecil Paget was himself a locomotive engineer, does not lessen the significance of the change.

The position of the Locomotive Running Superintendent on the SE&CR might have been a difficult one, with its responsibility to three different

people but, largely through the delightful personality of Jones himself, it worked well and was in fact continued for many years after the grouping. Liaison between the respective staffs was close and friendly at all levels, especially in later years when they came to occupy adjacent offices at Waterloo. The tense situation arising from McColl's previous activities was dealt with firmly and tactfully and the loyalty with which the Chief Clerk came to serve his new chief rather suggests that he had assumed control simply because he saw clearly that a firm hand was needed and that no one else was prepared to wield it. In the last years at Ashford McColl's character mellowed considerably even to the extent of revealing a dry Scots humour beneath that rather forbidding crust.

In 1913 and for a few years subsequently Maunsell certainly had enough to absorb his energies quite apart from the responsibility of running. Within six months of his arrival at Ashford he had made an exceedingly clean sweep and gathered round him instead a team of young and able engineers, who served not merely the South Eastern and Chatham, but who proved the backbone of the enlarged CME's department when amalgamation took place in 1923, and continued so until Maunsell retired. Almost the whole success of Southern Railway locomotive practice up to 1937 can be traced back to the momentous reorganization that took place at Ashford in the early months of 1914. In the British locomotive world the altogether outstanding event of the previous ten or twelve years had been the establishment of the famous eight new standard designs on the Great Western Railway, accompanied by advances in principle and detail which had maintained that company in the forefront of British practice for more than thirty years. By 1911 the last of the new standard designs was completed, and with a slackening of pressure on the new work side at Swindon some of those who had been closely concerned with important developments were looking for fresh opportunities of a 'new work' character elsewhere.

Maunsell for his part seems to have realized earlier than most other British engineers the extreme importance of Churchward's work, and there was a strong Great Western flavour about the new team he recruited. First and foremost came G.H. Pearson, Carriage Works Manager at Swindon and formerly Assistant Locomotive Works Manager, to be Assistant Chief Mechanical Engineer and Works Manager at Ashford. As assistant to him C.J. Hicks from Inchicore was appointed. Surtees was due for retirement, and James Clayton was selected to succeed him as Chief Locomotive Draughtsman. This was an appointment of particular interest and importance. After serving his time with Beyer, Peacock & Co Ltd, Clayton, when a young man of twenty, joined the SE&CR as a draughtsman under Surtees, but in search of experience and advancement he left the railway in 1903. Soon afterwards he became privately associated with Sir Cecil Paget in connection with the design of the celebrated experimental 2-6-2 locomotive No 2299. He joined the Midland Railway in 1905 and from 1907-14 was Chief Assistant in the locomotive drawing office at Derby.

Thus under Maunsell's leadership there were brought together two locomotive engineers, not merely able in themselves, but who severally had been associated with the two greatest railway engineering figures of the day—Pearson with his pioneer work under Churchward and Clayton from his most intimate association with the dynamic, brilliant personality of Paget. To reinforce this distinguished opening pair Maunsell recruited the rest of his team almost exclusively from Swindon. L. Lynes was appointed Chief Draughtsman of the Carriage and Wagon section, H. Holcroft was appointed as an assistant with the particular task of reorganizing and extending the entire works layout at Ashford. The new staff had, however, scarcely been gathered at Ashford before war was declared in August 1914 and all schemes for new locomotives and new works soon had to be shelved. The South Eastern and Chatham, together with all other British railways, was taken over by the Government and the Railway Executive Committee was brought into being to co-ordinate the work of the numerous independent companies. Maunsell was appointed Chief Mechanical Engineer to the REC and one of his first tasks was, strange to say, the rehabilitation of Belgian rolling stock which had been evacuated in the face of the German advance. By that time it was ensconced behind the Allied line in France, but immobilized by the lack of stores and spare parts. Ashford was made the depot for manufacture of parts for these Belgian locomotives and as no drawings were available they had to be made from actual samples. The work was naturally of extreme urgency and was given priority over any new developments Maunsell and his staff had in mind.

Provision of spare parts for the Belgian engines was only a part of the war work at Ashford and Maunsell as CME to the Railway Executive Committee had the task of supplying the Railway Operating Division and the military railways in France and other theatres of war with a wide variety of stores. All this involved the sending out of enquiries, placing of orders, inspection and so on, and for the work the responsi-

bility at first fell mostly upon Clayton. Later, as the prospects of extending Ashford works receded, Holcroft was brought in to relieve Clayton and as things became thoroughly organized it became possible to devote some time to new locomotive designs. So, despite the stress of wartime conditions, an excellent prototype was little by little evolved.

The 'N' Class 2-6-0, as it eventually took shape, was, however, not the first new locomotive to be completed during the war period. After taking up his appointment Maunsell discovered that although a total of 66 0-4-4 passenger tank engines of the 'H' Class had been authorized and ordered only 64 had been completed, the last one in 1910. Under the previous regime many parts for the remaining two engines had been 'lost' in the works, no doubt they had been borrowed as spares for the other engines of the class, but from whatever cause the building of the last two engines had never gone ahead. Any kind of irregularity was abhorrent to Maunsell and the story is told that he just turned Ashford works upside down to get the missing parts 'found' and the engines constructed. They were completed in the early months of 1915, and took the running numbers of 16 and 184, though naturally not in 'glorious technicolor'!

During the 1914-18 war occupation of the SE&C line became as important as we have known it in more recent times, and the demands of that period served to accentuate a need which had been growing for some time. Freight traffic tended to be concentrated at Ashford on the one hand, and Hither Green on the other, and heavy 'block' loads were worked between these two points. Intermediately, remarshalling took place only at Paddock Wood. The relative severity of the gradients between Hither Green and Tonbridge called for some reduction in the maximum rostered load below the tonnage that could be worked over the easy line through the Weald of Kent, but in order to reduce occupation of the line as much as possible it was desirable to operate heavy trains, and to run them non-stop over the 21.3 miles from Paddock Wood to Ashford.

The 'N' Class 2-6-0 engine was designed primarily to meet this demand, but with the 'general utility' attributes of the 2-6-0 type in mind, and its success in this respect on the Great Western, London, Brighton and South Coast and Great Northern Railways already evident, the 'N' Class was designed to be suitable for working passenger trains, heavy seaside excursions, Tattenham Corner race specials and so on. The broad principles of the design—taper boiler, high working pressure, top feed and long-lap valves—were almost pure Great Western but in Clayton's working out of the detailed design many features of Midland practice were incorporated, such as the large diameter smokebox and the shape of the chimney, cab

and tender. The arrangement of the top feed differed from that of the Great Western. What appeared to be a dome on the boiler was actually a casing for the trays of the top feed system. The trays were helical in form, and the whole affair rapidly became known at Ashford as the 'helter-skelter lighthouse'. After its incorporation on the first of the 2-6-0s this arrangement was tried out on one of the 'B' Class Stirling 4-4-0s No 13.

In view of the Great Western flavour in the 'N' Class engine due to Pearson's influence, it is interesting to compare the leading dimensions of the class with those of Churchward's '43XX' Class 2-6-0s. The Belpaire firebox had the top and sides slanting downwards and inwards towards the back plates and the regulator was in the smokebox, though an important difference lay in the adoption of Walschaert's gear arranged outside. When the prototype engine, No 810, was completed at Ashford in the summer of 1917 details of the motion were published, but then little significance was attached to the length of the valve travel, $6^7/_{16}$ in. In actual fact No 810 and the companion 2-6-4 tank engine No 790 proved to be two of the most outstanding locomotives built for service in this country since the pioneer work of Churchward in 1903-7. Their rather gaunt lines and austere finish were, however, not likely to appeal to those whose minds dwelt upon the ornate creations of the pre-1914 era.

2-6-0 Mixed Traffic Locomotives

Railway	GWR	SE&CR
Class	4300	810
Cylinders (in)		
Diameter	18½	19
Stroke	30	28
Maximum valve travel (in)	6¾	$6^7/_{16}$
Boiler		
Small tubes		
Number	209	175
Outside diameter (in)	1⅝	1¾
Large tubes		
Number	14	21
Outside diameter (in)	5	5⅛
Wheel diameter (ft in)	5 8	5 6
Heating surfaces (sq ft)		
Tubes	1,228.0	1,390.6
Firebox	122.9	135
Superheater	215.8	203
Total	1,566.7	1,728.6
Grate area (sq ft)	20.56	25
Boiler pressure (psi)	200	200
Total engine weight (tons)	62	59.4
Nominal tractive effort (lb)	25,670	26,040

In the case of the Great Western design the original

The first 'K' Class 2-6-4, No 790, built at Ashford in July 1917. (The late W.J. Reynolds.)

The Maunsell top feed apparatus on a Stirling 'B' Class 4-4-0. This was originally fitted to No 34 in June 1919, but the boiler was afterwards transferred to No 13, as seen here. (The late W.J. Reynolds.)

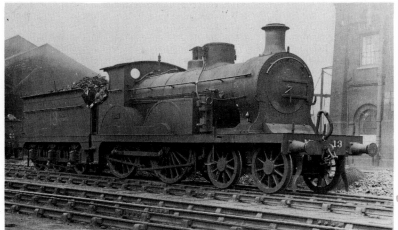

The prototype 'N' Class 2-6-0, No 810, at Bricklayers Arms shed. (The late W.J. Reynolds.)

boiler proportions and superheater as given above were slightly modified in later variations of the same class; the total engine weight as later standard was 65 tons 6 cwt.

The Maunsell superheater was first introduced on No 810 wherein the regulator was incorporated in the superheater header. The layout of the elements was a clever piece of designing, in which any element could be detached from the header and withdrawn without interference with any other element. This facility is of course provided for in the standard Swindon superheater, but with only two tiers of elements. On the SE&CR engine No 810 there were three tiers. At first the heating surface of the superheater was kept small, in conformity with Great Western practice, but in later engines of the class the elements were extended to almost the full length of the flues and the heating surface was increased from 203 to 285 sq ft. No 810 was very thoroughly tested on the road. Numerous indicator diagrams were taken, and on the SE&CR freight duties these showed excellent characteristics. Optimum power output was attained at a little over 50 mph when working at 25 per cent cut-off, then the indicated horsepower was approximately 1,000. The characteristic curves of boiler and cylinder performance are also reproduced.

The period following the armistice of November 1918 was one of uncertainty, both in the railway world and in the country at large. The Government of the day, to avoid large scale unemployment at Woolwich Arsenal, decided to build locomotives for the home railways, on which serious shortages had developed during the war. Even then the prospect of nationalization was in the air, and the Association of Railway Locomotive Engineers had been asked to see what could be done towards the production of new standard designs. Nothing tangible in the way of

finished designs resulted from their deliberations, though as will be told later this phase was an important one for Maunsell and his assistants. To enable the Government building programme to be started Maunsell's 'N' Class were selected as a standard, and a first order for one hundred was placed. When the outcome of long negotiation came to be grouping, and not nationalization, no one of the four groups made any bid to purchase the Government-built engine and so work came to a standstill after fifty had been erected. Eventually these fifty were purchased at a reduced price by the Southern Railway.

The prototype 2-6-4 tank engine No 790 was intended originally to form the basis for a class to take over all the principal passenger train workings on the South Eastern and Chatham Railway, including the boat trains. As the new Billinton 4-6-4 tank engines on the Brighton line were planned to run from Victoria to Portsmouth Harbour with no need of replenishing of the water supply en route, it was considered that the new SE&CR 2-6-4 tank, with all the expected economy in performance from the Great Western features in her design, would be able to do even better on the shorter runs from London to Dover. At first, with only one engine available, it was not possible to make very comprehensive tests, in any case the only runs possible during the first year of existence of engine No 790 to and from the Channel Ports were with troop trains. When the time came for planning for multiplication of the design, in 1921, it was necessary to make some regular trials to gauge the capability of the engine in relation to existing types which it would have to supersede, if it were to take general express passenger duties on the SE&CR. By that time also the rebuilt and superheated 'D' and 'E' Class 4-4-0s were in use on the Continental boat trains, and while reference to them to some extent anticipates the

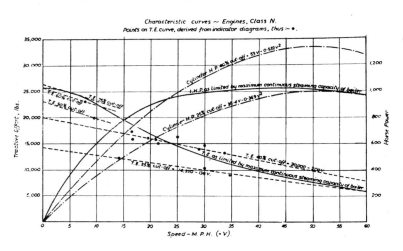

Left *Power output curves for SE&CR 'N' Class locomotives.*

Above right *The 'K' Class 2-6-4 tank No 790 on a horsebox special. (H. Gordon Tidey.)*

following chapter some overlapping is inevitable to complete the preliminary account of the prototype 2-6-4 tank engine of 'K' Class.

The trials that began in October 1922 were not over the full boat train route, but only west of Ashford, outward on the 8.40 am to Cannon Street and returning on the 3 pm from Charing Cross. On these trials No 790 was matched against an 'L' Class superheater 4-4-0 No 761, and a rebuilt and superheated 'D' Class 4-4-0. The working times of the two trains were as follows:

8.40 am up

Distance (miles)		Time (minutes)	Speed (mph)
0.0	ASHFORD	0	—
21.3	Paddock Wood	24	53.3
5.3	TONBRIDGE	9	35.3
7.4	Sevenoaks	15	29.0
20.2	LONDON BRIDGE	29	40.2

3 pm down

Distance (miles)		Time (minutes)	Speed (mph)
0.0	LONDON BRIDGE	0	—
20.2	Sevenoaks	32	37.8
7.4	TONBRIDGE	12	37.0
26.8	ASHFORD	32	50.3

While the 'K' Class 2-6-4 tank had been one of the proposed new standard types of post-war SE&CR motive power, one can discern that behind the scenes there had been some heart-searching in the intervening years, between the construction of the prototype and the time when it was prepared to issue a bulk order for more. When the results of these trials of 1922 were examined I should not be surprised if there was some further heart-searching, because putting the most favourable light on these results they were not exactly flattering to the 'K'.

Both 4-4-0 engines ran six return trips from Ashford to London. It was originally intended that three would suffice but the 'D1' proved to have some defects that affected the coal consumption, so a re-run was needed. After all the results were studied it was appreciated that the 'K' Class engine gained something in terms of the coal consumption per gross ton mile as compared with the two 4-4-0 tender engines, as the total engine weight in working order was 82.6 tons, against 90.3 tons for the 'D1' and 97.7 tons for the 'L'. Accordingly the results for the 'K' Class were adjusted to give an equivalent value for a tender engine. All three engines observed the booked running times on every occasion, though on the sharply-timed sections between Ashford and Tonbridge the 4-4-0 engines generally made the faster running. In particular, the 'L' Class engine No 761 did very well. On the up journey the tare loads hauled varied between 203 and 253 tons, and on the down between 221 and 282 tons.

SE&CR: Engine trials November 1922

Class	Engine number	Total coal per train mile (lb)	Load (tons tare)	Coal per ton mile (lb)	
'L'	761	54.35	235	0.164	First series
'D1'	735	61.85	243	0.192	
'K'	790	50.81	232	0.163	
'D1'	735	57.3	239	0.177	Second series
'L'	761	55.19	235	0.168	
'K'	790	53.60	232	0.162	No 790 as 2-6-0
'L'	761	54.7	235	0.165	Mean of two 'L' Class trials

At this stage in the locomotive history of the Southern it is the comparison between Classes 'L' and 'K' that is most significant. The work of Class 'D1' is discussed in detail in the following chapter. The valve setting of Class 'L', as recommended by Joynt at Inchicore, was not exactly in line with the latest British practice as introduced at Ashford on the advice of Clayton and incorporated in the 'N' Class Moguls and the 'K' Class 2-6-4 tank. Yet the 'L' Class 4-4-0 No 761 ran the latter new engine within the merest fraction of equalling her for the best coal consumption record of the trials as well as making the fastest intermediate running. Mr Maunsell's assistant, H. Holcroft, rode on the footplate throughout all these trials and in one of his books he was at pains to draw conclusions over the unexpected outcome. He wrote: 'The moral to be drawn from the test between the three classes of engines is that the efficiency of the boiler counts for more than that of the cylinders. The 'L' Class boiler had larger firebox heating surface than either of the other two boilers so that more of the heat of combustion was taken up through radiation,

resulting in lower temperature in firebox and in gases entering the tubes. As its working pressure was lower the temperature of the boiler water was also lower, so giving a larger thermal head through the plates and by convection in the tube area. Consequently the temperature of the smokebox gases was lower, as reflected in lower degree of superheat. Combustion efficiency was higher through the deep firebox and uniformity of thickness of fuel on the grate.'

On the 'K' Class engine the valve gear was in line with modern practice, and this contributed to rather higher cylinder efficiency. Holcroft evaluates the two locomotives thus: 'L' Class, boiler efficiency seventy per cent, cylinder efficiency ten per cent, overall thermal efficiency seven per cent. For the 'K' Class the respective figures were, boiler 64 per cent, cylinders eleven per cent and overall, also seven per cent. The respective efficiencies come into prominence later in this book, with the account of the development of the 'King Arthur' Class. Despite the somewhat unfavourable results of the 1922 trials authority was given for construction of twenty more 'K' Class in 1923, but there was a long delay in getting these engines finished as Ashford works was too busy to erect them. Some of the finished parts were sent to Brighton, after grouping, and the rest to Armstrong Whitworth at Newcastle, for erection by contract. These additional 'K' Class engines, both from Brighton and Newcastle were not available for traffic until 1925.

9. Boat train engines—new style

With the production of the 'K' Class 2-6-4 tank engine, No 790, the SE&CR had the prototype for a potentially fast passenger type having a tractive effort considerably higher than that of the 4-4-0 tender engines then working on the system, but due to a variety of circumstances no further engines of 'K' Class were built until after grouping, nor were they as economical as was anticipated. The end of the war in 1918, and the desire to restore regular passenger services to the Continent via Dover and Folkestone, brought a locomotive problem of some urgency. With the intensification of suburban services at Charing Cross and Cannon Street in view, together with electrification, it was decided that all Continental boat-train traffic should in future be worked from Victoria. The connections between the former SER and LC&DR lines at Chislehurst already provided a number of alternative routes to Dover, including those via Maidstone and Ashford, and via Chatham, Faversham and Canterbury, and these were available when, owing to late arrivals of the steamers, the regular paths via Ashford and Tonbridge had been missed.

The accompanying sketch map shows the elaborate system of routes that are available. The principal route is that passing through Herne Hill, Knockholt and Tonbridge, though the Catford loop-line is often used for relief trains in the outward direction. For inward bound trains the alternative route via Maidstone is often followed, while at times of very heavy outward traffic I have known second and third por-

tions of the regular trains to be worked via Chatham and Canterbury. The operating arrangements were very carefully worked out to avoid delay and congestion to ordinary traffic in the event of late arrivals of the cross-channel steamers. An up boat train running no more than 10 minutes late on the main line via Tonbridge might well cause a good deal of dislocation, and so for every scheduled departure time from Dover or Folkestone provisional paths were laid down covering every amount of late running. No special arrangements had to be made for each case, an up boat train takes the first provisional path available from the time it is ready to start. To fit in with other traffic some of these bookings necessarily involve slower running, quite apart from that involved in any case over the heavy gradients of the Maidstone route or in the ascent of Sole Street bank in case of a diversion via Canterbury and Chatham. From the viewpoint of locomotive performance however the main interest centres upon the working of the regular down boat expresses and especially the popular 11 am from Victoria—the service that eventually developed into the world-famous 'Golden Arrow'.

The exclusive use of Victoria as the boat-train terminus, however, meant that all such trains had to pass over the former LC&D line at some stage in their journey, and from this line the most powerful passenger engines, the 'L' Class 4-4-0s, were prohibited on account of their weight. The heaviest engines permitted over any of the Chatham lines were the Wainwright 'E' Class 4-4-0s. The normal for-

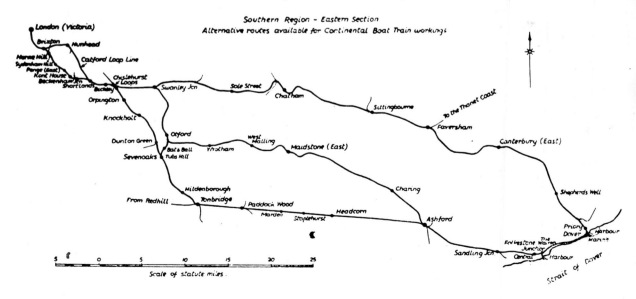

Below left *Boat train routes.*

Right *Dover Harbour, showing location of Admiralty and Prince of Wales piers. (Dover Harbour Board.)*

mation of the post-war trains was to be 300 tons tare and this was definitely beyond the capacity of the Class 'E' engines, 250 tons was about their limit on the timings laid down. The two superheated 'Es' 36 and 275, could have tackled 300-ton trains, but they also were too heavy, having a maximum axle-load of 18 tons 10 cwt against the 17 tons 12 cwt of the non-superheater 'E' Class. The Civil Engineer had already envisaged a comprehensive programme of bridge-strengthening and track-renewal which would permit the running of much heavier engines, but this work could not be completed for some years. In the meantime, the operating department was naturally averse to the regular double-heading which would have been necessary if reliance had been placed on existing types and so Maunsell set about the difficult task of producing an engine of 'L' Class capacity, but weighing no more than a non-superheated 'E'. He had to effect a weight reduction of at least nine per cent on that of the 'L' Class engines.

The problem was solved by an ingenious rebuilding of the 'E' Class engine No 179. It was truly a rebuild. Some engines nowadays termed rebuilds retain little more than the frames and wheel centres of the original locomotives, but in No 179 the boiler barrel and dome were used, as was most of the 'E' Class motion. The new design was built up as a blend of 'N' Class and 'E' Class practice, with the eminently practical result that no additional stocks of spare parts were required at the running sheds, since everything was interchangeable either with 'E' or 'N' Class standards. In planning the work Clayton's earlier experience of the rebuilding of Midland 4-4-0s at Derby was of importance, and certainly the work was very

quickly and cheaply done. The basic principle of the new design was very simple, namely to provide a larger grate, greater capacity for burning coal and high degree superheat, and to replace the original slide valves by larger diameter piston valves having ample port openings and longer travel. This formula for a fast and successful engine sounds familiar enough today, but its significance was hardly, if at all, appreciated outside Swindon and Ashford in 1919.

The new cylinders had the same diameter and stroke as the old ones, 19 in by 26 in, and so the nominal tractive effort of the engine was unchanged. but with 10-in diameter piston valves and the advantages of the modified motion those cylinders had such a capacity for taking steam, and using it effectively, that care had to be taken not to work beyond the capacity of the boiler. At 25 per cent cut-off the port opening to steam was no less than 0.5-in against the 0.33-in, at the same cut-off on the Great Western two-cylinder 4-6-0s. The increased firegrate area, in combination with relatively short flue tubes made the boilers very free in steaming however, and at the same time steam temperatures after passing through the superheater ranged between 650°F and 700°F. The superheater, smokebox regulator, collector pipes, boiler mountings and firebox stays were of the same type as used on the 'N' Class, and the 'helter-skelter lighthouse' was accommodated in the original dome. The chassis was stripped of all superfluous weight, the coupled wheel splashers were narrowed to the minimum width, the heavy tool boxes in the cab were removed and the cast-iron dragbox replaced by a fabricated-steel one. The engineman had been accustomed to use the wooden lids of the tool boxes as seats, and to compensate them for this loss Maunsell provided tip-up seats for both driver and fireman, as on the 'N' Class 2-6-0s.

In external appearance the modified No 179 had more than a passing likeness to the Midland Class '2' superheater rebuilds, not only in the cut-away running plate and the shape of the cab, but in many constructional details, where Clayton followed Midland practice. The chimney, as on 2-6-0 and 2-6-4 tank engines, looked like a shortened version of the later Derby pattern, and anticipated by some seven years the appearance of the true Midland short chimneys which became so familiar on the later compounds and standard Class 4 goods engines. No 179 was rebuilt at Ashford and completed in April 1919. At first she was painted black instead of the wartime grey but when, after successful trials, it was decided to convert more of the 'E' Class and ten were sent to Beyer, Peacock & Co in 1920, the grey painting was retained. Comparative dimensions of the Class 'E' engines before and after rebuilding are given in the accompanying table.

Class	'E'	'E1'
Cylinders (in)		
Diameter	19	19
Stroke	26	26
Valves	Slide	10 in diameter piston
Heating surfaces (sq ft)		
Tubes	1,396	322.25 (large tubes) 827.6 (small tubes)
Firebox	136	127.13
Superheater	—	228
Total	1,532	1,504.98
Grate area (sq ft)	21.15	24 sq ft
Boiler pressure (psi)	180	180
Weights in working order (tons cwt)		
On bogie	17 7	19 0
On drivers	17 12	17 10
On trailing coupled	17 6	16 0
Total engine	52 5	52 10

At various times when locomotives having a long valve travel in full gear were introduced many engineers feared that the increased travel would result in excessive wear. In service, however, such engines are run with the motion well linked up, and the actual valve travel at, say, 60 mph will be little if at all greater than that of an engine with the old conventional valve motion on which drivers often kept the cut-off at 35 per cent, or more, throughout the trip. The 'E1' Class

were usually run at about 25 per cent, though they could be pulled up to about eighteen per cent before they began to 'kick'. The valve travel in full gear was 6½ in, the steam lap was 1⅝ in and the exhaust clearance ⅛ in. In working the 300-ton boat expresses they were an outstanding success, once the men had got used to the long sloping firegrate. They had to be fired just as one saw on large modern 4-6-0s and 'Pacifics' with a thick fire in the back corners and under the door, gradually tapering to a relatively thin layer under the arch. They needed close attention throughout the run, for the natural vibration of the engine tended to shake the fire down, and care had to be taken to maintain the ideal formation.

Coming to their work on the road I have before me details of 36 runs on down Continental boat expresses with tare loads varying between 288 and 301 tons, in which every one of the ten Beyer, Peacock & Co rebuilds is represented. The timing for the 78 miles from Victoria to Dover Marine was at first 103 and then 100 minutes, the quickening was effected entirely by the resumption of normal speed running through the Folkestone Warren after the line had fully consolidated following the great landslip of December 1915. These trains were allowed 46 minutes pass to pass, for the 41.4 miles from Tonbridge (passed at 20 mph) to Folkestone Junction. On one occasion this was cut to 41¾ minutes in recovering time lost by delays earlier in the run. On the earlier journeys, in November and December 1921, small amounts of time up to 3 minutes were lost on the complete run from London to Dover through steaming troubles developing, but after mid-December 1921, in this comprehensive series of recordings, there is no instance of time lost due to engine problems. On two notable occasions the 70-minute allowance for the 59.5 miles from Bickley Junction to Folkestone Junction was cut to 65½ and 65 minutes by engines No 497 and No 19 respectively, the latter including a signal check at Knockholt which cost about 1½ minutes in running. Having regard to the severe nature of the road between Bickley Junction and Knockholt, and to the heavy slack through Tonbridge, these were remarkable runs with trainloads of 300 tons. On another occasion No 511 took a similar load over the old Chatham route to Dover, 78.4 very difficult miles in 107½ minutes.

The work throughout on this latter run was extraordinarily good, especially that between Faversham and Dover, over long adverse gradients of 1 in 100, with the severe speed restriction through Canterbury, and the need for reduced speed on the final descent towards Dover. In everyday running the 'E1' Class engines were capable of sustaining continuously an output of 900 to 1,000 indicated horse-

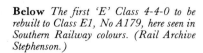

Right *SE&CR post-1919 Continental Pullman boat train near Bickley, hauled by rebuilt and superheated Class 'E1' 4-4-0 No 67. (Author's collection.)*

Below *The first 'E' Class 4-4-0 to be rebuilt to Class E1, No A179, here seen in Southern Railway colours. (Rail Archive Stephenson.)*

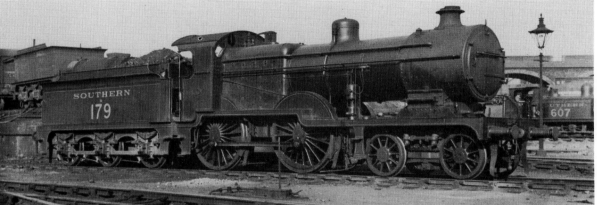

SE&CR: Victoria-Dover Marine down boat trains: Class 'E1' 4-4-0 engines

Date	Engine number	Load (tons tare)	Actual time (m s)	Delays
24.11.21	511	294	102 15	—
29.11.21	19	294	105 30	Engine not steaming well
30.11.21	67	294	105 30	Brakes dragging
1.12.21	511	294	106 00	Engine not steaming well
5.12.21	511	294	100 15	—
6.12.21	19	294	99 45	Signal check Knockholt
9.12.21	19	294	102 30	—
16.12.21	507	294	102 00	Signal check Sydenham
6.2.22	511	296	101 00	—
9.2.22	163	294	102 30	Signal check Tonbridge
10.2.22	163	301	100 30	—
16.6.22	504	291	102 00	—
30.8.22	507	291	106 15	Permanent way slack Bickley, engine not steaming well
16.4.23	506	300	101 00	Signal check Beckenham Permanent way slack Paddock Wood
30.4.23	506	289	99 15	Signal check three times
10.8.23	497	289	99 00	Signal check Brixton

power at 60 mph and contemporary records suggest that they ran equally well with a partly-opened regulator and cut-off of 25 to 30 per cent, as with full regulator and early cut-off.

Summary details of some boat train runs of 1921-33 are given in the accompanying table. These runs are selected as typical from the much larger collection previously referred to, and while they show generally close adherence to booked time there was not a great deal of margin with the full 300-ton load. On the run on 6 December 1921 engine No 19 was developing about 950 indicated horsepower for 42 minutes on end between Paddock Wood and Sandling Junction. Although this was probably an exceptional effort the power output demanded by the boat train workings was really high in relation to the size and nominal tractive effort of the engines. Details of this fine effort by engine No 19 are shown in the accompanying diagram, and it will be seen that the cut-off was thirty per cent throughout, and that the regulator was half open.

The average speed during this spell was 59 mph. The boiler pressure had been steadily maintained at 175 psi until the summit point near Chart was passed. There, as the water level had dropped a little, the second injector was put on for a short time and, with the regulator closed for a brief period following an adverse distant signal, the water level was quickly raised. After Smeeth matters were comfortably in hand and the firing relaxed. This was an extremely fine piece of running.

The steam distribution obtained with this particular layout of the Stephenson's link motion was so good that the optimum power output was equal to, if not slightly greater than, that of the 'N' Class 'Moguls', although the latter were considerably heavier engines and had a higher nominal tractive effort. The optimum ihp of the 'N' Class was about 1,000 at 25 per cent cut-off. The further diagram reproduced herewith shows a run with the 'E1' Class engine No 506 on the Dover-Birkenhead express,

Below left *Diagram run of engine No 19.*

Below *Diagram run of engine No 506.*

Right *Continental special near Chelsfield hauled by 'E' Class 4-4-0 No A175. (Rail Archive Stephenson — F.R. Hebron.)*

Below right *One of the 'D1' Class rebuilt and superheated 4-4-0s, No 735, in 1921. (The late W.J. Reynolds.)*

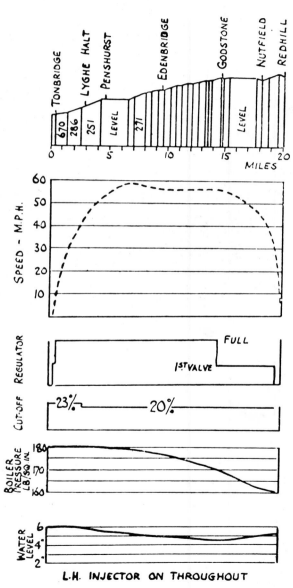

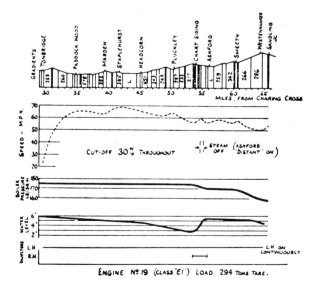

ENGINE N° 19 (CLASS 'E1') LOAD 294 TONS TARE.

when an output of 1,000 cylinder hp, or slightly over, was sustained throughout from Penshurst to Godstone, at an average speed of 56 mph while using no more than twenty per cent cut-off with full regulator. As the diagram shows, boiler pressure was fully maintained during this fine effort, until at Godstone the working was eased and the firing relaxed, since the engine was terminating at Redhill. The run of 19.6 miles was made in 26 minutes start to stop, against a booked time of 29 minutes; but if the initial effort had been continued beyond Godstone, another 1½ to 2 minutes could easily have been cut from the overall time.

The same engine put up another very good run on the corresponding eastbound train, then booked nonstop over the 46.1 miles from Redhill to Ashford. The load totalling 287 tons tare must have presented a variegated appearance as it included coaches, in pre-grouping colours, of SE&C, L&SW, Great Central and Great Western build. Down the initial descent from Redhill, cut-off was seventeen per cent, but increased to eighteen per cent at Nuffield. There was then no further change for 38 ½ miles, over which distance speed averaged exactly 60 mph. The first valve of the regulator was used from Nutfield on the gradual descent to Tonbridge, after which the main valve was just opened for the slightly harder stretch to Ashford. The total time for the 46.1 mile run from Redhill was 50 minutes, notwithstanding a signal check which involved a reduction to 40 mph through Tonbridge. The boiler steamed very freely throughout—from Edenbridge onwards, where the engine was periodically blowing off, the firedoor was opened and the damper partly closed. This running, on a very small regulator opening, was typical of the 'E1' Class.

The eleven engines of Class 'E1' were all stationed

at Battersea and worked mostly on the boat trains. Their success led to consideration of further rebuilding to improve the motive power situation on the Kent Coast line. There were thirteen non-superheated engines remaining, but these were in excellent condition and doing good work with lighter trains, and it was felt that it would be more advantageous to rebuild some of the 'D' Class engines which were older than the 'Es', as a greater advance in power could be obtained by converting 'D' Class engines to 'D1' than by rebuilding 'E' to 'E1'. Accordingly ten of the 'D' Class were despatched to Beyer, Peacock & Co in 1921 for rebuilding on the same lines as the 'E1' Class. These engines differed from the 'E' Class in having coupled wheels of 6-ft 8-in diameter against 6 ft 6 in and this made the tractive effort of the 'D1' Class, as the rebuilds were known, slightly less than that of the 'E1s'. Top feed was not used on the 'D1s' and the regulator kept in the dome.

In actual work on the road there was little or nothing to distinguish the performance of the 'D1' and 'E1' engines, and eleven more were rebuilt at

Ashford works—two in 1923, one in 1926 and eight in 1927. This rebuilding provided a stud of efficient modern engines which could be used at will anywhere on the old SE&CR system, and which put up some very fine running with the seaside expresses from Victoria to Margate and Ramsgate. Even in the later days of 'Pacifics' in the Southern Region of British Railways, the 'D1s' and 'E1s' were still used on fast passenger work. The run of the 5.22 pm from Cannon Street to Rochester, tabulated herewith, is an admirable example, made after nationalization, in 1948. The signal check at Hither Green Sidings box put the train 2 minutes late at Chislehurst, but with some fast running over the Chatham line and a top speed of 76 mph at Farningham Road the summit at Sole Street was passed nearly a minute early. The ascent from Farningham Road includes two definite breaks in the 1 in 100 grading at Fawkham Junction and a mile before Meopham, but it was nevertheless excellent work to clear the summit at 50 mph. A fast descent into the Medway valley, with a top speed of 78 mph, brought the train into Rochester nearly 4 minutes early.

Southern Railway: 5.22 pm Cannon Street-Rochester

Engine Class 'D1' 4-4-0 No 1509
Load 8 coaches, 254 tons tare, 275 tons full

Distance (miles)		Schedule time (m s)	Actual time (m s)	Speed* (mph)
0.0	CANNON STREET	0 00	0 00	
0.7	LONDON BRIDGE	2 30	2 47	—
3.7	New Cross	7 00	7 50	50
6.0	Hither Green	10 30	10 55	46
			signal check	
7.8	Grove Park		14 30	—
9.1	Elmstead Woods		17 10	—
10.1	Chislehurst	16 30	18 50	42
11.0	St Mary Cray Junction	18 30	20 27	—
12.4	St Mary Cray		22 12	60
15.3	Swanley	23 30	24 56	56
18.1	Farningham Road		27 48	76
21.0	Fawkham		30 15	62
23.5	Meopham		33 05	50/53
24.5	Sole Street	35 00	34 16	50
28.5	Cuxton Road Box	40 00	37 53	78
30.6	Rochester Bridge	44 00	40 17	
31.3	ROCHESTER	45 30	41 46	

Above left Rebuilt 'D1' 4-4-0 No A749 leaving Victoria on a Kent Coast express. (Rail Archive Stephenson — F.R. Hebron.)

Left Relief Continental boat express, via Maidstone east line near Bromley, hauled by Class 'E1' 4-4-0 No 1507 and 'F1' rebuilt 4-4-0 No 1233. (H.C. Casserley.)

Net time 39 minutes 45 seconds
*By stop watch

Below Up relief, all-Pullman, Continental boat express near Bromley hauled by 'D1' Class 4-4-0 No 1246. (H.C. Casserley.)

Up express from Dover to Charing Cross in Folkestone Warren, hauled by 'E1' Class 4-4-0 No 1019 (new numbering). (O.S. Nock.)

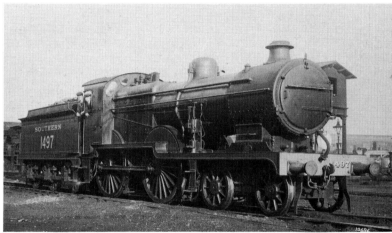

'E1' Class 4-4-0 No 1497 at Stewarts Lane shed. (The late W.J. Reynolds.)

Below *Up Kent Coast train climbing Sole Street bank, with Class 'E1' engine No 1019. (H.C. Casserley.)*

Reference has already been made to the bridge strengthening programme undertaken by the Civil Engineer. As this proceeded, successive relaxations on loading limits were made on certain routes, though generally speaking these were of most immediate importance to the Locomotive Running Superintendent. One such relation, however, led to a small though significant change on the 'D1' and 'E1' engines, and it came about in a rather roundabout way. One day in October 1923 the engine of the 11 am down Continental boat express failed with a broken crank-axle at Westenhanger. When the engine was towed into Ashford it was found that she was not an 'E1', but one of the superheater 'Es', No 275. Interest was naturally aroused as to what No 275 was doing on the boat train at all, and enquiries elicited the news that weight restrictions on the line between Bickley and Victoria had been relaxed sufficiently to permit of No 36 and No 275 being used. The Running Superintendent had been quick to take the opportunity of increasing his stock of boat-train engines.

The 'E1' Class was then reconsidered in the light of this relaxation and Maunsell put forward a proposal to increase the adhesion weight on the rear pair of coupled wheels by approximately one ton. This was accepted by the Civil Engineer and the change was made by reinstating the old cast-iron dragbox of the Wainwright 'E' Class, instead of the fabricated one used as a weight-saving device on the 'E1s' as originally built. The replacement was carried out on all engines of Classes 'D1' and 'E1' as they passed through the shops for general repairs. While on the subject of weight relaxation I may add that the Civil Engineer announced that he would be prepared to accept 'L' Class 4-4-0s on certain sections of the Chatham line from July 1924, subject to some special speed limits being observed, but in view of the supreme competence of the 'E1s' the use of 'L' Class engines was never adopted on the boat trains, and in any case by the summer of 1925 'King Arthurs' were permitted to run on the principal boat-train route from Victoria to Dover, via Tonbridge. It was, however, some little time before the 4-6-0 engines could

be used on the alternative routes, via Maidstone or Faversham, and in the summer particularly the 'E1s' continued to do great work. These little engines indeed rank among Maunsell's most interesting and successful designs.

The only slight reservations that can be made are on the grounds of thermal efficiency, in comparison with the 'L' Class, as a result of the trials with the 'K' Class 2-6-4 tank in 1922. Then however the usefulness of the 'E1' and 'D1' 4-4-0s had been proved beyond any shadow of doubt, and the results of the 1922 trials while very interesting, were of only academic value so far as train running was concerned. While in the trials the 'D1' Class engine romped along in a lighthearted manner, on a relatively short cut-off, and gave every impression of being completely master of the job, the sloping firegrate required much more careful attention throughout the run. The pull on the fire was stronger at the back of the grate than at the front, and the rate of combustion over the grate area had to be evened up by keeping the firebed thin in front to reduce resistance to incoming air from the ashpan, and thickening up the back part to increase it.

This deeper fire on the back part of the grate affected combustion efficiency to such an extent as to reduce the overall efficiency of these notable rebuilt engines to a lower figure than that of the 'L' Class. This reduction was also affected by the $\frac{1}{8}$ in of exhaust clearance given to the piston valves, resulting in early release and so in incomplete expansion. A free-running engine was obtained at the expense of a certain loss in cylinder efficiency. The use of short cut-offs in these engines increased the temperature range and gave higher superheat temperatures. Compared to the 'L' Class, while the latter showed an equal cylinder efficiency of ten per cent, the boiler efficiency due to the deeper grate and the better combustion was seventy per cent against no more than sixty per cent on the 'D1'. The overall efficiencies of these two 4-4-0 designs as thus revealed by the 1922 trials were seven per cent for the 'L' and six per cent for the 'D1'.

10. Overture to the Southern

At the beginning of the grouping era the Southern Railway was considerably slower off the mark than the other newly-formed companies. One gathered that there was some difficulty over the financial arrangements, and it should not be forgotten that there were four major companies involved in the amalgamation as in 1922 the South Eastern and the London, Chatham and Dover were still separate companies financially. At first the three major operating constituents, London and South Western, London, Brighton and South Coast and South Eastern and Chatham, continued independently, under their former General Managers, though after six months thus the co-ordination had proceeded far enough for the appointment of certain senior officers to be announced, though curiously enough not the new General Manager. In fact, however, Sir William Forbes of the Brighton and Sir Percy Tempest of the South Eastern were sufficiently senior in years of service as to be on the point of retirement. Forbes, indeed, had been General Manager of the LB&SCR since 1899, while Tempest had been Chief Engineer to the SE&CR since 1899 and General Manager since 1920, while still continuing to hold his former post as Engineer. As the youngest of the three, the way was seemingly clear for Sir Herbert Walker of the LSWR to assume the General Managership of the Southern in due course.

His appointment was confirmed as from 1 January 1924. It was a very important one so far as the locomotive and operating departments were concerned, because Sir Herbert took the keenest interest in all traffic matters—a little too keen at times for his chief officers! The 'key' appointments, as from 1 July 1923 were E.C. Cox as Chief Operating Superintendent, A.D. Jones as Locomotive Running Superintendent and R.E.L. Maunsell as Chief Mechanical Engineer, all significantly from the South Eastern and Chatham Railway. The post of Chief Engineer went to the veteran A.W. Szlumper of the L&SWR, but his deputy was George Ellson of the SE&CR who was soon to prove a grievous thorn in the side of the locomotive department. In July 1923 both Urie and L.B. Billinton retired, and though T.S. Finlayson at Eastleigh and B.K. Field at Brighton continued as Works Managers of their previous commands, the principal posts so far as the development of locomotive practice went to the ex-SE&CR men who had been gathered in Maunsell's first staff reorganization at Ashford in 1914. Clayton continued as Assistant to the Chief Mechanical Engineer and Holcroft as junior assistant. Pearson continued as Deputy Chief Mechanical Engineer of the Southern Railway, but he remained at Ashford while Maunsell himself, together with Clayton and Holcroft, moved to the new headquarters' offices at Waterloo, where they were accommodated conveniently adjacent to the chief operating officers, E.C. Cox and A.D. Jones.

It is important at this stage of passing from South Eastern and Chatham to Southern days, to touch upon contemporary affairs as they affected J. Clayton, who had been Chief Locomotive Draughtsman at Ashford, and H. Holcroft, for it was upon these two men that a big share in the responsibility for Southern locomotive development ultimately evolved. In 1928, as a young graduate, I listened enthralled to Maunsell when he delivered a lecture to the graduates section of the Institution of Mechanical Engineers on 'The Trend of Modern Steam Locomotive Design' and I remember too the gracious tribute he paid to Clayton and Holcroft at the conclusion of that lecture. I have referred, previously, to the attempts to prepare designs for new standard locomotives for general service on the British railways after the 1914-18 war. Although the idea of producing British standard designs was dropped, when it became known that grouping and not nationalization would be the outcome of deliberations on the future working of the railways, the period of discussion and committee work within the Association of Railway Locomotive Engineers was of some significance to the future practice of the Southern Railway. While all the railways had taken part, those most actively interested were the Great Northern, the Midland, the Lancashire and Yorkshire and the Great Western, while with Maunsell himself charged with the task of preparing the designs ultimately to be agreed upon, the South Eastern and Chatham was in something of a key position. As can well be imagined, there was, apart from the full sessions of the Association, a great deal of preliminary backstage work to be done, and much of this devolved upon Clayton.

While in these final years of the SE&CR Clayton had been in constant touch with leading personalities of the British locomotive world, it was above all his association with Churchward that was to bear the choicest fruit in after years. Of course Pearson had brought to Ashford a strong advocacy of Swindon practice, and it had been put into effect on the 'N' Class and 'K' Class engines. The 'N' Class cylinder design too had been to some extent adapted in the rebuilding of the Wainwright 'E' and 'D' Class 4-4-0s. But with increasing attention to workshop matters, Pearson's influence upon new locomotive design tended to lessen, while Clayton's increased. In 1919 Clayton had been promoted from Chief Locomotive

Draughtsman to Personal Assistant to the CME and his association with Churchward during those critical years led to an almost fervent admiration for Great Western practice, when he came to recognize the genius that lay behind it.

While Clayton, through the work of the ARLE was gaining this invaluable experience, Holcroft became associated, in a more roundabout way, with Gresley. It was in 1918 that the first Great Northern three-cylinder locomotive with conjugated valve gear was completed at Doncaster Works. The design was rather severely criticized from many quarters, but it was of particular interest to Holcroft in view of investigations he had made into three-cylinder locomotives while in the drawing office at Swindon. There he had invented a conjugated valve gear for which, on Churchward's instructions, a patent had been taken out in his name. As a sequel to the appearance of the GNR 2-8-0 engine No 461, Holcroft was invited to read a paper before the Institution of Locomotive Engineers, in 1918, on three-cylinder locomotives. The outcome of this paper was that Gresley adopted the simpler form of the conjugated valve gear advocated by Holcroft, wherein the placing of the middle piston valve horizontally beside the inclined cylinder, enabled the simple 2:1 lever mechanism to be used, while retaining horizontal outside cylinders.

At this time Holcroft was away from Ashford, and in charge of a Railway Executive Committee depot at Purfleet, which dealt with the inspection and dispatch of material for military railways on the Continent. While so engaged he was called into personal consultation by Gresley to discuss the cylinder and valve gear arrangements which in due course appeared on the GNR 2-6-0 No 1000. It was subsequently adopted as standard on all Gresley three-cylinder designs for the GNR and the LNER. Interest in three-cylinder locomotives had now been

well and truly aroused, and early in 1919 Holcroft was recalled from Purfleet and given the task of designing a three-cylinder variant of the SE&CR 'N' Class 2-6-0, in which a further infusion of Swindon practice can be noted. From this time onwards Holcroft gradually came to play the part of junior partner to Clayton, and after the grouping he was appointed an Assistant to the Chief Mechanical Engineer. At Waterloo a small section was established under Clayton's direct supervision to initiate all new designs. The schemes were than developed in the Eastleigh drawing office under T.S. Finlayson, who had come from the North British Locomotive Company to be Chief Locomotive Draughtsman in 1913. Maunsell strengthened this team of ex-L&SWR men by some transfers from Ashford, to introduce a leaven of SE&CR practice, and at all times Clayton maintained a fairly close supervision. On completion, all new locomotive drawings were sent to Waterloo to be scrutinized before submission for Maunsell's final approval.

The first Maunsell three-cylinder engine, 2-6-0 No 822, was interposed in the regular series of Class 'N' locomotives built at Ashford in 1922. The proportions were arranged so as to provide the closest possible comparison between No 822 and the standard engines—16-in diameter cylinders were used, and as this gave a slightly larger volume than that of two 19-in diameter cylinders, the boiler pressure was lowered to 190 psi during the period of the comparative tests, so as to make the nominal tractive efforts of both two- and three-cylinder engines the same. The valve chests of the outside cylinders were set inwards and the valves operated through rockers, as on the Great Western two-cylinder designs, which provided clearance for the links to the conjugated valve gear, which were attached to the rear end of the outside cylinder valve rockers instead of in front of the valves

SE&CR three-cylinder 2-6-0 No 822 as originally built with conjugated valve gear. (The late W.J. Reynolds.)

From top to bottom *The three-cylinder 2-6-0 No 822 on an up goods train at Grove Park. (H. C. Casserley.)*

The pioneer 'K' Class 2-6-4 tank engine No 790, when named River Avon, *in Southern colours. (H. C. Casserley.)*

The 'Sunny South Express' just after grouping, with some of the stock already in LMS colours, hauled by Class 'I3' 4-4-2 No 28, near Earlswood. (Rail Archive Stephenson — F. R. Hebron.)

One of the post-war 4-6-4 tanks, No 330, on a Brighton Pullman express near Earlswood. (Rail Archive Stephenson — F. R. Hebron.)

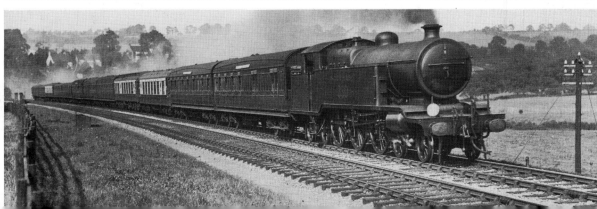

as in the Gresley three-cylinder 2-6-0s of the '1000' Class. By this method the factor of expansion of the valve spindles, which had to be taken into account on the Great Northern engines, was eliminated. The layout of the conjugated gear was carefully arranged so that the levers were clear of the steam chests and the valves could, therefore, be removed without dismantling any of the valve motion.

The structural design of the front end was an interesting and original piece of work. As in Churchward's two-cylinder engines, the cylinders were formed of two castings bolted together, but in the case of No 822 the dividing line between the two was, of course, not central, as one of the two castings had to include the inside cylinder and its steam chest. It is of interest that the American Locomotive Company adopted this method of construction when, in subsequent years, three-cylinder engines were tried out extensively in the USA. On engine No 822 the cylinder blocks were fitted into a gap in the main frame, and the top of the gaps in the frames were bridged by splice plates, tying the frames, cylinders and smokebox saddle together. The arrangement made a good solid job, and it was subsequently adopted in all Southern three-cylinder engines, other than the 'Schools', which latter had a front-end design based on the 'Nelsons'. Engine 822 was completed at Ashford Works in December 1922, just early enough, therefore, to be claimed as a South Eastern and Chatham engine.

She came prominently under review at the time of the Railway Centenary celebrations in 1925, when among other events, a paper was read by Mr Gresley, as he was then, on 'The Three-Cylinder High Pressure Locomotive' during the summer meeting of the Institution of Mechanical Engineers, held that year at Newcastle-on-Tyne. In this paper the SE&CR engine No 822 was illustrated and described. The ensuing discussion was opened by Clayton, and he quoted extensively from his experience of No 822. The results they had obtained at Ashford indicated that the three-cylinder arrangement gave some thirteen per cent increase in boiler efficiency; the figures were borne out by the monthly coal returns, by the way the coal appeared to be consumed in the firebox, and by the lesser amount of smoke. The economy in coal was, Clayton stated, due to the six lighter exhaust beats per revolution of the three-cylinder engine, which gave improved draught and firebox action over the two-cylinder engine. Furthermore, he strongly endorsed, as result of experience with No 822, Gresley's contention that the more even torque made it possible to increase the power of an engine, since the mean torque could be greater without risk of the engine slipping.

Clayton then described the phenomenon that has since become common knowledge regarding the conjugated valve gear, namely the over-running of the inside valve. Gresley, in his reply, told how he too had experienced the same trouble, though the measures to counteract its effect were not difficult to adopt. In any event the high power output, consistent performance and long mileages achieved by the Gresley 'Pacifics' on the LNER between 1923 and 1939, afford sufficient testimony that the conjugated gear was a practical proposition for engines engaged in some of the fastest and heaviest duties ever seen in this country. The trouble arises, of course, when wear develops in the pin joints, and this affects the outside valve gear as much as the inside one. If over-running of the valves occurs outside, it is faithfully reproduced inside by the combination levers and its effect magnified. With a well-tuned-up gear the inside cylinder receives a good distribution of steam, though as speed increases beyond 50 mph or so, there always seems a tendency for the ihp of the inside cylinder to increase above that of the outside ones.

The systematic tests of the 2-6-0 engine No 822 against two-cylinder engines of Class 'N' were carried out in regular goods service, but in passenger service at express speed the three-cylinder engine rode more smoothly, and it could be run with a wide open regulator at shorter cut-offs than the two-cylinder engines engaged in similar work. During trials conducted by the Bridge Stress Committee, No 822 attained a maximum speed of 79 mph with 5-ft 6-in wheels. Another interesting point in favour of the three-cylinder engine was that, due to the smaller cylinders, the overall width was reduced sufficiently to enable it to run over the Tonbridge-Hastings line where the side clearances are severely restricted. All in all, the building of engine No 822 constituted a notable and successful experiment. It convinced Maunsell, and Clayton, of the advantages to be derived from three-cylinder propulsion where running conditions were difficult and a high power-weight ratio was required, and paved the way for such notable engines as the 'Schools'.

While at the time of the Grouping, in January 1923, Ashford Works had an order for fifteen 4-4-0 engines generally similar to the 'L' Class, but of improved design, these had not been proceeded with because they cut across Maunsell's original plan of running the passenger service of the SE&CR eventually by the 'K' Class 2-6-4 tank engines. The 1922 trials from Ashford, and the good showing of the 'L' Class engine in its coal consumption against the 'K' had provided something of a jolt in the drawing office. However the go-ahead was ultimately given for building ten 'K' Class engines, although progress was at first so slow as to be non-existent. After the completion of the three-cylinder 'N' Class 2-6-0 No 822, new work at Ashford ceased for a while and interest turned to the activities of Brighton and Eastleigh. At the former, the feeling was one of sadness that the Works had seen its best days as a locomotive building centre. In the early autumn of 1923, after Colonel Billinton had retired, there was a great gathering at Brighton at which he was presented with a silver loving cup by the men who had been under his charge. In a speech of thanks he said that under the grouping scheme engine building would probably cease at Brighton, and that the war memorial 4-6-4 tank, *Remembrance,* would be the last new engine to be built there. That splendid engine, decorated with memorial plaques on each of the side tanks, was finished in grey instead of the usual Brighton sepia brown.

While not entirely new engines, a notable work in the last year of the old company was the rebuilding with a larger boiler, Belpaire firebox and superheater of one of the celebrated 'B4' Class 4-4-0s, No 55, designed by Billinton's father and forming one of the batch built in 1901 by Sharp, Stewart & Co which

were always known on the Brighton line as the 'Scotchmen'. The term rebuild when applied to locomotives usually implied that the frames, wheel centres, and part of the motion had been retained; indeed, in the case of the Maunsell 'E1' Class on the South Eastern and Chatham the boilers also were used. With the Brighton 4-4-0 No 55, however, precious little was left of the original. The basic plan was to use the boiler and firebox of the mixed 2-6-0s which had proved very successful. To do this meant lengthening the frames, and the extent that this was needed can be seen by comparing the line diagrams. The coupled wheelbase was increased from 8 ft 9 in to 10 ft, and the distance between the rear pair of bogie wheels to the drivers was increased from 7 ft 5 in to 8 ft 6 in. The framing at the front end was also made much deeper. The compensated suspension was retained, although the scale-beam levers had necessarily to be much longer, as shown on the diagram. New cylinders of 20-in diameter were used, with piston valves, and although the increased size of cylinders was the only dimension providing enhanced

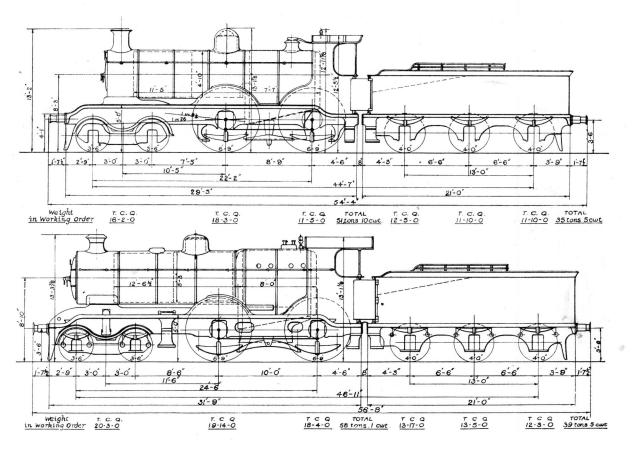

Below left *LB&SCR 4-4-0 before and after rebuilding.*

Above *The second 'B4' 4-4-0 to be rebuilt as Class 'B4X', No 60, at Redhill in 1926. (The late P. Ransome Wallis.)*

Right *The 4-6-2 tank No 325, formerly Abergavenny, in Southern colours, on an up stopping train from Brighton near Merstham. The train is mostly six-wheeled stock! (Rail Archive Stephenson — F.R. Hebron.)*

tractive effort over the original engine the use of piston valves with double-admission ports and superheated steam made for a potentially faster and more powerful engine on every count. This was quickly shown on trials made with No 55 in the late autumn of 1922.

The initial order was for twelve conversions, but the remainder were not put in hand until No 55 had been very thoroughly tried out, and it was not until after grouping that the others took the road. I have some special memories of the introduction of this class, designated 'B4X'. Not long after coming to London to begin my engineering studies at Imperial College I made the acquaintance of F.E. Mackay, then the doyen of railway train photographers, and acquaintance soon ripened into a lasting friendship. As might be imagined he had many contacts among serving railwaymen and he and I became very interested in the goings and comings of the prototype 'B4X' No 55 on the Brighton. One of his friends was in the locomotive works at Brighton, and learning of my own interest in train photography, for some weeks

in the early spring of 1923 he sent me a postcard advising what train No 55 would be working on the following Saturday. I got a reasonable shot of the second one of the class, No 60 in Star Lane cutting, south of Coulsdon, but I did not manage to meet No 55. For the record, the other ten 'B4s' that were rebuilt were numbers 43, 45, 50, 52, 56, 67, 70, 71, 72 and 73. All of them were still in service at the end of the Second World War, though the two that had been named, No 52 *Sussex* and No 70 *Devonshire* lost their titles early in the grouping era.

On the London and South Western, Eastleigh Works was continuing with Urie's programme of modernizing the Drummond express passenger 4-4-0s by fitting the Eastleigh superheater. One of the 'L12' Class had been so equipped as early as 1915, but the rest of them were not so treated until after the war, and the whole of the class were modernized by the end of 1922. The rebuilds formed a welcome reinforcement to the 'D15' Class on the Bournemouth service. In 1921 there had been some welcome accelerations and augmenting of service facilities,

Ex-L&SWR Class 'L12' 4-4-0, rebuilt and superheated and fitted with six-wheeled tender, at Reading (The late P. Ransome Wallis.)

Two superheated 'T9' class 4-4-0s, No 337 and No 302, on a heavy express for Portsmouth passing Raynes Park. (Rail Archive Stephenson — F. R. Hebron.)

The Royal Train engine, 'T9' Class No 119, at Portsmouth Harbour station. (O. S. Nock.)

including provision of buffet cars on most of the few trains that did not include a full restaurant car service. Compared to the trains of pre-war days the loads were much heavier, generally more than 50 to 100 tons more so on the sharpest-timed trains. I had some relatives living at Bournemouth at the time, and I enjoyed some good runs up to Waterloo on the 8.45 am express which was often hauled by the rebuilt 'L12' Class engines in the early 1920s, with loads of about 320 tons. The heavier trains on the service, like the 6.30 pm down from Waterloo, were usually worked by the 'D15' Class and they often loaded up to nearly 400 tons, a formation unheard of on this route in the days when the 'Paddleboat' 4-6-0s worked the crack trains.

Having completed the superheating of the 'D15' and 'L12' Classes Urie turned to the celebrated 'T9' 4-4-0s, and in 1922 engine No 314 was rebuilt with an Eastleigh superheater, extended smokebox and a tall stovepipe chimney. Though the appearance of the engine was not improved thereby the performance, excellent though it always was in every way, was enhanced to such an extent that eventually all 66 engines of the class were so modernized. The earlier rebuilds were equippped with the Eastleigh superheater, but as the process continued, some years after grouping, the later conversions had the Maunsell superheater and those treated earlier were remodified later. It was not until 1929 that the whole class had been completed. A number were transferred to the Brighton and South Eastern sections, to supplement rather than to replace existing engines, and the esteem in which the class in itself was held by the Running Department was shown by the occasions when, even in the late 1930s, 'T9s' were chosen to haul the Royal Train. When King George VI and Queen Elizabeth paid their memorable visit to Canada and the USA in 1939, not long before the outbreak of the Second World War, their train was hauled from Waterloo to Portsmouth by the 'T9' 4-4-0 No 718. The sister engine No 119 was used to haul the Royal Train conveying King George V and Queen Mary to Portsmouth for the Silver Jubilee Naval Review in June 1935. All 66 engines of the 'T9' Class were still in service when the Southern Railway was incorporated in British Railways in January 1948.

The last class of locomotive that could be ascribed to R.W. Urie was the modified version of the 'H15' mixed traffic 4-6-0, first introduced in 1913, and then notable as marking the first change from the practice of Dugald Drummond. The series of engines numbered 482-491 gained the reputation of being very speedy, indeed in pre-war express passenger traffic they seemed able to match the 'Paddleboats'. The new batch of 'H15' Class, built at Eastleigh in 1924, differed in outward appearance by having the slightly coned boiler as used on the 'N15' express passenger 4-6-0s, and with the running plate carried rearwards level to the cab. A novelty, for the first time on an Eastleigh-built engine, was the crosshead pump for the vacuum brake system. This had long been a feature of the Great Western locomotives and its incorporation on an ex-L&SWR class could have been an example of the permeation of Clayton's influence on new Southern designs, bearing in mind his admiration of Swindon practice following his wartime association with Churchward. The pump was prominently mounted on the left side of the engine below the cross-head guides, unlike the Great Western arrangement which in the case of the four-cylinder engines was between the frames.

The additions to class 'H15' in 1924 included only ten completely new engines namely numbers 473-478 and numbers 521-524. The class was completed by the rebuilding of the five original Drummond four-cylinder 4-6-0s numbers 330-334, which could be distinguished by their larger boilers and consequently shorter chimneys and boiler mountings, and by their inside-framed Drummond bogie tenders. The rebuilds of the 1905 engines 330-334 were completed between October 1924 and January 1925. They also had the vacuum brake crosshead pump. These additions to the 'H15' created a little confusion with the 'King Arthurs', with the first of these latter coming out from Eastleigh almost immediately after the rebuilt 330-334 series. But as will be discussed in the ensuing chapter there was all the difference in the world between the capability of the two classes. One or two of the new 'H15s' were drafted to the Bournemouth route with results that could only be called depressing in the extreme. I was not in a position to analyse the locomotive work from a technical angle at that time, but so far as times and speeds were concerned, as could be noted by an observer travelling as an ordinary passenger, the work was generally inferior to that of the 'D15' 4-4-0s. Fortunately these engines were not retained on express passenger work for very long.

A few years later, when the 'King Arthurs' had taken over regular working of the Continental boat trains between Victoria and Dover Marine someone in Locomotive Department headquarters at Waterloo, studying current records of train performance and comparing it with that on the West of England main line considered that the heavy gradients of the boat-train route and the frequency of speed restrictions had an inhibiting effect on 'King Arthur' Class running and a locomotive with a smaller driving wheel would be more suitable. As a result a test was carried out with an 'H15' Class 4-6-0, No 478, outward on the 2 pm boat train from Victoria, with a medium load of 301 tons tare. Although the engine

Above *Drummond 0-6-0 No 306, rebuilt and superheated, on an up goods train at Seaton Junction. (O.S. Nock.)*

Left *Urie mixed traffic 4-6-0 Class 'H15' No 522, one of the batch built just after grouping. (H.C. Casserley.)*

was worked hard, using full regulator and cut-offs of forty per cent continuously from Tonbridge to passing Folkestone Central, the average speed was no more than 50 mph and the performance generally was much inferior to what had been done with 300-ton trains at the time when the 'E1' Class 4-4-0s were working the boat trains. On the Bournemouth trains, my own opinion was that the 'H15' Class were inferior to the 'D15' 4-4-0s. On a typical run, with a gross load of 305 tons, engine No 524 starting from Southampton passed Basingstoke in 42¾ minutes, and then ran very poorly on to Esher, averaging not more than 57 mph over this wholly favourable 33.2 miles of line. Although signal checks came afterwards the net time from Southampton to Waterloo was as much as 98 minutes for the 79.3 miles. An explanation for the generally poor showing of the post-war batch of the 'H15' Class is offered in the next chapter.

11. The 'King Arthurs'

The years immediately following the grouping of the railways in 1923 witnessed a steady increase in passenger train loads in most parts of Great Britain. On the Southern the Traffic Manager intimated that locomotives would be required capable of maintaining a start-to-stop average speed of 55 mph with train loads up to 500 tons. This envisaged the restoration of the crack timings of London and South Western days between Waterloo and Bournemouth, Waterloo and Salisbury and Salisbury and Exeter, but with 500-ton trains, as compared with the maximum of about 350 tons worked prior to the decelerations made during the First World War. It is to be feared, however, that the prospect of 500-ton express passenger trains on any section of the Southern Railway did not represent a practical proposition from the traffic working point of view. The main line platforms at Waterloo accommodated a maximum of thirteen coaches if the train engine was not to foul the tracks of the outgoing lines from the adjoining platform. The space for the locomotive that had brought in the empty stock had also to be accounted for. With a thirteen coach train on the western section of the line the maximum tare load would be 420 not 500 tons. It was the same with the boat train platforms at Victoria. However, authority

was given for twenty engines of an entirely new type to be built, and by the close of 1923 preliminary designs for the locomotive that eventually emerged as the 'Lord Nelson' were in hand.

However the production of a locomotive of an entirely new design, and moreover one which came to include several novelties in construction, is not a rapid process, and events combined to compel the building of new express passenger engines at an earlier date. For one thing the Western Section was short of really capable engines. The passenger stud was headed by the twenty two-cylinder 4-6-0s of Robert Urie's 'N15' Class; then there were the ten Drummond four-cylinder 4-6-0s of Class 'T14' (Paddleboats); ten Urie 6-ft 4-6-0s (Class H15): ten 6-ft Drummond four-cylinder 4-6-0s (448-457 Class, used mainly west of Salisbury) and six Drummond 4-6-0s, 330 to 335, with 6-ft wheels, one of which had been rebuilt by Urie as a two-cylinder engine. An order for ten 6-ft 4-6-0s of similar design to the 'N15' was in course of completion at Eastleigh in 1923 and these engines, as referred to in the foregoing chapter, were put into passenger traffic in 1924.

Prior to grouping an order had been given to Eastleigh works for the reconstruction of the 448-457 series of four-cylinder Drummond 4-6-0s as two-cylinder engines, but at the end of 1923 no steps had been taken to put the work in hand and in view of the shortage of express engines Maunsell decided to modify the original scheme for this reconstruction

One of the Eastleigh-built 'King Arthurs', No 452 Sir Meliagrance, *with a Drummond tender at Nine Elms shed. (Real Photographs Co Ltd.)*

by retaining the Drummond engines, and only scrapping them when the new 6-ft 7-in in 4-6-0s with the 'N15' boiler were ready. On these latter the front end was to be modelled on Ashford lines. Under Clayton's close supervision the new cylinder design was worked out, including large ports, large steam chest volume and long travel valves, while the cylinders themselves were made 20½-in diameter by 28-in stroke, to work in conjunction with a higher boiler pressure than that used in the LSWR 'N15s'—200 psi instead of 180 psi. The decision to replace rather than rebuild the Drummond engines meant that the latter could remain in traffic through the summer of 1924, when the motive power situation was expected to be critical. Only the tenders, and such items as the engine bogies were to be used in the replacements.

So far as ex-L&SWR motive power was concerned, the Urie 'N15' Class of 6-ft 7-in 4-6-0 was proving a disappointment. Complaints were received by the Chief Mechanical Engineer of the unsatisfactory working of these engines. They were massive, built in the battleship tradition of the Drummond school, but although they could run very fast on occasions they were never really free in steaming and could not sustain a high output of power. Recorders taking notes of the running of these engines from the carriage, and having no access to footplate data were often perplexed at the apparently poor work. Some of these recorders sought to put the blame upon the enginemen for slack or inefficient working, but while this stigma might have applied to some railways, in the 1920-35 period no line of that time was served better by its drivers and firemen than the Western Section of the Southern. The footplate traditions built up in the days of Dugald Drummond had been sustained and strengthened in Urie's time—no body of men had been better schooled in the art of handling their engines than those of the L&SWR and one may be fairly sure that no-one could have got better work out of the Urie 'N15s' than the top link drivers at Nine Elms, Salisbury, Bournemouth and Exmouth Junction.

On one particular journey from Waterloo to Salisbury, engine No 753, with a load of no more than 280 tons, was in such straits for steam when passing Oakley summit that no higher speed than 47 mph was run for miles on the ensuing down grade towards Andover—with the train already behind time. It was on account of erratic and indifferent work of this kind that the Running Department approached Maunsell, and early in 1924 a comprehensive series of tests was begun upon engine No 742 while running in ordinary passenger service between Waterloo and Salisbury. On a typical run made with the engine in its original condition, with 5⅛ in diameter blastpipe top, boiler pressure could not be maintained higher than 140 psi throughout the critical uphill section from Weybridge to the deep cutting west of Pirbright Junction, and on what is normally a fast section from Farnborough to Basingstoke pressure fell to 100 psi. The occurrence of these trials in the spring and summer of 1924 and the appearance of the new 4-6-0s early in 1925 has suggested a close connection between the two. Actually there was very little connection—Maunsell had to 'make something' of the Urie and the road trials of No 742 were still in full swing when the front-end design of the new 4-6-0s was complete in April 1924.

Modification to the Urie 'N15' first took the form of increasing the area of the steam and exhaust ports and the provision of ⅛ in exhaust clearance. This improved the steam flow through the cylinders, but still the steaming remained indifferent. The smokebox arrangements for the new 4-6-0 (which included modified chimney and blastpipe), were then applied to No 742 and proved extremely successful, so much so that a typical run during the final series of tests the boiler pressure was consistently maintained at 170 psi to 180 psi for 75 miles on end, during which time the indicated horsepower was continually over 1,000 and rising at times to over 1,200. The engine was indeed transformed, and, it should be noted, without alteration to the valve motion which had a travel of 5⅛ in in

The Urie 'N15' 4-6-0 No 742 undergoing indicator trials on the 11 am ex-Waterloo West of England express in 1924. (Loco Publishing Co.)

One of the 'Scotch Arthurs', No 763 Sir Bors de Ganis, *at Stewarts Lane. (The late W.J. Reynolds.)*

full gear and a steam lap of 1 in. With this vindication of the boiler and smokebox modification proposed for the new engines the work at Eastleigh was pushed ahead in earnest, and simultaneously arrangements were made for the remaining Urie 'N15s' to be brought into line with No 742.

In the early autumn of 1924 plans for the summer service of 1925 discussed between the various officers concerned made it clear that the stock of express locomotives would be inadequate to meet the programme. The design of a new locomotive to meet the prophetic '500-ton-55 mph' standard was progressing, but there was no prospect of the first of these engines appearing before 1926, and it was decided therefore to put on order a further twenty of the Maunsell 'N15s' and have them built by contractors. Drawings were available, patterns could be lent, and there was a prospect of having at least some of these engines before the summer service started. But the preliminaries were going to take time, the specification had to be drafted to be sent out with the invitations to tender. So, after allowing time for the various firms to make their estimates, more than a month had elapsed and it was not until December that the order for twenty locomotives was placed with the North British Locomotive Company. The 'Scotchmen', as these latter engines became known on the Southern, were built in record time, and the first four engines were delivered in May 1925. In the meantime in February 1925 the first of the new engines replacing the Drummond 4-6-0s 448-457 was completed.

The new 6-ft 7-in 4-6-0 locomotives, which took the running numbers of those they replaced, provided a small, but very definite example of the undercurrents that were flowing in the first years of the department of the Chief Mechanical Engineer of the Southern Railway. It was hardly likely that a hard bitten old Scot like Jock Finlayson would meekly knuckle under to all the precepts of design propounded by James Clayton, in the small headquarters drawing office set up by Maunsell at Waterloo, particularly when his own drawing office at Eastleigh was reinforced by men from Ashford. Clayton certainly dictated the details of the front-end design of the new 4-6-0s, differing from the Urie 'N15' Class in having 20½-in by 28-in cylinders instead of 22 in by 28 in and a boiler pressure of 200 psi instead of 180 psi. More importantly they included the front-end features of the 'N' Class SE&CR 'Moguls' with long valve travel and long laps. When the details were submitted for his scrutiny at Waterloo Clayton apparently did not think to check the lateral clearances, with the result that the cab and platform widths were built to the L&SWR gauge and so were too wide to run on either the Brighton or the SE&CR lines! However care was taken in drafting the specifications for the contractor-built engines of the same class that they conformed to a loading gauge profile that was applicable to all three sections of the Southern Railway.

Prior to the completion of these engines a decision had been taken by the Board that in future all express passenger locomotives of the Southern would be named, and in view of the company's close association with the West of England it was decided that the 'N15' Class should be named after personalities and places connected with the legend of King Arthur and the Round Table. As a piece of publicity it was a stroke of genius, for these fine names brought that touch of individuality that mere numbers can never convey, and at once the engines of the 'King Arthur' Class became firm favourites with the travelling public. The first of the Eastleigh engines, No 453, was named *King Arthur* while the rest of the 448-457 series and the 'Scotchmen' were with one exception named after the Knights of the Round Table. The Urie 'N15s', which were also included in the class, were named after other associations with the legend, No 742, for example, became *Camelot*. The exception among the new engines was No 454, named *Queen Guinevere*.

The 'King Arthurs' rank among the great designs of the day. It should be emphasized too that the completion of engine No 453 took place three months before the historic locomotive exchange of May 1925, between the Great Western 'Castles' and the LNER 'A1' Pacifics, an event which is often quoted as the starting point in modern British locomotive development. The refinements of front-end design, including a valve travel in full gear of as much as $6^9/_{16}$ in were incorporated on a locomotive built in the massive traditions of Eastleigh. In this latter respect Finlayson not only put on the Drummond cab and made the width over the platforms to the South Western standard, but the old Drummond tenders were used. The 'Scotchmen', of which the original order was increased to thirty, were built to the composite loading gauge, had Urie tenders and cabs similar to those of the 'N' Class 2-6-0s. For the normal tractive effort of 25,320 lb at 85 per cent boiler pressure the

Top *'The Golden Arrow' Pullman boat express leaving Victoria, hauled by No 767,* Sir Valence. *(Real Photographs Co Ltd.)*

Above *Up 'Atlantic Coast Express' near Earlsfield, hauled by engine No 775,* Sir Agravaine. *(Real Photographs Co Ltd.)*

total engine weight of 81 tons was perhaps on the heavy side—one ton more, in fact, than that of the Great Western 'Castles' which had a tractive effort of 31,625 lb. Clayton once tackled Finlayson on this very point, asking why he could not get the weight down a little, but old 'Jock' would not be drawn further than to remark that he supposed 'the spec-eefic gr-r-ravity of steel was differ-r-rent at Swindon!'

At first the distribution of the new engines at the various sheds was fairly defined by batches. The 'Eastleigh Arthurs' No 448-No 457, were seen on the West of England trains, as they were mostly shedded at

Right Iseult, *one of the Urie-built 'N15' Class 4-6-0s of the LSWR, was later fitted with an improved front end and assimilated to the 'King Arthur' Class. She is seen here at Basingstoke Shed in April 1956. (R.C. Riley.)*

Right *The pre-war Bulleid livery of the Southern Railway shown on the restored* Lord Nelson *at Carnforth in 1980 while she was on loan from the National Railway Museum for working special trains of the Cumbrian Coast and Settle-Carlisle lines. (R.C. Riley.)*

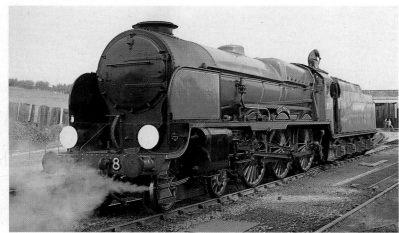

Below Lord Nelson *in steam on the Settle-Carlisle line. (D.C. Williams.)*

'Merchant Navy' No 35015, Rotterdam Lloyd, *passing Factory Junction, Battersea, with the down 'Golden Arrow'. (R. C. Riley.)*

Above *No 928,* Stowe, *in the earlier Southern livery. Seen here near Freshfield on the Bluebell Railway. (D.C. Williams.)*

Left *Another view of* Lord Nelson, *this time at Bold colliery. (D.C. Williams.)*

Salisbury and Exmouth Junction, No 763-No 772 went to Stewarts Lane for the Continental boat expresses, No 773-No 782 were at Nine Elms and No 783 to No 792 at Bournemouth. It was with these last ten locomotives that I had most of my earlier experiences with the 'King Arthur' Class. Looking back over the many logs I compiled between 1925 and 1930 I cannot say that any of them contained very outstanding or spectacular work. They were quietly efficient. The Bournemouth drivers of those days seemed content to work easily uphill and to allow their engines to run freely on the easier stretches. I travelled frequently too, behind Nine Elms men on the Sunday evening train leaving Bournemouth at 7.05 pm. It was always

very heavy, and again the usual practice was to go quietly up from Southampton to Litchfield and then to run very fast east of Basingstoke.

The capacity of the 'King Arthurs' for very fast and heavy work was shown in some trials with engine No 451 *Sir Lamorak* on which indicator diagrams were taken. On 20 November 1925, with the normal ten-coach train of the Atlantic Coast Express, the driver was instructed to work the engine 'a bit heavy' in order to get some good fat diagrams. The result was an arrival at Salisbury 16 minutes early, catching the station staff totally unprepared to deal with the train! An abbreviated log of this journey, as recorded from the footplate by Mr Holcroft is given below:

Southern Railway: Waterloo-Salisbury

Engine Class 'N15' 4-6-0 No 451 *Sir Lamorak*
Load 10 coaches, 281 tons tare, 295 tons full

Distance (miles)		Schedule time (m s)	Actual time (m s)	Average speed (mph)
0.0	WATERLOO	0 00	0 00	—
3.9	CLAPHAM JUNCTION	7 00	6 30	36.5
24.4	Woking	28 00	25 30	64.6
47.9	Basingstoke	54 00	45 30	70.4
66.4	Andover	73 00	61 00	71.8
83.8	SALISBURY	92 00	76 00	69.4

'King Arthur' Class

Built by L&SWR as Urie 'N15' Class and subsequently named

736 *Excalibur*	746 *Pendragon*
737 *King Uther*	747 *Elaine*
738 *King Pellinore*	748 *Vivien*
739 *King Leodegrance*	749 *Iseult*
740 *Merlin*	750 *Morgan le Fay*
741 *Joyous Gard*	751 *Etarre*
742 *Camelot*	752 *Linette*
743 *Lyonesse*	753 *Melisande*
744 *Maid of Astolat*	754 *The Green Knight*
745 *Tintagel*	755 *The Red Knight*

Eastleigh replacements of the Drummond 6-ft 4-6-0s 'G14' Class

448 *Sir Tristram*	453 *King Arthur*
449 *Sir Torre*	454 *Queen Guinevere*
450 *Sir Kay*	455 *Sir Lancelot*

451 *Sir Lamorak*	456 *Sir Galahad*
452 *Sir Meliagrance*	457 *Sir Bedivere*

Engines built by North British Locomotives Ltd, 1925

763 *Sir Bors de Ganis*	778 *Sir Pelleas*
764 *Sir Gawain*	779 *Sir Colgrevance*
765 *Sir Gareth*	780 *Sir Persant*
766 *Sir Geraint*	781 *Sir Aglovale*
767 *Sir Valence*	782 *Sir Brian*
768 *Sir Balin*	783 *Sir Gillemere*
769 *Sir Balan*	784 *Sir Nerovens*
770 *Sir Prianius*	785 *Sir Mador de la Porte*
771 *Sir Sagramore*	786 *Sir Lionel*
772 *Sir Percivale*	787 *Sir Menadeuke*
773 *Sir Lavaine*	788 *Sir Urre of the Mount*
774 *Sir Gaheris*	789 *Sir Guy*
775 *Sir Agravaine*	790 *Sir Villars*
776 *Sir Galagars*	791 *Sir Uwaine*
777 *Sir Lamiel*	792 *Sir Hervis de Revel*

Above *Up Bournemouth express near Hook hauled by engine No 787 Sir Mendadeuke. (The late M. W. Earley.)*

Below right *The first 'Arthur' fitted with a smoke deflecting shield, engine No 772 Sir Percivale. (The late W.J. Reynolds.)*

As a compliment to the foregoing effort, with a fairly light train, the same engine put up some magnificent running on another indicator trial with the 11 am from Waterloo to Salisbury on which a load of fourteen coaches was taken, 440 tons tare. The run was made in 93 minutes start to stop, and the data quoted below shows that the performance of the engine was highly efficient.

Trial run: 13 April 1926

Load (tons tare)	440
Average speed (mph)	54.0
Average indicated horsepower	1,113
Average gradient, rising	1 in 3,160
Coal per train mile (lb)	42
Coal per indicated horsepower hour (lb)	2.2
Calorific value of coal (BTU per lb)	13,690

The indicated horsepower quoted above is the mean of sixteen cards taken during a period of 86 minutes. The regulator was full open for the whole of that time, and the actual maximum indicated horsepower recorded was 1,241 at 59 mph when the engine was working in 22½ per cent cut-off. Although this test was carried out without a dynamometer car, and without the precision characterizing present-day indicator trials there is no reason to doubt the general run of the result. The overall performance as represented by the coal consumption per indicated horsepower hour is certainly excellent.

About the same time a very interesting exchange of 'King Arthur' Class engines took place between the Eastern and the Western Section of the Southern Railway. It was desired to compare the relative diffi-

culties of working on the Salisbury and Dover roads, and so one engine was chosen from Stewarts Lane and Nine Elm sheds and these two engines were worked with their regular crews on both routes. After preliminary exchanges to enable the drivers to learn the 'foreign' roads each engine made six trials on each road. The two engines were taken for trial without any special preparation, and this ensured that the tests were conducted in ordinary service conditions. To Dover and back the 10.45 am boat train from Victoria was to be worked, returning with the 3.30 pm or the later timing dependent on the arrival of the boat. On the Western section the trains worked were the down and up Atlantic Coast Expresses. As the trials were held in the winter when loads on the West of England route were at their minimum to make a true comparison between working on the two routes it was arranged to add empty coaches between Waterloo and Salisbury, and return, to make the loads up to that conveyed daily on the 10.45 am boat train from Victoria to Dover, usually 415 tons tare.

The most careful provisions were taken for the comparison to be made on equal terms. Hard Yorkshire coal from Dalton Main Colliery was used every day, and samples taken each day when the competing engines were being coaled and a chemical analysis made. Before each set of trials the boilers were to be washed out; steam was to be raised from cold water on the first day, and from warm water on the five subsequent days. The engines were lit up three hours before the departure time from the yard except on the first day when the boiler was cold, then the time allowed was four hours. The minimum quantity of coal for the double journey was weighed on to the tender. A reserve supply of one ton was to be carried throughout the trials at the back of the tender. This was boarded off by a partition, and was not to be used except in emergency. Both engines used had necessarily to be of the 'Scotchmen' batch, No 768 *Sir Balin* from Stewarts Lane shed and No 778 *Sir Pelleas* from Nine Elms. It is unncessary to expand on all the supplementary precautions that were taken to ensure that the fairest possible comparison was made, but it was obviously taken very seriously as a night watchman was appointed at each of the sheds to see that no interference with either of the engines should take place during the night!

All this was to no avail however. Although a responsible officer of the Locomotive Department was deputed to ride on the footplate of each engine throughout the trials, Rogers the Test Engineer on No 778 and Holcroft himself on No 768, no attempt was made to secure uniformity in driving practice. The result was that the Nine Elms man on No 778 drove in the style of Dugald Drummond, with regulator wide open for all the hard work and the gear well linked up, whereas the Stewarts Lane man rarely linked up as far as 25 per cent cut-off and used a partly opened regulator for much of the time. The trials resulted in not so much as a comparison between routes as between engines and crews. To use a colloquialism, the result was a 'push-over' for Nine Elms, as the coal consumption figures in the following table show. On the Dover road engine No 778 used less coal than she did on her own line from Waterloo to Salisbury.

'N15' Trials on Eastern and Western Sections

Route	Engine number	Average load (tons tare)	Coal used per double trip including standing (lb)	Coal per train mile (lb)	Booked average speed (mph)
Victoria-	768	412	9,237	59.5	45.9
Dover	778	410	7,588	48.6	45.9
Waterloo-	768	414	8,904	53.2	54.5
Salisbury	778	420	8,084	48.2	54.5

On one run with the Atlantic Coast Express No 768 worked a train of 418 tons tare, and about 430 tons gross to Salisbury in 91 minutes in spite of a permanent way check between Oakley and Overton. The passing times were 7¼ minutes to Clapham Junction, 29¼ minutes to Woking, 54 minutes to Basingstoke and 72½ minutes to Andover. Cut-offs were varied between 23 and 27 per cent, but it was only between Woking and Battledown Junction that the regulator was full open. The engine steamed well throughout, with pressure never less than 190 psi, but the superheat temperatures were mostly below 600°F. The above details suggest that the Dover road is the harder of the two, seeing that the driver most familiar with it showed a considerably heavier coal consumption 'at home' rather than over the strange route, although the Nine Elms driver was remarkably consistent in his coal consumption. Even the slower timing of the 'Golden Arrow' indicates clearly the less favourable nature of the Eastern Section road. Personally I never found performance on the boat trains very enterprising, and the accompanying log of the 10.45 am in 1926 is perhaps typical.

Birkenhead-Bournemouth express on the GWR line between Reading West and Southcote Junction. The engine is No 788 Sir Urre of the Mount. *(The late M.W. Earley.)*

Southern Railway: 10.45 am Continental Boat Express

Engine Class 'N15' 4-6-0 No 768 *Sir Balin*
Load 412 tons tare, 435 tons full

Distance (miles)		Schedule time (m s)	Actual time (m s)	Speed (mph)
0.0	VICTORIA	0 00	0 00	—
4.0	Herne Hill	9 00	9 15	—
5.7	Sydenham Hill	—	12 55	26.0
8.7	Beckenham Junction	17 00	17 20	—
12.6	Bickley Junction	24 00	23 40	32.0
14.9	Orpington	29 00	28 15	—
17.7	Knockholt	33 00	33 10	27.5
21.7	Dunton Green	—	38 55	57.5
23.2	Sevenoaks	40 00	40 40	47.0
28.1	Hildenborough	—	45 50	70.5
30.6	TONBRIDGE	48 00	48 45	slack
35.9	Paddock Wood	54 00	55 20	61.5
40.5	Marden	—	59 55	57.0
43.0	Staplehurst	61 00	62 35	—
46.3	Headcorn	—	65 55	—
51.5	Pluckley	—	72 10	47.0
57.2	ASHFORD	75 00	78 10	61.0
61.5	Smeeth	—	82 40	—
65.3	Westenhanger	—	87 10	47.0
66.5	Sandling Junction	87 00	88 40	
71.0	FOLKESTONE CENTRAL	—	93 15	
72.0	Folkestone Junction	93 00	94 15	
78.0	DOVER MARINE	102 00	101 40	

Waterloo-Bournemouth and Weymouth Express at Battledown Junction. The engine is No 747 Elaine *with the author on the footplate. (The late M. W. Earley.)*

During the coal trials against engine No 778, the Stewarts Lane engine No 768 made a much better run than the one tabulated, though the timing was done in less detail. With a load of 418 tons tare and about 450 tons gross, Tonbridge was passed in 49¾ minutes, after permanent way checks. Then came some fine running, with a time of 20¼ minutes from Paddock Wood to Ashford and 9½ minutes on to Sandling Junction—a total of 85½ minutes, from Victoria—and with a brisk finish Dover was reached in 98¼ minutes. The engine was run with full regulator throughout from Tonbridge to Sandling Junction and the cut-offs were 33 per cent in accelerating from the Tonbridge slack, 25 per cent from Paddock Wood, 27 per cent from Chart Siding, 30 per cent from Ashford and 33 per cent from Smeeth. This was heavy for a 'King Arthur' and in view of the coal consumption rather suggests that this particular engine was not in the best of condition.

Some years afterwards when travelling by the up Atlantic Coast Express I was interested to see this same engine back on at Exeter and, in the hands of Driver Davey of Exmouth Junction, she made one of the finest runs I have ever clocked with a 'King Arthur'. We began steadily up that difficult start on 1 in 100 slope to Exmouth Junction, and then with the engine going into complete silence we swept down the 1½ miles of 1 in 100 past Pinhoe to reach 68 mph at Broad Clyst. On the long ascent to Honiton Tunnel—13.2 miles of it with only two very short breaks—the big load of 445 tons told against the engine, but it was nevertheless very fine work to climb from Broad Clyst to Milepost 153½ at an average speed of 43 mph, and the attainment of 60 mph on the mile of 1 in 100 descent after Sidmouth Junction showed that there was no nursing of the engine. Once into Honi-

ton Tunnel, with the heavy pulling over, the run became a characteristically exciting experience, with very rapid accelerations from each successive summit, with the speed often all but doubled in 2½ to 3 miles. Crewkerne was a case in point, where the engine accelerated from 42 to 82 mph in 2¾ miles. The average speed from Milepost 153½ to Wilton, 67.5 miles, was 58.8 mph.

Seaton Junction-Exeter

Train 12.24 pm
Engine 'N15' Class 4-6-0 No 455 *Sir Lancelot*
Load 12 coaches, 362 tons tare, 385 tons full

Distance (miles)		Actual time (m s)	Speed (mph)
0.0	SEATON JUNCTION	0 00	—
0.8	Milepost 148½	2 30	21.0
1.8	Milepost 149½	5 15	22.0
2.8	Milepost 150½	7 53	23.0
3.8	Milepost 151½	10 15	26.0
4.8	Milepost 152½	12 32	26.0
5.8	Milepost 153½	14 40	29.0
7.0	Honiton	16 15	58.0
10.3	Milepost 158	19 05	78.25
11.6	SIDMOUTH JUNCTION	20 45	—
—	—	—	—
0.0		0 00	
3.7	Whimple	5 40	65.5
7.4	Broad Clyst	8 35	79.0
9.3	Pinhoe	10 10	62.5
11.1	Exmouth Junction	12 25	—
12.2	EXETER	14 55	

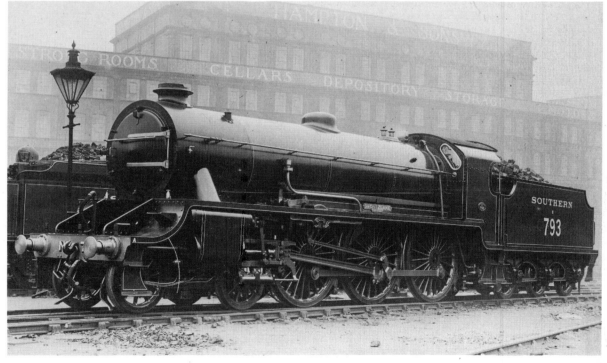

Left *Ocean Liner boat train from Southampton Docks to Waterloo at Battledown flyover, hauled by engine No 788* Sir Urre of the Mount. *(The late Derek Cross.)*

Below left *The first of the 'King Arthurs' built for the Brighton line, with six-wheeled tenders, No 793* Sir Ontzlake. *(The late W.J. Reynolds.)*

In referring to 'King Arthur' performance over the Salisbury-Exeter line it is sometimes imagined that the fast climbing of many of the steeper banks is entirely due to impetus. In a further table is shown a really excellent example of a start against the worst of all these banks, and the way the engine gathered speed with its load of 385 tons, against the 1 in 80, was most impressive. Then, as usual, came the customary swift downhill accelerations. The train was well on time, or no doubt still faster work would have been done from Honiton. On the other hand the Urie engines never seemed quite so strong on the banks as the 'King Arthurs' proper, although they too ran very fast downhill. In the 1930s I travelled several times behind No 744 *Maid of Astolat,* and twice she came within an ace of 90 mph between Honiton and Exeter. The run tabulated herewith, shows part of a trip on the 3 pm from Waterloo when we reached well over 80 mph on each of the principal descents, and very nearly bagged a fourth at Yeovil Junction. But up Honiton Bank, whereas No 455, starting a heavier train from a dead stop at Seaton Junction, reached 26 mph on entering Honiton Tunnel, No 744 had fallen to 23½ at this point, even though she passed Seaton Junction at 68 mph!

Templecombe-Sidmouth Junction

Engine 'Urie' 'N15' 4-6-0 No 744 *Maid of Astolat*
Load 10 coaches, 323 tons tare, 350 tons full

Distance (miles)		Actual time (m s)	Speed (mph)
0.0	TEMPLECOMBE	0 00	—
1.5	Milepost 113½	5 08	33.0
6.1	Sherborne	10 03	83.5
—	Wyke Crossing	—	75.0
10.7	YEOVIL JUNCTION	13 37	79.0
12.0	Sutton Bingham	15 31	64.5

Distance (miles)		Actual time (m s)	Speed (mph)
14.3	Milepost 126½	16 58	56.0
16.0	Hardington Box	18 33	71.0
19.5	Crewkerne	21 43	58.0
21.6	Milepost 133½	24 20	34.5
27.5	Chard Junction	30 00	77.5
32.6	Axminster	33 53	85.0
35.8	Seaton Junction	36 24	68.0
38.6	Milepost 150½	39 40	36.0
40.6	Milepost 152½	43 57	23.5
41.6	Milepost 153½	46 16	28.25
42.8	Honiton	47 45	60.0
46.1	Milepost 158	50 30	82.0
47.4	SIDMOUTH JUNCTION	52 15	

A further fourteen 'King Arthurs' were built at Eastleigh in 1926 for the Brighton section. To suit the existing turntables these engines were fitted with six-wheeled tenders in place of the big double-bogie Urie type fitted to the 763-792 series.

Engines built at Eastleigh in 1926 for Central Section

793	*Sir Ontzlake*	800	*Sir Meleus de Lile*
794	*Sir Ector de Maris*	801	*Sir Meliot de Logress*
795	*Sir Dinadan*	802	*Sir Durnore*
796	*Sir Dodinas le Savage*	803	*Sir Harry le Fise Lake*
797	*Sir Blamor de Ganis*	804	*Sir Cador of Cornwall*
798	*Sir Hectimere*	805	*Sir Constantine*
799	*Sir Ironside*	806	*Sir Galleron*

In later years many of those engines originally allocated to Continental boat train workings received six-wheeled tenders and on two runs that I enjoyed over the Brighton line before electrification both the 'King Arthurs' concerned had begun their careers as boat train engines. In a later chapter and in constituting also a farewell to the Brighton 4-6-4 tank engines on this service, I have set out details of some runs on the world famous 'Southern Belle', the inspiration for so many other all-Pullman trains, not merely in accommodation but in name: 'Bournemouth', 'Thanet', 'Devon', the 'Eastern Belle' of the LNER and even Mr Punch's ever-memorable 'Suffix Belle' which covered the 91½ miles from High Dudgeon to Pelting St Giles in 63 minutes and on which passengers were not allowed to bring their own food!

12. South Eastern vicissitudes

Despite the outstanding success of the 'King Arthur' Class engines one always had the feeling that they were not in line with the planned development of the locomotive stud as envisaged by Maunsell himself and enthusiastically supported by Clayton and Holcroft. It had been a disappointment to them that Ashford Works had been unable to proceed at once with the erection of the 'K' Class 2-6-4 tanks, the parts for which had been manufactured in 1923, and that it was only by putting the job out to contract that the first nine engines had been completed by the late summer. Even so, these engines were not allocated to their originally planned duties on the Kent Coast express trains, but to the Brighton main line. The prototype engine, No 790 built in 1917, was also transferred from the South Eastern to form a link of ten working from Brighton shed.

The new engines, which from the outset were named after rivers, were dual braked for working with the Westinghouse-fitted LB&SCR stock. They were put to work, strangely enough, on what may have been called the second line duties of Brighton shed on the coast-wise runs to and from Portsmouth, and the London duties on the lesser trains. No logs of their running appeared in the 'British Locomotive Practice and Performance' feature of *The Railway Magazine,* and the only photograph of one of them was a rather indifferent shot of the morning Newhaven boat train emerging from Balcombe Tunnel. The tenth of the new 2-6-4s, No 890, was built at Ashford with three cylinders and conjugated valve gear—she was completed in 1925. Shortly after this another batch of ten, No 800 to No 809, were erected at Brighton Works. The class were named as follows:

790	*River Avon*	800	*River Cray*
791	*River Adur*	801	*River Darenth*
792	*River Arun*	802	*River Cuckmere*
793	*River Ouse*	803	*River Itchen*
794	*River Rother*	804	*River Tamar*
795	*River Medway*	805	*River Camel*
796	*River Stour*	806	*River Torridge*
797	*River Mole*	807	*River Axe*
798	*River Wey*	808	*River Char*
799	*River Test*	809	*River Dart*
	890	*River Frome*	

In the London and South Western style of painting, which was adopted as standard for Southern Railway locomotives, they looked exceedingly well. But while the original plan in SE&CR days had been to standardize the 2-6-4 tank type for passenger duties up to, but not including the boat expresses, the very considerable increase in weight of some of these trains made it necessary to provide engines with higher water capacity. Thus the number of turns on which engines of the 'K' Class could be usefully employed became rather more limited than had at first been envisaged, and after the completion of the 800-809 batch, arrangements were made for the construction of further batches as 2-6-0 tender engines with 6-ft diameter coupled wheels. The standard design was thus maintained, but in a form in which longer runs could be undertaken where necessary. As strengthening of the bridges had by then taken place, the 'K' Class engines were permitted to run on the Chatham and Maidstone lines, as well as on the main line from Charing Cross to Dover.

Thus engaged in regular passenger work, a disturbing characteristic of their running became more and more apparent. Like many big tank engines they were somewhat given to rolling, and while this was generally attributed to weak spots in the road, the men were naturally reluctant to let them show their paces and frequently braked round curves where rolling regularly took place. When only one engine of the class was running, the prototype No 790, reports from drivers of bad spots were quickly attended to, and no complaints were made about the engine itself; but with Nos 800-809 running as well, the track deteriorated faster under these heavy engines than normal maintenance could cope with and these 'bad spots' tended to develop. As the Brighton-built batch were completed they were allocated to the South Eastern line and the first of them were shedded at Redhill. The second of these, No 801 *River Darenth,* was the subject of a 'flap' of no mean order in the publicity department at Waterloo. My good friend the late Maurice W. Earley secured a beautiful photograph of this engine in the late summer of 1926 leaving Reading on the SE&CR line with the Birkenhead-Dover through express. His picture graced the pages of *The Railway Magazine* and copies were also sent to Waterloo. My friend Cuthbert Grasemann was then a new recruit to the Advertising and Publicity Department, which was then under J.B., now Sir John, Elliot. Grasemann was in charge of planning for poster advertising, and Earley's photograph of *River Darenth* caught his eye. He had it very much enlarged, and enlivened by some such caption as 'South for Sunshine' it soon decked many a Southern station. However, hours, it seemed to Grasemann, after that poster's first appearance he received a peremptory summons to Elliot's presence, to accompany him down to the station—tail between legs, as it were—to see what our trains looked like before he produced any more posters! For Earley's photo-

Class 'K' 2-6-4 tank engine No 797 River Mole *at Victoria (Brighton side). (The late W.J. Reynolds.)*

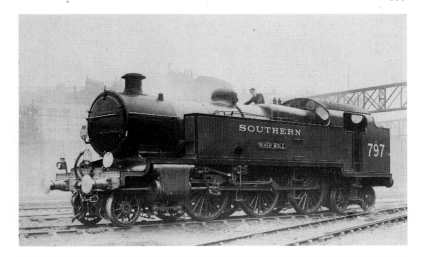

Three-cylinder 'K' Class 2-6-4 tank engine No 890, River Frome, *with conjugated valve gear. (Late W.J. Reynolds.)*

Birkenhead-Dover express shortly after leaving Reading, hauled by 'K' Class 2-6-4 tank No 801, River Darenth. *(The late M.W. Earley.)*

graph, while it showed an ex-SE&CR 'birdcage' corridor 'brake' next to the engine consisted otherwise of Great Western stock as far as the eye could discern!

The batch of 'K' Class engines based at Redhill were not called upon for much real express work. They, and the three-cylinder engine No 890, seemed to spend much of their time on the Reading locals, continuing with those trains northward from Redhill over the Brighton line to London termini. They seemed to evade the cameras of photographers, for the records of their goings are indeed few and far between. Mr Cecil J. Allen logged one of the Brighton-based engines on one of the Eastbourne trains, non-stop to Lewes, but it was an indistinguished run with a moderate load—nothing that an old non-superheated 'B4' 'Scotchman' could not have achieved in my first days of travelling over the route. In the early summer of 1927 five of the Redhill-based engines were transferred to Dover, Nos 800-804, and their places taken by five of those hitherto shedded at Brighton. While the latter transfer might well have suggested that at Central Section locomotive headquarters these engines were not held in very high esteem, the basing of the former Redhill engines at Dover made their use on the lighter Kent Coast express workings a possibility.

The South Eastern and Chatham, in company with the Brighton had used shingle ballast, laid on a foundation of ash, and while this had given satisfactory results in the past with relatively light locomotives, there were increasing signs that it was inadequate for modern requirements. In 1927, a number of definite complaints about rolling were received regarding certain engines of the class, and three derailments occurred, in two of which the three-cylinder engine No 890 was involved. Then, on 24 August 1927 came the disaster near Sevenoaks, when engine No 800 left the road on the curve between Dunton Green and Sevenoaks station, and a portion of the derailed train became blocked and smashed against the central pier at Shoreham Lane Bridge. The casualty list was a serious one, and all the 'K' Class engines were withdrawn from service, pending the Ministry of Transport enquiry. It is important to emphasize that although the engine actually concerned was relatively new, and had covered little more than 40,000 miles in traffic, the design dated back to 1917 and was one expressly prepared for the fastest passenger traffic on the South Eastern and Chatham Railway. After the accident both engines and track immediately came under suspicion. In the course of the Ministry of Transport inquiry, conducted with his usual skill by Colonel Sir John Pringle, it was revealed that there had been several reports of bad riding by the 'K' Class 2-6-4 tank engines, indeed there had been three cases of derailment, all on the Swanley-Maidstone-Ashford line. Although this itself was a secondary line it was nevertheless one used frequently for conditional boat train workings. At a very early stage in the inquiry the suspicions began to shift from the engine to the track, and the assistance of Mr H.N. Gresley, Chief Mechanical Engineer of the LNER was sought in carrying out some independent riding tests on Southern locomotives.

Colonel Pringle considered it desirable to obtain full and independent information regarding the riding qualities of the Southern Railway 'River' Class tank engines of both two-cylinder and three-cylinder varieties. With the agreement of the parties concerned, trials were conducted between Huntingdon and St Neots on the LNER main line, and on these trials Mr Gresley made a very full report. The trains hauled consisted of two coaches and the LNER dynamometer car, and some very fast running was made by the 'K' Class engines Nos 803 and No 890. The maximum speeds attained were between 77 mph

Three-cylinder 2-6-0 No A890 after conversion from 2-6-4 tank type, still with conjugated valve gear. (The late W.J. Reynolds.)

and 83 mph, and on a first class road both engines rode with admirable smoothness. Gresley commended No 803 as 'a very steady, comfortable riding engine' and while No 890 was rather more lively on its springs, which may have been due, in part, to the centre-line of the boiler being 3 in higher than on the two-cylinder engine, she too came through the tests without the slightest adverse comments. It was No 890 which reached the highest speed in the trials on the LNER namely 83¼ mph—yet another tribute to the free running qualities of the three-cylinder engines.

Following upon these trials, Sir Herbert Walker asked that a similar series of trials should be carried out with the same engines over a section of the Southern Railway, and accordingly on 16 October 1927 runs were made on the L&SWR line between Woking and Walton. The veteran Sir John A.F. Aspinall, former Chief Mechanical Engineer, and later General Manager of the Lancashire and Yorkshire Railway, was present at these trials and as on the LNER Mr Gresley rode on the footplate on each one of the test runs. Here the rolling was severe and in his report Gresley considered that at speeds of 70 mph and over the rolling was greater than he thought to be safe for regular working on roads in a condition similar to that of the Southern Railway between Woking and Walton. It was thought that the rolling was caused by irregular depression of the road, apparently due to the sleepers not being properly packed and to defective drainage. To provide a comparison with the running of the 'K' Class tank engines with that of the express passenger engines working the boat trains and also the fastest trains running on the Eastern Section of the Southern Railway arrangements were made to also include a 'King Arthur' Class 4-6-0 in trials conducted both on the LNER main line and on the L&SWR line between Woking and Walton.

The engine tested was No 782, *Sir Brian,* and Gresley was not impressed. On the LNER at speeds of 75 mph to 81½ mph the engine ran steadily without any roll or lurch; but the vibration on the footplate was so severe that it was impossible to obtain any record with the accelerometer, used for measuring the lateral and vertical acceleration in a roll or lurch. On the Southern a maximum speed of 86 mph was registered. Gresley reported: 'The vibration was, if anything, worse than on the London and North Eastern. At the places where rolling occurred with the tank engines, there was considerable rolling and lurching with the tender engine, and the riding can be described as being very rough and uncomfortable'.

No doubt some of these sentiments were passed on to Bullied, who was then his personal assistant, which may have accounted for his marked antipathy towards the 'King Arthurs' when he took up office on the Southern. Gresley paid a glowing tribute, however, to the design of both two-cylinder and three-cylinder tank engines, and expressed the opinion that on a good road, such as that of the LNER where they were tested, they could be run safely at any speed which they could attain. As a result of this report, however, and of the criticism made of permanent way generally on the Southern Railway, the directors decided to replace the shingle ballast with Meldon granite on all main lines and to improve the drainage throughout. It was a long and costly process, and rather than hold the 'River' Class idle until it was completed, they were converted into tender engines and included in Class 'U'. The first of these latter engines were already on the road, but reference to their work is made in a later chapter. The names borne by the 2-6-4 tanks were not revived.

At the time of the grouping of the railways, in 1923 the South Eastern & Chatham had an order outstanding for fifteen new 4-4-0 express engines of simi-

Class 'N' 2-6-0 No A860 at Mortehoe, on the Ilfracombe branch. (The late M.W. Earley.)

Hastings train near Orpington, hauled by 'L' Class 4-4-0 No A771. (Rail Archive Stephenson — F.R. Hebron.)

lar weight and capacity to the 'L' Class. Following the successful rebuilding of the Wainwright 'D' and 'E' 4-4-0s, as described earlier, a new design would have followed on the same lines. However no complaints had been received from the Running Department about the original 'L' Class 4-4-0s, as they were capable of dealing successfully with the existing loads and timings. A scheme for improving the valve gear had been worked out by the Chief Mechanical Engineer's department, at the time however the shops were so busy with routine repairs that the plan was pigeon-holed. When the fast 80-minute expresses between Charing Cross and Folkestone Central were put on, in the summer of 1921, the Running Department of the SE&CR pressed for more Class 'L' 4-4-0s. This cut across Maunsell's standardization policy in which it was proposed to use the 'K' Class 2-6-4 tanks for work of this kind, but tests with the prototype engine No 790 showed that on fast runs of almost 70 miles in length their tanks' capacity would leave very little margin.

So far as the new 4-4-0s were concerned grouping had the effect of postponing their construction indefinitely, and for the first five years of its operation the 80-minute Folkestone service was run by the original 'L' Class 4-4-0s. Providing the loads did not

much exceed 200 tons they could manage this 52 mph booking satisfactorily. With short lap valves, and a somewhat hamstrung front-end these 'L' Class engines had to be run at about 40 per cent cut-off with a narrow regulator opening. They were well suited to the haulage of heavy loads at 45 mph to 50 mph but faster running, as needed on the main line, was obtained only by lengthening the cut-off to provide more exhaust opening, and of course this meant working with a partly closed regulator. However they were economical on coal consumption and were popular with their crews.

They showed up well on the Hastings line, on which the severity of the curvature in places entails many speed restrictions to 40 mph or so. There are few opportunities on this route for sustained fast running, such as that regularly made between Westenhanger and Tonbridge on the main line. For some reason, which those who were most familiar with the 'L' Class never seemed able to fathom, No 761 was the most free-running of the lot, and in *The Railway Magazine* for September 1922 details are given of a run with this engine, and a load of 215 tons gross, on which speed averaged 66 mph from Smeeth to Paddock Wood, with maximum speeds of 72½ mph through Ashford and again at Headcorn. But even on

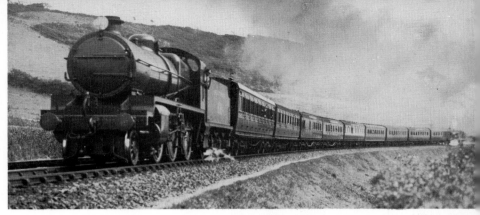

Waterloo-Ilfracombe express climbing Mortehoe bank with 'N' Class 2-6-0 No A839 and an 'M7' 0-4-4 banking at the rear. (The late M.W. Earley.)

'N' Class 2-6-0 No A838 climbing the 1 in 36 bank from Ilfracombe towards Mortehoe with a local train. (The late M.W. Earley.)

this run, when time was kept to Charing Cross, the engine was nearly a minute down on schedule on passing Tonbridge—40.5 miles from Folkestone Central in 41 minutes 55 seconds. Recovery took place on the hilly stretch up to Knockholt, where of course the engine was easily master of so relatively light a train.

There were occasions, as at holiday week-ends, when train loads were much heavier. The following are examples of running in the years 1923, 1924 and 1925 on the Folkestone non-stops.

Engine number	775	761	775	777
Load (tons tare/full)	310/340	255/275	263/285	312/340
Direction	Down	Up	Up	Up
Net overall time (minutes)	83	81¾	79	88

The run up of No 775 was certainly a very fine one, with Tonbridge (40.5 miles) passed in 41 minutes 15 seconds from the start and speed averaging 68 mph from Smeeth to Paddock Wood, but the other journeys tell their own tale. What finally forced the issue

was the introduction of heavy corridor stock in place of the old SE&CR non-corridors. This sent the regular load of certain trains over the 300-ton mark and made an improved type of locomotive essential. The 'K' Class tank engine was clearly unsuitable.

When authority was given to go ahead the need had become so urgent that time did not permit of a thorough redesign to produce an engine on 'E1' lines. Ashford was not able to undertake the work, and the new engines had to be built by contractors. The course adopted was to use the existing drawings, patterns and templates of the 'L' Class and introduce only those modifications which could be readily accommodated. It was not possible, without redesigning the cylinders, to give longer steam chests with direct ports and 1⅝-in lap as on the 'E1' rebuilds. In accordance with the scheme which had been pigeon-holed some years earlier, the valve travel was increased to the maximum that the existing design of steam-chest would permit, by the adjustment of the eccentrics, and alteration of the rocking lever arms. Thus the steam lap was increased from ⅞ in to 1³/₁₆ in. Another improvement was to use the Class 'N' chimney and smokebox arrangement. This was tried out first on one of the existing 'L' 4-4-0s, No 779, and the proportions were settled by experiment

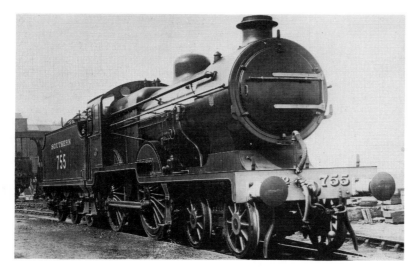

before incorporation in the 'L1' design. The new engines used a higher boiler pressure of 180 psi and smaller cylinder diameter, thus the tractive effort was the same as for the 'L' Class.

The rearrangement of the cab was much more extensive in the case of the 'L1' than on the 'King Arthur'. Instead of the large tool boxes with wooden tops, built up over the trailing coupled wheels, which made standing room limited on the 'L' Class engines, the 'L1s' had tip-seats for the driver and fireman, as on the 'E1', 'D1' and 'N' Classes. Thus the driver could stand directly behind the front window, in a comfortable stance, instead of having to lean across the toolbox, the fireman had more room to swing his shovel. The tenders were similar to those of the 'N' Class.

Fifteen engines, 753 to 759 and 782 to 789, were built by the North British Locomotive Co in 1926. Originally all engines of the constituent companies of the Southern Railway retained their old numbers. To avoid confusion these numbers were prefixed according to the works at which they were maintained. Thus engines of the former SE&CR had the prefix 'A', Brighton engines were 'B' and the ex-LSWR types were prefixed 'E'. New locomotives of types derived from pre-grouping designs were numbered in the corresponding series, so that the 'King Arthurs', derived from the L&SWR 'N15' Class, were prefixed 'E', while the 'L1' 4-4-0s were prefixed 'A'. At a later date the ex-SE&CR engines had 1,000 added to their numbers and the ex-Brighton types 2,000, so that the 'L1' Class eventually became 1753 to 1759 and 1782 to 1789.

The new 4-4-0s were an immediate success, and although their nominal tractive effort was no greater than that of the 'L' Class and the boiler was the same

in each case, they were able to manage the 80-minute Folkestone trains with loads of 300 tons, against the 200-225 tons which represented about the maximum with which timekeeping could usually be relied upon with the older engines. Indeed, excellent runs have been recorded with 'L1' Class engines loaded up to no less than 350 tons. One such run that I noted personally remains vividly in my memory for the silent way in which the engine, No 787, worked into speed between Ashford and Tonbridge. On this journey there was a heavy slack through Ashford, but afterwards we put up an average of 67.8 mph over the 10.4 miles from Headcorn to Paddock Wood with a load of 355 tons.

Studying the details of many runs with the 80-minute Folkestone trains it is evident that the superiority of the 'L1' Class over 'L' was almost entirely over the fast running section between Tonbridge and Sandling Junction. The new engines did not show up the same advantage in the hill climbing. This of course was understandable, seeing that the nominal tractive effort of both classes was the same and the 'L' Class had never been deficient in 'power to pull'. Although the speed worthiness of the 'L1' Class was shown in many runs on the Folkestone trains in the years 1926-31, before the 'Schools' took over, these engines were never in the top flight of inside cylinder 4-4-0s—nor could they be expected to be seeing that their design was very much a hasty adaptation of the 'L' Class. Nevertheless they held the fort on the Folkestone flyers most worthily, until the loads in the holiday seasons began to rise well over the 300-ton mark. Some examples of the speed they made on the fast stretch from Smeeth to Paddock Wood 25.6 miles are set out below.

Engine number	753	783	755	784	758
Gross load behind tender (tons)	275	305	305	320	340
Average speed (mph)	70.7	72	70.2	68.4	72
Maximum speed (mph)	75	75	74	74	76.5

In view of the success of the 'L1' engines it might be imagined that some alterations would be made to the original 'L' Class as opportunity permitted. So far as I am aware, however, no such change was made to the valve motion, though as some of the 'L' Class acquired Maunsell chimneys there may have been changes in the smokebox. Be that as it may, in the years just before the Second World War the 'L' Class engines were putting up some very fast running on

occasions. Out of many logs sent me by various friends in pre-war years there is no more remarkable example than that on the 8.11 am from Ramsgate to Ashford. I have tabulated the log of the run as between Minster and Ashford, and to those who do not know this route it will probably come as something of a surprise to learn that the general tendency of the gradients is rising all the way! After a rapid start on the level speed was eased to 45 mph at Grove Ferry over the curves, but in the next 2¼ miles speed was worked up to 75 mph and was held at 75-76 mph up the 1 in 579 to Sturry. Then between Canterbury and a point some 1½ miles beyond Chilham the gradients are steadily rising; indeed this stretch ends with 1½ miles at 1 in 220-176-200. Here a speed of 60 mph was sustained till the crest was reached and the engine streaked away to 74 mph on the level at Wye. This was a most exhilarating little run.

Minster-Ashford

Train 8.11 am Ramsgate to Ashford
Engine Class 'L' 4-4-0 No 1774
Load 4 coaches, 128 tons tare, 135 tons full

*slack over reverse curve

Distance (miles)		Schedule time (m s)	Actual time (m s)	Speed (mph)
0.0	MINSTER	0 00	0 00	
5.0	Grove Ferry		6 12	45*
7.1	Chislet		8 25	75
9.1	Sturry		10 00	76
11.5	CANTERBURY WEST	13 00	12 34	
0.0		0 00	0 00	
3.0	Chartham		4 55	58
5.2	Chilham		7 10	60
9.9	Wye		11 48	74
			signal check	
14.2	ASHFORD	20 00	17 55	

An interesting direct comparison between Classes 'L' and 'L1' might be made from the two runs from Whitstable to Bromley tabulated herewith. Certainly on the basis of these times the 'L1' did, with 350 tons, much the same as the 'L' did with 230. But without knowing how the two engines worked one cannot draw any reliable conclusions. But Mr S.A.W. Harvey, a regular correspondent at that time, sent me an analysis of all the runs he had timed with super-heater 4-4-0s of the inside-cylinder varieties on Sole Street bank prior to 1940. This analysis makes most interesting reading. The long incline is commenced at reduced speed—usually about 30 mph through

Rochester—and impetus would not ordinarily be exhausted by the time Cuxton Road box is passed. But the average speed over the 4 miles from this signal box to Sole Street station gives a very good guide to the sustained effort on the bank. In this analysis, 47 runs with 'L' Class engines give results little better than those of the superheater 'D1' and 'E1' rebuilds, and the best 'L' ascent is eclipsed by the best 'E1' effort. But on every account the 'L1' performances are the best of all; the climbing of engine No 1786 with 350 tons was certainly excellent. I have worked out the point-to-point average speeds on the comparative runs of engines 1762 and 1786.

Whitstable-Bromley South

Date				June 1939		August 1935	
Class				'L'		'L1'	
Engine number				1762		1786	
Load (tons tare/full)				221/230		323/350	

Distance (miles)		Schedule time (m s)		Actual time (m s)	Average speed (mph)	Actual time (m s)	Average speed (mph)
0.0	WHITSTABLE	0	00	0 00	—	0 00	—
				signal check			
7.1	Faversham	10	00	12 23	34.4	10 17	41.2
11.1	Teynham			17 45	44.8	15 18	47.9
14.4	Sittingbourne	18	00	20 45	66.0	18 14	67.3
17.5	Newington			24 00	57.3	21 40	54.3
20.2	Rainham			26 28	65.8	24 20	60.8
—						signal check	
23.2	Gillingham			29 14	65.3	28 10	47.0
24.8	CHATHAM	30	00	31 14	48.0	31 10	32.0
25.4	Rochester			31 56	51.2	31 57	45.8
26.2	Rochester Bridge			33 02	43.5	33 07	41.2
28.2	Cuxton Road			36 12	37.9	36 07	40.0
32.2	Sole Street	43	00	42 45	36.6	43 15	33.6
33.2	Meopham			44 05	45.0	44 48	38.9
35.7	Fawkham			46 28	62.9	47 32	54.3
—						signal check	
38.6	Farningham Road			48 56	70.2	51 14	47.1
—						signal check	
41.4	Swanley Junction	53	00	52 02	54.2	63 50	—
				permanent way slack			
44.3	St Mary Cray			53 36	48.7	67 32	47.0
—				signal check			
45.7	St Mary Junction			58 08	32.9	69 20	43.3
—				signal check			
46.5	Bickley Junction	59	00	61 42	13.5	70 05	63.9
47.1	Bickley			63 00	27.6	70 48	51.2
48.2	BROMLEY SOUTH	62	00	64 56	—	72 35	—
Net time				57 15		58 15	

Continental boat express near Orpington Junction, hauled by engine No 764 Sir Gawain. *(Real Photographs Co Ltd.)*

4-4-0 Performance on Sole Street Bank
Cuxton Road Box-Sole Street: 4 miles

Engine class	'D1'	'E1'	'L'	'L1'
Number of runs timed	11	17	47	11
Average gross load (tons)	225	230	250	320
Average speed (mph)	31.4	32.0	31.2	28.9
Best run:				
Load (tons tare)	275	255	280	350
Time (m s)	7 08	6 27	7 13	7 08
Average speed (mph)	33.6	37.2	33.3	33.6

In the last year of the Southern Railway, 1947, I enjoyed an excellent run on the footplate of an 'L1', No 1758 on the 4.57 pm mail train up from Ashford, running to London Bridge via Redhill. The load was a moderate one of 275 tons gross behind the tender and with it the engine ran very freely. The driver made frequent changes in cut-off to suit the rise and fall of the road, and this took us along at a fine even pace, as the effects of each rise were anticipated and cut-off lengthened before speed had begun to fall. Once into speed the cut-off was varied between 22 and 28 per cent, and our progress was such that Milepost 35¾ (a mile short of Paddock Wood), 20.4 miles from Ashford, was passed in 21¼ minutes from the start. Beyond this point a long engineers' slack delayed our run into Tonbridge. From the restart, up steadily rising gradients of 1 in 266 and 1 in 251, 30 per cent cut-off was used at first, with the regulator wide, though not fully opened. Edenbridge, 9.2 miles, was passed in 13¼ minutes, at 54 mph, but after this, with the train getting ahead of time the steaming was eased. Altogether I found No 1758 a very lively, good steaming engine. After Redhill, with load reduced to 180 tons, the effort required was relatively small.

13. The 'Lord Nelson' Class

In September 1923, barely two months after his appointment as Chief Operating Manager of the Southern Railway, Mr E.C. Cox, announced that the future standard for main-line express trains was to be a load of 500 tons tare. This extraordinary target was to apply not only to the West of England and Bournemouth routes of the former L&SWR, but also to the Continental boat trains and to the Kent Coast Services by both the Chatham and South Eastern routes. As if this was not enough, in the way of optimistic forecasting of traffic density, it was stated that such trains would require to be worked, apparently on all routes, at start-to-stop average speeds of 55 mph. My recollection of those days, when I was an engineering student in London, was that this breathtaking remit was taken as 'one of those things' amid the euphemistic 'ballyhoo' surrounding some of the publicity generated by the grouping of the railways. In any event the best times offered in 1923 from London to Salisbury, 54 mph, Southampton 51 mph, Folkestone 53 mph, and Margate 48 mph generally showed a standard far below a 55 mph average, let alone maintenance of it with such loads as 500 tons. In any case loads of that magnitude were rare anywhere on the railways of Great Britain at that time.

Nevertheless in mid-October 1923 instructions were given to the newly constituted CME's department to proceed with the design and construction of twenty new engines that would be a start to this ambitious specification. No locomotive engineer could resist such a challenge, but after the first flush of exhilaration at such a prospect, which would put the Southern Railway abreast, if not ahead of the most powerful express passenger designs then existing in the country there was a pause. At that time the Great Western 'Castles' and the LNER 'Pacifics' of Gresley and Raven design represented the greatest advances in power on British railways, and rather surprisingly the folks at Ashford then felt the new Southern locomotives would have to be of no more than the same capacity to meet the new traffic requirements. Two questions at once arose, should the new engine be of 4-6-0 or 4-6-2 type and should it have three cylinders or four? Maunsell was open-minded but Clayton, impressed by the 'Castle', thought that a 4-6-0 with narrow firebox would do the job and be cheaper to build. While the quality of coal likely to be available on the Southern would not be up to that regularly used then on the GWR the distances to be run on the Southern were not so long and in Clayton's opinion a wide firebox was not called for on this account. Regarding the number of cylinders, experience with the SE&CR 2-6-0 engine No 822 had pointed clearly to the advantages arising with the use of six exhaust beats per revolution instead of four; Clayton was so far impressed with Churchward's practice as to favour four cylinders, though the GWR 'Castles' and 'Stars', with normal crank setting, gave only four beats per revolution. His junior partner, Holcroft, following up his historic work on three-cylinder locomotives had, in 1920, carried his advocacy still further with a paper on 'Four-Cylinder Locomotives', read before the Institution of Locomotive Engineers. In that paper he had put forward a proposal for cranks at 135°, giving eight exhausts per revolution, and coupled with this the design of a conjugated valve gear so that only two sets of motion would be needed for the four cylinders. Use of the 135° setting would enable Clayton to have four cylinders, but at the same time gain the advantage of softer blast and more than even turning moment. To put the 135° crank arrangement to the test, though without conjugated valve gear, one of the remaining 6-ft Drummond 4-6-0s, No 449, which had earlier been fitted with a superheated boiler, was selected for trial. A set of coupled wheels was prepared at Eastleigh, in which the angle of cranks of the driving wheels was altered to 135°, and the balance weights suitably adjusted in all wheels of the set. After the performance of the engine had been recorded with the cranks having the normal 180° setting, the engine was lifted in the shops and the set of wheels with the 135° setting substituted. With this sole alteration No 449 was then sent back into traffic. The resulting performance was so much in favour of the alteration that a definite decision was made to adopt the 135° crank setting for the new engines.

Further design work on the new four-cylinder 4-6-0 was deferred during the summer of 1924 as at that time the new Chief Mechanical Engineer's headquarters office at Waterloo was in process of establishment, with accompanying upheaval in the personal affairs of all concerned. In the early autumn in 1924 work began in earnest on the scheming out of the design, but before giving his final decision on the type of engine Maunsell was anxious to obtain some first-hand observations of the locomotive work on other lines. On 1 October 1924, Clayton rode from Paddington to Plymouth on No 4076 *Carmarthen Castle* with the Cornish Riviera Express. Ten days later he rode on a Gresley 'Pacific', with the Flying Scotsman from Kings Cross to Grantham. Any doubts that might have existed were dispelled by Clayton's footplate trips on these two engines and a definite decision was taken to make the new Southern engine a four-cylinder 4-6-0. These observations of Clayton's on the relative merits of two famous designs were to be amply confirmed less than a year later, in the interchange trials of 1925, though in support of the Gresley 'Pacifics' it should be said that it was not until 1926 that modifications were made to the valve gear which transformed their general running and their coal consumption.

Design work on the new engine was again held up in the late autumn of 1924, when the pressing needs of the Traffic Department for the summer service of 1925 made it necessary to abandon for a time the project of having twenty new engines authorized to the '500-ton—55 mph' specification. The preparation of detail drawings for a new engine and the subsequent making of patterns and templates would alone occupy some twelve months, whereas adding to the number

Drawing of a 'Lord Nelson' Class 4-6-0.

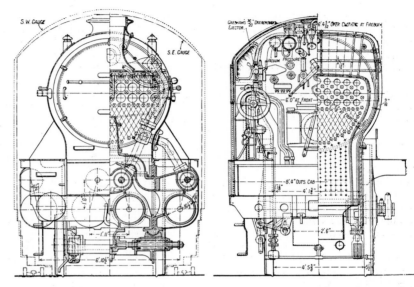

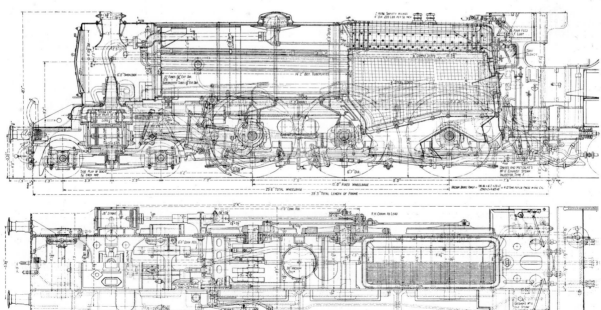

of an existing design would enable construction to start once the necessary material was on hand. Therefore as described in Chapter 11 a further batch of improved 'N15' Class 4-6-0s ('King Arthurs') was built by outside contractors. But once the detailed contract specifications for these latter had been prepared, for the various builders to tender, attention was once again turned to the new four-cylinder 4-6-0, and after running conditions on all routes concerned had been examined on the 500-ton 55 mph basis it was estimated that a locomotive capable of a sustained output of 1,500 indicated horsepower would meet a case. This would have seemed a serious underestimate of the power required for such a specification, but in the event traffic did not require such an output. The leading dimensions were settled as: cylinders 16½-in diameter by 26-in stroke, coupled wheels the standard 6 ft 7 in and working pressure 220 psi. This provided a nominal tractive effort of 33,500 lb, the highest of any British express passenger engine at that time. Piston valves with long lap were of course included, 1½-in lap and 6½-in travel in full gear.

Although the general outline of the design came from an appraisal of the Great Western 'Castle', very little similarity can be seen in the working out of the details—far less than in the 'N' Class Moguls as compared with the GWR '43XX' type. In the new Southern 4-6-0 all four cylinders were practically in line—this gave very short and direct steam passages, but with a divided drive this resulted in the outside connecting rods being 11-ft centres against 6-ft 11-in centres for the inside ones. Four separate sets of valve gear were used. The original length of boiler between tube-plates in the Waterloo design was shortened at the request of Eastleigh for the practical reason of making the tube length the same as that of the 'King Arthurs' and so save stocking an additional size of tube. Consequently the boiler barrel was 1 ft shorter than that of the 'Castle', although in the Belpaire

firebox that rounding of the outer shell, so carefully developed at Swindon, was to a large extent reproduced. The trapezoidal shape tapering inwards from the front was not adopted, and with a straight barrel the water space outside the tubes at the firebox tubeplate was considerably less than on the 'Castle'. A regulator in the dome, and the feed introduced through clack valves on the side of the boiler served to emphasize the lack of similarity between the Eastleigh and Great Western designs. The degree of superheat was considerably higher in the Maunsell engine.

Very great care was taken in design to keep the weight down, and Clayton had to exercise strict supervision at Eastleigh to prevent the traditional heavy-handedness of the ex-L&SWR draughtsmen from getting the upper hand. Certain parts which would normally be left as forged or cast were machined to keep the weight down, but when the prototype engine came well within the estimated figure this latter refinement in construction was not adopted on the further fifteen engines of the class. The connecting rods and motion were made very light by the use of 'Vibrac' high-tensile alloy steel. The extent to which weight was kept down is shown in the total for engine in working order, 83½ tons, against the 81 tons of a 'King Arthur' which had a nominal tractive effort only 76 per cent of the 'Nelson' figure. All in all the new 4-6-0 represented a thoroughly original and handsome design. The prototype was built at Eastleigh, and completed in August 1926. With the highest tractive effort of any British passenger engine the Souther Railway Publicity Department made the most of their opportunities for boosting 'the most powerful British locomotive' and the very name bestowed *Lord Nelson*, was symbolical of Southern readiness to take on all comers. A first-class impression was certainly created, both in railway circles and outside.

The *Lord Nelson* after completion was engaged in work of an experimental kind, until April 1927, so far as the engine itself was concerned, though these trials

were conducted on service trains with consistently reliable time-keeping. At an early date it was clear she was an extremely free-running engine as speeds of 90 mph were touched on several occasions and although much of this early work was done with poor quality foreign coal, due to the prolonged coal strike of that year, the steaming was good, including that on such a duty as the 10.45 am Golden Arrow from Victoria to Dover. None of these early runs however made demands even remotely approaching the 500 ton—55 mph standard.

Between Waterloo and Salisbury trial runs were made in December 1926, with the normal ten-coach formation of the Atlantic Coast Express, 316 tons tare. On a down journey the engine was worked in sixteen per cent cut-off throughout. With one brief intermission, near Hook, the regulator was kept full open for the continuous work gradually against the collar to the summit 53½ miles out of Waterloo. This point was passed in 57 minutes and Porton (78.3 miles) was passed in 80 minutes. Adverse signals delayed the finish, with a dead stop for 1¾ minutes, but arrival in Salisbury was a little before time in 90¼ minutes from Waterloo (83.8 miles). On the following day with the up train departure from Salisbury was 10¼ minutes late and opportunity was taken to make some fast running. The adverse start to Oakley, 31.4 miles from Salisbury, was made in 33½ minutes, after which 37.6 favourable miles on to Esher occupied no more than 29½ minutes, an average of 76½ mph. This might have been still faster, as the engine developed 90 mph with ease, but at that time the standard of permanent way construction and maintenance on the constituent sections of the Southern Railway had not reached the high levels afterwards sustained, and the engine tended to pitch at low rail joints. The regulator had accordingly to be eased at times. On this trip 66 miles were run in the first hour from Salisbury, and in spite of three signal checks Waterloo was reached in 83 minutes (83.8 miles).

On these two trips water consumption was 31 gallons per train westbound and 30 gallons eastbound. The estimated coal consumption was 37 lb per train mile westbound and 34½ lb eastbound, in both cases using imported coal. On the up journey the cut-off was between 20 and 25 per cent up the initial stiff climb to Grateley, and 15 per cent thereafter. One point noticeable during the early trial runs of the *Lord Nelson* was the response of the engine to different methods of driving. The Western Division men, working faithfully in the Drummond tradition, used a wide-open regulator and early cut-offs; men from the former SE&CR, handling the engine on heavy boat trains, rarely opened the main regulator valve more than halfway and kept cut-off at about 25 to 30 per cent. Yet there seemed little to choose between the results obtained, as had been the case with the *King Arthurs* and was later to be shown on the *Schools* Class 4-4-0s. Purely from the user's point of view there is a great deal to be said for an engine that responds equally well to the vagaries of individual enginemen. In running the winter ten-coach load of the Atlantic Cost Express, the engine was of course working well below its maximum designed capacity.

By far the most important among these early trials was one on Sunday 10 April 1927, when a special train of sixteen coaches, 521 tons tare, was run from Waterloo to Exeter and back. Indicator diagrams were taken only on the down journey. No dynamometer car was available, and so the results had all to be based on the indicated horsepower obtained. Sixteen indicator cards were taken between Waterloo and Salisbury and a further nineteen between Salisbury and Exeter. Unfortunately although details of the speeds, cut-offs, steam chest pressures and indicated horsepower were published many years later in Holcroft's book *Locomotive Adventure,* the locations of those observations were not stated—one is left to guess at these from the speeds. No detailed logs were com-

Left *The* Lord Nelson, *when newly built in 1926. (The late W.J. Reynolds.)*

Right *The* Lord Nelson *at Nine Elms, fitted with front end shelters for indicator tests. (The late W.J. Reynolds.)*

piled. The booked time from Waterloo to Salisbury was as follows; leaving at 8.52 am:

Distance (miles)		Time (m s)	Average speed (mph)
0.0	WATERLOO	0 00	—
3.9	Clapham Junction	7 00	33.5
13.3	Hampton Court Junction	17 30	54.0
32.2	Sturt Lane Junction	37 30	53.4
47.8	Basingstoke	54 00	57.0
50.3	Worting Junction	57 00	50.0
66.4	Andover	72 00	64.5
82.7	Tunnel Junction	87 30	63.5
83.8	SALISBURY	90 00	—

The actual time made was 96¼ minutes, due to a diversion to slow line running between Earlsfield, through Wimbledon and back on to the fast line at Raynes Park. An analysis subsequently published, for only the Waterloo-Salisbury run gave the following details:

Distance (miles)	83.8
Booked time (m s)	90 00
Actual time (m s)	96 15*
Average indicated horsepower	1,292
Average cut-off with full regulator (per cent)	22
Average boiler pressure (psi)	210
Average steam chest pressure (psi)	200
Coal per train mile (lb)	66.5
Water per train mile (gallons)	44
Coal per sq ft of grate area per hour (lb)	105
Coal per indicated horsepower hour (lb)	2.68

The average of ten indicator cards, once they got really going after the initial delays gave a fine record of 1,397 indicated horsepower, but one would have liked the actual locations, to be able to study the horsepower figures in relation to the gradients.

The feeling that something was missing from the overall picture was even more pronounced when it came to the continuation west of Salisbury. The booked time for the run of 88 miles was 103 minutes, with a stop of one minute intermediately at Sidmouth Junction. The timing to this latter station, 75.8 miles, was 87 minutes, an average of 52 mph, against which one may recall that the pre-war average in London and South Western days from Salisbury to Exeter was 55 mph. To make that average with the *Lord Nelson* test train would entail cutting five minutes from the Salisbury-Sidmouth Junction time. From the details of the indicator cards subsequently published in Holcroft's book one can gather that they had something of a struggle to get up Honiton bank with that 520-ton load. It is clear that an indicator card was taken near Axminster, when speed was being worked up for an all-out charge at the bank. The maximum indeed was the highest on the entire journey from London, 84 mph. The details of this card and of the five following ones were as follows:

Speed (mph)	Cut-off (per cent)	Steam chest pressure (psi)	Indicated horsepower
84	15	186	1,336
65	17	185	1,172
36	37	170	1,334
26	38	176	1,145
20	40	175	1,050
12	57	162	736

When boiler pressure was near to its maximum on

*Includes one signal stop and two severe crossover slacks

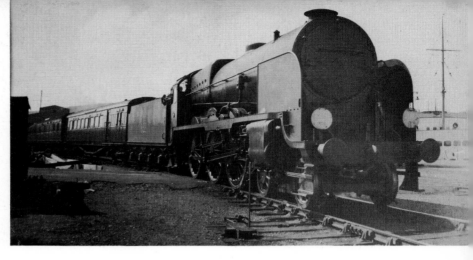

Left Inward bound Continental boat express leaving Folkestone Junction sidings behind engine No 856, Lord St Vincent. (*The late W.J. Reynolds.*)

Right Engine No 858, Lord Duncan, on the quay at Dover Marine. (*O.S. Nock.*)

this engine the steam chest pressure was about 200 psi, as it had been all the way from Waterloo to Salisbury. There was considerable variation westward, and it seemed that the severe pull up Honiton bank took its toll, finally lowering the speed to 12 mph. In any case there did not seem to be any margin with a 520-ton load. With no delays west of Salisbury the 88 miles to Exeter were covered in 102¼ minutes inclusive of the one brief scheduled stop at Sidmouth Junction. No other intermediate times were quoted, but it is clear that the average speed fell a good deal lower than the 55 mph average. Nevertheless it was a rousing effort, and one can appreciate the need for Rodges and his test engineers relaxing, 'on the cushions' on the way back. Unfortunately the published report gave no details of the coal consumption on the heavily-graded section of line west of Salisbury.

For some time prior to the test run the engine had been working on the Western section, principally between Waterloo and Salisbury, but soon afterwards it was transferred back to the Eastern section, where most of the preliminary running, in 1926, had been made. Holcroft reported on several of these runs, on the earliest of which the engine was being worked by Driver Francis, of Eastleigh, with a Battersea driver, Stuckey riding as pilotman. Soon however the latter took over as regular driver of the *Lord Nelson,* and he resumed after the engine was transferred back to Stewarts Lane shed after the 520-ton test run on 10 April 1927. When Mr Cecil J. Allen had a footplate run on the engine working the 10.45 am Pullman boat train, before that train had been named 'The Golden Arrow', it was clear that the Battersea methods of working the engine had superseded those of Nine Elms. Driver Stuckey, despite having a 460-ton load behind him, never opened the regulator to more than one half, and was running for most of the way to Dover with a considerably narrower opening than that.

Victoria-Dover

Train 10.45 am Boat Express
Engine 4-6-0 No 850 Lord Nelson
Load 14 vehicles, 432 tons tare, 460 tons gross

Distance (miles)		Schedule time (m s)	Actual time (m s)	Speed(†) (mph)
0.0	VICTORIA	0 00	0 00	—
4.0	Herne Hill	9 00	8 45	41
5.7	Sydenham Hill		12 00	31½
7.2	Penge		14 30	48
8.7	Beckenham Junction	17 00	16 25	40*
10.8	Bromley		19 30	37/46
12.6	Bickley Junction	23 00	22 15	30*
13.3	Orpington Junction	25 00	23 50	25*
14.9	Orpington		26 25	45
17.6	Knockholt	32 00	31 05	33½
21.6	Dunton Green		36 05	61½

Distance (miles)		Schedule time (m s)	Actual time (m s)	Speed(†) (mph)
23.1	Sevenoaks	39 00	37 45	45
—		permanent way slacks twice		25
30.6	TONBRIDGE	47 00	47 25	30*
35.9	Paddock Wood	53 00	53 45	69
40.5	Marden		58 05	62½
43.0	Staplehurst	60 00	60 15	70½
46.3	Headcorn		63 10	61½
51.6	Pluckley		68 05	67
55.1	Chart Siding		71 30	62½
57.2	ASHFORD	73 00	73 25	66
—		permanent way slack		25
61.5	Smeeth		78 40	
65.2	Westenhanger		83 25	46
65.4	Sandling Junction	84 00	85 00	66
72.0	FOLKESTONE JUNCTION	89 30	90 30	55*
72.9	Warren Halt		91 30	64½
77.6	Dover Junction		96 25	15*
78.0	DOVER MARINE	98 00	98 10	

*Permanent speed restrictions
†Maximum and minimum speeds by stop watch

It was one of the marked characteristics of Southern footplate work that after the amalgamation of the three railways and the introduction of new standard types that no attempt seems to have been made to rationalize driving methods, in the same way that Dugald Drummond insisted on, and that the close liaison between Churchward and his running inspectors ensured the same situation on the Great Western. Of course it may well be pointed out that in both these instances the footplate men and the inspectors were under the direct control of the Chief Mechanical Engineer, whereas on the Southern, derived from the later SE&CR practice the Running Superintendent was an independent officer. It was fortunate that most of the Maunsell locomotives ran equally well however they were driven, though not necessarily with equal economy, as could be seen from the coal trials with the 'King Arthurs' described in Chapter 11. The details recorded by Cecil J. Allen on his footplate run with *Lord Nelson* provided a good typical example of the heaviest boat train working until the beginning of the Bulleid era. The trade depression of the early 1930s, and the general drift in Continental traffic away from the luxury daytime service precluded any spectacular acceleration such as were envisaged in the Operating Departments announcement of 1923.

When Maunsell was thoroughly satisfied with the prototype ten further engines of the 'Lord Nelson' Class were built at Eastleigh in 1928-29, and five more towards the end of 1929. The only alteration

made was a slight modification of the inside cylinders to give a better lead to the exhaust steam at the base of the blast pipe. These engines were named after famous British admirals of the past, and very high the class as a whole ranked in popular esteem. Their names were:

851	*Sir Francis Drake*
852	*Sir Walter Raleigh*
853	*Sir Richard Grenville*
854	*Howard of Effingham*
855	*Robert Blake*
856	*Lord St Vincent*
857	*Lord Howe*
858	*Lord Duncan*
859	*Lord Hood*
860	*Lord Hawke*
861	*Lord Anson*
862	*Lord Collingwood*
863	*Lord Rodney*
864	*Sir Martin Frobisher*
865	*Sir John Hawkins*

In all round service, the 'Lord Nelson' boiler was never quite so free in steaming as that of the 'King Arthurs', yet when the locomotives were competently handled their running could be exceptional. They were, however, the only Southern express engines in which the fire grate was partly level and partly sloping. While generation after generation of Great Western enginemen had learned to fire such a grate with conspicuous success, there were, on the Southern, ultimately only sixteen engines of the 'Lord Nelson' Class, and not all the enginemen concerned had the opportunity to become wholly familiar with them. Very similar troubles were experienced on the former London and North Western Railway when the 'Claughton' Class was introduced in 1913.

During Maunsell's time five engines of the class were subjected to various modifications:

(a) No 859, *Lord Hood,* was fitted with 6-ft 3-in coupled wheels instead of 6-ft 7-in to see if smaller driving wheels would be beneficial in the working of Continental boat trains on the heavily-graded Eastern Section.

(b) No 860, *Lord Hawke,* was fitted with boiler barrel longer than standard, providing additional heating surface of 131 sq ft. This was actually the original Waterloo design, with 10-in longer tube than that common to the standard 'Nelsons' and the 'King Arthurs'.

(c) No 857, *Lord Howe,* was fitted with round-topped firebox and combustion chamber. This alteration however had no bearing on the 'Nelson' design itself. In 1933 a 'Pacific' was under consideration, and No 857 was made the 'guinea pig' for trying out some new practices proposed for the 'Pacific' boiler, including a combustion chamber.

(d) No 865, *Sir John Hawkins,* had the crank setting altered from 135° to the conventional 90°. This alteration was typical of Maunsell's willingness to try out practical suggestions put to him to improvements in design. In this case the idea was that a four-cylinder engine with cranks at 90° might accelerate a train better than one

Top right *Engine No 860,* Lord Hawke, *at Waterloo preparing to leave with the Bournemouth Belle. (British Railways.)*

Middle right *Engine No 860,* Lord Hawke, *on a down West of England express near Winchfield. (The late M.W. Earley.)*

Right *Rearward shot of engine No 855,* Robert Blake, *on a down Continental boat express near Bromley. (H.C. Casserly.)*

Left *Engine No 862, Lord Colling-wood, fitted with 'Kylchap' blastpipe in 1934. (The late W.J. Reynolds.)*

Below *Engine No 859, Lord Hood, fitted with 6-ft 3-in coupled wheels instead of the standard 6 ft 7 in (The late W.J. Reynolds.)*

Above *Engine No 857, Lord Howe, fitted with enlarged round topped boiler and combustion chamber on Continental boat train near Bromley. (H.C. Casserley.)*

Left *Engine No 865, Sir John Hawkins, leaving Waterloo with the Bournemouth Belle. (C.R.L. Coles.)*

having the 135° setting. Negative results, as in the alterations to engines 859 and 860, served to confirm his faith in the original design.

(e) No 862, *Lord Collingwood*, was fitted with Kylchap blastpipe and double chimney. For some reason this change seems to have been markedly unsuccessful.

Yet another variation had been considered in 1931, of converting a 'Lord Nelson' into a four-cylinder compound, with 250 lb pressure and poppet type valves, but although authority was actually given to carry out this conversion it was not proceeded with.

None of the experimental modifications of 'Lord Nelson' Class engines showed any particular advantage over the standard design, in fact two of the poorest runs I ever experienced were with engine 859, on the up 'Golden Arrow', and with 865 on the down 'Bournemouth Belle'. Despite the 6-ft 3-in coupled wheels of No 859 the climbing from Tonbridge to Sevenoaks Tunnel with no more than 377 tons tare was such that 17¼ minutes were spent over this 7½ miles of ascent. Yet on the previous day the same engine had done excellently on the outward bound 'Golden Arrow', running at 72 mph steadily on level track with a trailing load of 445 tons. On the other hand none of the modified engines were altered back to their original condition. Despite the variation in their tractive performance on the road the 'Lord Nelsons' were extremely reliable from the running shed point of view, and in the discussion upon Mr C.S. Cocks's paper before the Institution of Locomotive Engineers in 1948 a high tribute was paid to them on their freedom from trouble and lightness in maintenance by Mr Pelham Maitland, who, as Nine Elms Shed Superintendent, had all of them in his immediate charge at some time or another.

For a time engines of the 'Lord Nelson' Class worked through from Waterloo to Exeter, with a change of crew at Salisbury, but on the Western end of the line they never seemed to come into their own. They ran extremely fast on the favourable stretches, but from records published from time to time in *The Railway Magazine* the uphill work was rarely, if ever, up to the best 'King Arthur' standards. The run tabulated herewith, with engine No 850, is about the best I have seen with a 'Nelson' between Salisbury and Exeter. At the 'high spots'—Gillingham, Sherborne, Axminster, Sidmouth Junction, and Broad Clyst it will be seen that speeds were 81, 83½, 80, 84 and 90 mph respectively; but the uphill speed of 30 mph at Hewish summit, and 21 mph at Honiton Tunnel did not suggest any real mastery of the load, though without a record of the engine working one cannot attach too much significance to the details of passing times and speeds.

Right *Inward bound Continental boat express in the Folkestone Warren with the 6 ft 3 in 'Lord Nelson' No 859,* Lord Hood. *(The late M.W. Earley.)*

Right *Engine No 864,* Sir Martin Frobisher, *on up Continental boat express near Bromley. (H.C. Casserley.)*

Salisbury-Exeter
Engine 4-6-0 No 850 *Lord Nelson*
Load 12 cars, 389 tons tare, 410 tons full

Distance (miles)		Schedule time (m s)	Actual time (m s)	Speed (mph)
0.0	SALISBURY	0 00	0 00	—
2.5	Wilton		6 25	—
—			slack	—
8.3	Dinton		15 55	—
12.5	Tisbury		21 25	55.0
17.5	Semley		27 35	43.5
21.6	Gillingham		31 00	81.0
28.4	Templecombe	33 00	37 10	—
30.8	Milborne Port		40 00	46.0 (minimum)
34.5	Sherborne		43 15	83.5
39.1	YEOVIL JUNCTION	44 00	46 45	73.0/77.0
41.3	Sutton Bingham		48 50	51.0 (minimum)
47.9	Crewkerne		55 20	72.0
49.7	Milepost 133¼		58 05	30.0
55.9	Chard Junction		64 00	78.0
61.0	Axminster		68 00	80.0
64.2	Seaton Junction		70 30	67.0
70.0	Milepost 153½		81 35	21.0 (minimum)
71.2	Honiton		83 10	60.0
75.8	Sidmouth Junction	85 00	86 55	84.0
79.5	Whimple		89 50	72.0 (minimum)
85.1	Pinhoe		93 45	90.0
86.9	Exmouth Junction	95 00	95 20	—
88.0	EXETER	98 00	97 45	—

Net time 94 minutes 30 seconds

A criticism of policy, rather than engineering design, has been made in that with only sixteen engines available there were insufficient to make up wholly 'Lord Nelson' links in the season of heaviest traffic, either on the boat trains, or on Western Division workings from Waterloo. During the winter months there were usually sufficient 'Lord Nelsons' at Stewart's Lane to work all the regular boat trains. The utilization was not high, normally consisting of a single return trip to Dover, or Folkestone Junction six days a week for each engine in the link. At one time it was intended there should be a total of 31, but the Directors cut the order for the third batch from twenty to five owing to heavy expenditure on electrification schemes. Con-

sequently with only sixteen engines instead of 31, loadings had to be arranged that, in the event of 'Nelsons' not being available, the trains were within the capacity of 'King Arthurs'. This meant that the larger engines were always working within their optimum capacity, except when the additional tractive effort was employed to make up lost time. Yet on the everyday 'form' displayed in the years 1932-37 on trains within 'King Arthur' capacity it seems very doubtful if the 'Lord Nelsons' could regularly have risen to the heights of performance put up in the trial run of 10 April 1927—in other words the 500 ton—55 mph standard.

14. Maunsell mixed-traffic and shunting classes

It would be easy for a lineside observer to assume that the Southern was almost wholly a passenger line. Heavy freight trains were conspicuous by their absence, at any rate during the daylight hours, and transfer goods trains between the London yards had to be kept well out of the way at times of the suburban rush hours. From the time he came to England from the Great Southern and Western Maunsell did not build a single purely freight locomotive, and in what was left of the pre-grouping years the same can be said of his colleagues on the Brighton and the South Western Railways. The first large mixed traffic engine for which he was saddled with responsibility had been the 'H15', built in 1924, but that had been a pre-grouping Eastleigh design and not a very brilliant one at that. When the time came for building more of the Urie 5-ft 7-in 4-6-0s of the 'S15' Class their front end was modified on the lines of the 'King Arthur' Class, and they proved excellent engines. Fifteen of the modified 'S15s' were built in 1927 and another ten added in 1936. They worked the heavy night express goods trains between Exeter and Nine Elms, and from Southampton and Nine Elms.

One summer night I had a footplate pass to ride the 7.38 pm up from Exeter on the 'S15' Class engine No

826. From the start the load was no more than light, only sixteen loaded four-wheelers and a bogie brake van; but after the non-stop to Templecombe our train was made up to one of ninety axles, amounting to a gross load of about 500 tons behind the tender. Over the sharply undulating line to Salisbury the engine did well, getting away smartly on the falling gradient from the start and attaining a speed of 48 mph before beginning the rise to Buckhorn Weston Tunnel. The regulator was then opened well on to the second valve, about three quarters over on the quadrant plate, and with 35 per cent cut-off this took our 500-ton load up to the tunnel without speed falling below 31 mph. Then down to Gillingham, reaching 52½ mph, before tackling the 4-mile rise to Semley on gradients mostly around 1 in 100. The cut-off remained unchanged, but half way up the regulator was opened still wider, and with the exhaust rousing the echoes we topped the summit at 24 mph. It was then plain sailing down to Salisbury, and with cut-off shortened to 20 per cent we rode smoothly down on easy steam, not exceeding 50 mph and keeping exactly our booked time from Templecombe, 28.4 miles in 47 minutes. I had hoped that we might have got another 'S15' for the non-stop run to Nine Elms, but instead we got a

'S15' Class 4-6-0 No 834, fitted with an ex-'Lord Nelson' Class high capacity eight-wheeled tender. (The late W. J. Reynolds.)

'S15' Class 4-6-0 No 824 after fitting with smoke deflector shields. (The late W. J. Reynolds.)

very much run-down 'King Arthur'. She did the job all right, but we had an extremely rough ride!

By the year 1928 the gradual development of fast passenger train service on many parts of the Southern Railway system led to a demand for further locomotives of an intermediate character. The duties were of the kind for which Pearson, in SE&CR days, had advocated the use of tank engines. One is inclined to think that he viewed the proposition from the 'shop' angle, rather than that of the running man, seeing advantages such as there being no tenders to fill up the works' sidings. However his frequent assertions that tank engines did not need turning were not borne out in practice. On the Southern, as everywhere else, if they had the time and opportunity enginemen would invariably turn their engines rather than run bunker first for an appreciable distance. There was also the factor of water capacity. While tank engines may have managed the lightly-loaded Portsmouth expresses of the Brighton in pre-grouping days, it was a different matter altogether with the heavy Isle of Wight boat trains over the steep gradients of the Portsmouth direct line. Not long after the construction of the prototype 'K' Class engine, No 790, a test was made in October 1917 with the 1.40 pm boat train non-stop from Charing Cross to Folkestone Junction, 70.9 miles. The load consisted of four Pullman cars, six non-corridor bogies and a six-wheeled van, 310 tons tare. The schedule time of 102 minutes was kept, in spite of a bad signal check at Hildenborough, but so far as water supply was concerned it was a close thing.

An inspector was riding on the footplate, and a very careful watch was kept throughout; but after leaving Charing Cross with full tanks they finished with only 150 gallons left. This showed a total consumption of 1,850 gallons, 26 to the mile. While this was quite good in the haulage of a train that probably weighed quite 340 tons gross, the average speed of this wartime service—barely 42 mph—was low compared with what would be required in normal express service. In later years the 'K' Class engines managed the Can-

non Street-Ashford non-stop run quite comfortably, though this distance of 55 miles allowed a consumption of about 35 gallons per mile—a very big difference from 26. Furthermore on the 1917 run with the 1.40 pm boat train steam heating was not in use.

After some consideration the new intermediate passenger engines of 1928 were built as a tender engine version of Class 'K'—a 2-6-0 with 6-ft coupled wheels, designated Class 'U'. The design is generally similar to the 'N' Class mixed traffic engines, though with 6-ft coupled wheels against 5 ft 6 in, and a large number of parts are interchangeable. The 'U' Class engines were permitted to run up a maximum speed of 70 mph and they were well suited to all classes of passenger working excepting only the heaviest and fastest duties, which were allocated to 4-6-0s. Thirty engines of this class were built new in 1928-1931, and carried the running numbers 1610-1639. After the Sevenoaks disaster of 1928, when one of the 'K' Class 2-6-4 tanks were derailed at full speed, these latter tank engines were eventually converted to Class 'U'. It is sometimes assumed that Class 'U' came into being as a result of Sevenoaks but this is not so, the decision to build no further 'K' tanks, and to have 6-ft 2-6-0s instead was taken some time previously, and the first engines of Class 'U' were actually in service before the accident to the 'K' Class tank engine occurred. The three-cylinder 2-6-4 tank No 890, Class 'K1' did however become the prototype of the three-cylinder 2-6-0 passenger engines. Like the other 2-6-4 tanks she was rebuilt in 1928, and at first she retained the conjugated valve gear. The 'U1' Class proper, twenty engines built at Eastleigh in 1931 and numbered 1891 to 1910, had three independent sets of Walschaert's valve gear. Reference to them is rather anticipating the general theme, but it is convenient to deal with the entire group of engine classes that were

Three-cylinder 2-6-0 Class 'U1' No 1902 on an excursion from the GWR line to the Kent Coast near Bromley. (H. C. Casserley.)

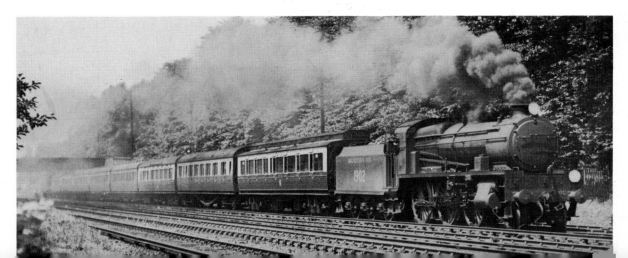

derived from the South Eastern and Chatham proto-type 2-6-0 and 2-6-4 tank. As the remainder of the group were of the three-cylinder type, some account is needed as to how the second phase of three-cylinder propulsion came into being on the Southern Railway.

This second phase was notable for the introduction of the 'Schools' Class express passenger 4-4-0s, in 1930, of which a good deal more will be said in the next chapter. In that class three cylinders were used so that a higher tractive effort might be obtained, without greater adhesion weight, through utilizing the more even turning effort on the driving axle resulting from six exhausts per revolution. So far as the 6-ft 2-6-0s were concerned it was hoped to get more rapid acceleration from rest, since in theory one could develop a higher tractive effort without risk of slipping. The 'U1' engines had cylinders of 16-in diameter by 28-in stroke, against 19-in diameter by 28-in stroke in Class 'U' and the nominal tractive effort, at 85 per cent, boiler pressure was 25,385 lb against 23,865. The long piston stroke in relation to cylinder diameter rendered the 'U1' engines very suitable to working with short cut-offs and while officially they were permitted to run up to a maximum of 70 mph, in actual fact they often ran a great deal faster. Among notes of a large number of runs in my records there are two cases of 80 mph and many examples of free running up to 75 mph or so.

Both in Maunsell's time and since, engines of Class 'U' and 'U1' undertook much of the less spectacular passenger working. They had the Waterloo-Portsmouth service before the introduction of the 'Schools' on that route and at one time the 5.5 pm from London Bridge to Eastbourne was a regular 'U1' job. The reduced width over the cylinders made it possible to use the 'U1' engines on the Hastings line but the numerous curves caused undue flange wear,

Bournemouth-Birkenhead express passing Reading West Junction hauled by three-cylinder 2-6-0 Class 'U1' No 1894. (The late M.W. Earley.)

and the same trouble was experienced west of Exeter, where some of these engines were used for a short time. They did much of their best and most reliable work on semi-fasts, particularly on the Chatham main line. The 'semi-fast' was a mere figure of speech in the case of these 2-6-0s, between stops their running was fully up to the Kent Coast express standards. In more recent times 'U' and 'U1' Class engines have undertaken the working of through trains from northern and western lines to the Kent Coast. One summer Saturday in 1950, for example, No 31907 took over the haulage of a Wolverhampton-Ramsgate train, nominally non-stop from Banbury to Ramsgate, via Maidstone, Ashford and Canterbury. Actually the Western Region handed over to No 31907 at Kensington (Addison Road) and the 'non-stop' was further interrupted at Maidstone where the engine was watered and remanned. As a further example of good work in the last steam days No 31894 had the 12.15 pm Birmingham express out of Brighton, and with a heavy train of 350 tons ran the 40.4 miles to East Croydon in 50½ minutes.

One of the fastest runs of which I have details was made in 1938 by 'U1' engine No 1907 on the 1.30 pm from Bromley South to Chatham, with a heavy load of 360 tons. The severe uphill start to St Mary Cray junction 2½ miles, including 1½ miles at 1 in 95-100 from the immediate start, was covered in 7¼ minutes. Then some really fast running followed, with an average of exactly 60 mph from St Mary Cray Junction to Sole Street, 13.5 miles. Although this stretch includes the fine racing descent to Farningham Road, where 76 mph was attained, there is more adverse than favourable going. The crest of the bank, near Sole Street, was cleared at the exceptional speed of 56 mph. A top speed of 76 mph was again reached descending to the Medway valley, and Cuxton Road signal box, 20 miles, was passed in 24¼ minutes from Bromley South. Despite a signal check at Rochester Bridge, Chatham, 23.4 miles, was reached in 30¼ minutes start to stop. With such a load as 360 tons this was an excellent piece of work, and shows that the

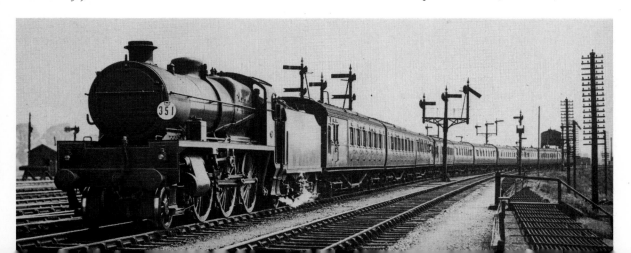

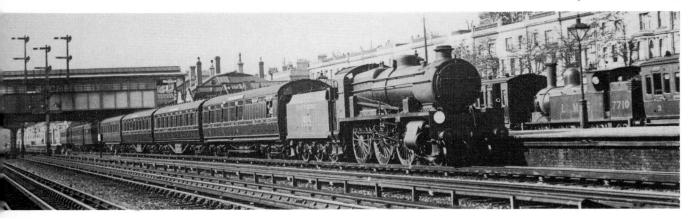

Above *The SE&CR portion of the 'Sunny South Express' at Addison Road, hauled by three-cylinder 2-6-0 Class 'U1' No 1905. (H.C. Casserley.)*

Left *Bournemouth-Birkenhead express between Southcote Junction and Reading West hauled by a 'U' Class 2-6-0. (The late M.W. Earley.)*

Below right *Three-cylinder 2-6-0 No 1890 near Bromley. It had been rebuilt from a 2-6-4 tank engine after removal of conjugated valve gear. (H.C. Casserley.)*

'U1' engines were capable of express passenger performance, beside their more regular duties on semifast trains.

On the Portsmouth direct line, when 98 minutes was the allowance for non-stop trains over the 73.6 miles from Portsmouth town to Waterloo, the 'U1' engines handled trains up to 350 tons successfully. Records available show that here they were restrained more nearly to their official maximum speed of 70 mph on falling grades, whereas in later years, when the timing was cut to 90 minutes, the 'Schools' Class ran frequently up to 85 mph on favourable stretches. At the same time while both the 'U' and 'U1' engines were classified as 'passenger' they are often used on freight trains.

Some typical examples of 'U1' running, principally on the Chatham line, are:

Route	Engine number	Gross load (tons)	Mileage	Actual time (m s)	Net time (m s)	Maximum speed (mph)
Chatham-Bromley	1908	305	23.4	32 55	33 00	72
Rochester-Bromley	1890	355	22.8	36 50	36 45	68
Chatham-Bromley	1897	265	23.4	35 30	35 30	70
Victoria-Chatham	1902	290	34.3	52 02	51 00	66
Ashford-Paddock Wood	1907	235	21.3	24 53	24 45	68
Sevenoaks-London Bridge	1907	235	20.2	27 35	26 45	65
Bromley-Faversham	1908	340	41.0	57 01	52 45	72

Right *Bulleid 'Q1' Class 0-6-0, No 33038, at Stewarts Lane Shed in October 1959, prior to working the empty stock of the 'Bournemouth Belle'. (R.C. Riley.)*

Right *An unrebuilt 'Merchant Navy' Class 4-6-2, No 35001, Channel Packet at Stewarts Lane Shed. Built in 1941, she was the first of her class and survived until 1964. (R.C. Riley.)*

Below *'Merchant Navy' No 35030 as rebuilt by British Rail. She is seen at Weymouth Shed in June 1967 with nameplates removed shortly before the electrification of the Waterloo-Bournemouth line and the end of steam on the Southern Region. (R.C. Riley.)*

A BR-rebuilt 'West Country', No 34013, Okehampton, *seen at Cannon Street in 1958 before the demolition of the ornate overall roof. (R.C. Riley.)*

Above *An unrebuilt 'West Country', No 34069* Hawkinge, *taking water at Yeovil Junction with a down freight. (R.C. Riley.)*

Left *No 35023* Holland Africa Line *at Exmouth Junction Shed on 5 July 1957. (R.C. Riley.)*

Over the switchback road of the North Kent line these are excellent runs for a relatively small-powered locomotive. Their 'express passenger' capabilities over a more favourable road are well illustrated by the run from Ashford to Paddock Wood. The detailed logs of three runs from Bromley South to Chatham, with loads of more than 300 tons are given in a separate table. Of these, the first, behind No 1897, was unchecked. Speed rose to 74 mph at Farningham Road, but after passing Sole Street on time, at 47 mph, the engine was run very easily down to Rochester, and speed at no time exceeded 50 mph. By contrast No 1901 lost 2 minutes by adverse signals in the early stages and did not exceed 70 mph at Farningham Road then after passing Sole Street at 46 mph the engine was let fly and speed touched a full 80 mph before Cuxton Road. The third run was the best of the three—No 1907 lost about a minute by adverse signals before Bickley Junction, but then she ran splendidly. 76 mph was attained through Farningham Road, Sole Street was cleared at 56 mph and 76 mph reached again on the descent to Rochester.

A further example of high speed running by a 'U1' is given in the tabulated details of the 8.20 pm up from Faversham, in 1939, between Rochester and Bromley South. In consideration of the load the ascent to Sole Street was quite undistinguished, but then the engine raced away to reach 80 mph at Farningham Road. This characteristic of moderate uphill work and very fast running on favourable stretches is common to many engines with modern long-travel valves and Walscheart's gear, the 4-4-0s with Stephenson's gear tend to show up better on the banks.

Bromley South-Chatham

Run number			1	2	3
Engine number			1897	1901	1907
Load (tons tare/full)			304/325	320/345	340/360
Distance (miles)		Schedule time (m s)	Actual time (m s)	Actual time (m s)	Actual time (m s)
0.0	BROMLEY SOUTH	0 00	0 00	0 00	0 00
—			—	—	signal check
1.7	Bickley Junction	5 00	5 03	5 25	6 00
3.9	St Mary Cray		7 42	8 12	8 55
6.8	Swanley Junction	11 00	10 48	11 28	12 00
—			—	signal check	—
9.6	Farningham Road		13 28	15 55	14 35
12.5	Fawkham		16 05	19 20	17 00
15.0	Meopham		19 08	23 05	19 40
16.0	Sole Street	21 00	20 23	24 25	20 43
20.0	Cuxton Road Box		24 58	28 10	24 15
22.0	Rochester Bridge	29 30	27 40	30 55	27 07
22.8	Rochester		28 50	32 12	28 30
—			—	—	signal check
23.4	CHATHAM	32 00	30 23	33 20	30 20
Net time (m s)			30 30	31 30	28 45

Rochester-Bromley South

Engine Class 'U1' 2-6-0 No 1909
Load 225 tons tare, 245 tons full

Distance (miles)		Schedule time (m s)	Actual time (m s)	Speed (mph)
0.0	ROCHESTER	0 00	0 00	
0.8	Rochester Bridge		2 20	—
2.8	Cuxton Road Box		6 45	—
6.8	Sole Street	14 00	14 42	31
7.8	Meopham		16 10	60
10.3	Fawkham		18 45	—
13.2	Farningham Road		21 07	80
—		permanent way slack		—
16.0	Swanley Junction	24 00	24 45	—
18.9	St Mary Cray		28 40	—
21.1	Bickley Junction	31 00	31 35	—
—			signal check	
22.8	BROMLEY SOUTH	34 00	34 45	

After World War 2, during a period of the summer service, engines of this class were at one time drafted from the Eastern Section of Southern Region to Nine Elms shed for working the Saturdays-only service from Waterloo to Lymington. On this duty the main-line engine was turned at Brockenhurst as the turn-table there cannot accommodate any longer engine and tender than the 'U1'. When I was privileged to observe from the footplate the working of this particular service, the engine was, by a coincidence, the same one that featured in several fine pre-war journeys mentioned earlier in this chapter, No 1907, afterwards renumbered 31907. The trains concerned were the 9.42 am down from Waterloo and the 1.46 pm up from Brockenhurst. The scheduled times and the actual performances may be summarized as follows:

	Down	Up
Distance (miles)	92.9	92.9
Total booked time (m s)	140 00	138 00
Booked running time (m s)	126 00	127 00
Number of booked stops	5	3
Average booked speed (mph)	44.5	44.2
Total actual time (m s)	151 30	154 30
Total running time (m s)	138 30	146 00
Net running time (m s)	127 00	126 30
Average actual speed (mph)	44.2	44.3
Number of signal checks	4	3
Number of signal stops	2	2
Load of train tons tare	324	324
Load of train tons gross	370	365

The performance can therefore be considered as a satisfactory one, on an overall basis, but circumstances combined to make it a great deal better than would otherwise appear. First of all, the engine had last been shopped for general repairs in June 1950, 26 months before the date of my trip and since this general overhaul she had covered a little over 75,000 miles. In spite of this, however, her general condition was good, she rode easily and well up to the maximum attained speeds of 70 mph and 72 mph and the only indication of mounting mileage was a certain amount of play between the axle-boxes and guides apparent when running with steam shut off.

The major factor that governed the finer points of performance was that neither the driver nor the fireman had previously ever worked on an engine of this class. The 'U1' is, however, a very simple and straightforward one to manage, and the driver quickly adopted full regulator working with the gear well linked up, running mostly at 20 per cent cut-off. The fireman, like many a keen youngster with whom I have ridden, tended to overfire at times and to have a core of partly burnt coal just under the door. With so heavy a train a fairly thick fire was necessary, and when it was well burned through the engine steamed very freely. All in all the crew did very well, and that they were able to do so, as strangers, on an exacting duty, stands much to the credit of the design. The train itself, it should be added, was loaded almost to capacity—with corridors and guards vans accommodating many passengers there must have been at least 800 on board during the outward trip, hence the heavy increase of gross load behind the tender, over tare load.

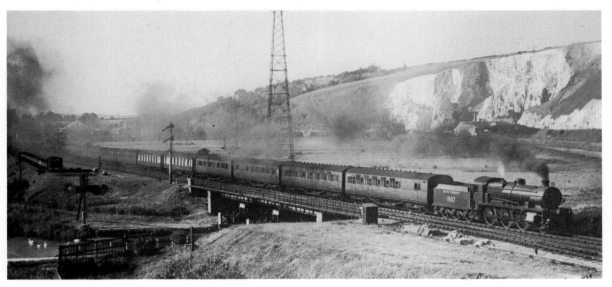

Victoria-Eastbourne Pullman car express near Lewes, hauled by three-cylinder 2-6-0 Class 'U1' No 1907. (O.J. Morris.)

While quite a number of logs have been compiled with trains hauled by engines of Class 'U1' the two-cylinder variety, Class 'U' do not seem to have come within the ken of 'stop-watchers' to anything like the same extent. A run of No 1635 is probably not a very good example of their work, though it is interesting in another way as being routed via the Catford loop line. As far as Shortlands, where the Chatham main line is rejoined, No 1635 had done adequately with this substantial train, though the loop is graded somewhat more easily than the main line by avoiding the heavy accent from Brixton to Sydenham Hill tunnel. But after Shortlands the work was disappointing. At Mary Cray, where the 'U1' No 1907 was doing 68 mph, No 1635 was doing no more than 54 mph. Speed fell to 34 mph at Swanley, where No 1907 was doing 58, and the top speed through Farningham Road was only 62 mph. Then there was a distinct improvement, as Sole Street was cleared at 44 mph, but this really came too late and the train was nearly 3 minutes late into Chatham.

By contrast another engine of the class in her 2-6-4 tank days made a smart run on the 3.15 pm express from Victoria to Eastbourne. The load, it is true, was no more than 250 tons, and again No 799 *River Test*, went easily uphill. But this time there was some fast work on the favourable stretches, with speeds of 75 mph at both Horley and Haywards Heath, and Lewes (50.2 miles) was reached practically on time in 65½

minutes from Victoria, despite three slight signal checks. The net time was 62 minutes. This run was timed by Mr Cecil J. Allen.

The last variety of what may be termed the Southern 'Mogul' family was the Class 'W' 2-6-4 goods tank engine of 1931. This was a reversion to the style of the 'K' tanks, but with 5-ft 6-in coupled wheels. To provide a high and even starting torque the engines were fitted with three cylinders, with details and motion interchangeable with Class 'U1'. The nominal tractive effort at 85 per cent boiler pressure is the high one of 29,452 lb and renders the class very suitable for short hauls with heavy trains, as with inter-region freights between Old Oak Common and Hither Green yards. As in the 'U1' Class all three cylinders drove on to the middle pair of coupled wheels. Such cross-London routes involve sharp gradients leading to fly-over junctions, which may well have to be climbed immediately after a signal stop. Good braking was likewise needed for the descents, and not only had the coupled wheels a high percentage brake force, but the bogie was braked—an unusual feature nowadays. The Class 'W' engines have been most successful in dealing with this particular traffic. To summarize the 'Mogul' group; the same design of boiler, with 200 psi working pressure, was used on Classes N, N1, U, U1 and W; the cylinders and motion of the three-cylinder 'N1' engines, of which five were built in 1930, was the same as 'U1' and 'W'. The prototype three-cylinder engines, 822 (Class N1) and 890 (Class K1) originally had conjugated valve gear which was later removed, though the 'K1' engine, after conversion to the 2-6-0 type and transference to Class 'U1' ran for some time with

Three-cylinder 2-6-4 Class 'W' short-distance heavy tank engine No 1914. (The late W.J. Reynolds.)

Three-cylinder 0-8-0 Class 'Z' shunting tank engine No 951. (The late W.J. Reynolds.)

the original valve gear. Ultimately the 'Mogul' family on the Southern consisted of 172 engines—eighty of Class N, six of 'N1', fifty of Class 'U', 21 of Class 'U1' and fifteen of Class 'W'.

There is a further interesting three-cylinder design to be mentioned at this stage, the 'Z' Class 0-8-0 shunting tank. The need was felt for a small number of powerful engines for work in hump and other marshalling yards, and to have sufficient side-play at the leading and trailing wheels to permit of a 4½ chain curve being negotiated. A good design was worked out making extensive use of standard parts. Thus the cylinders were interchangeable with Classes 'N1' and 'U1' and the boiler was a Brighton standard. The grate area was small, only 18.6 sq ft, but the aim of the design was to provide a boiler of large steam and water capacity, to store heat for periods of waiting, and to minimize blowing off. With 4-ft 8-in coupled

wheels, three cylinders, and the high nominal tractive effort of 29,380 lb at 85 per cent boiler pressure, these engines did their work with quiet efficiency.

Their quietness, indeed, was much appreciated by those who lived near heavily-worked marshalling yards, the 'Z' Class engines were practically immune from slipping and the softness of their exhaust was noticeable. Some of these engines were in service at the important marshalling yard beside the main line at Eastleigh. There trains had to be shunted against a rising gradient of 1 in 250, but the 'Z' Class engines experienced no difficulty in propelling the heaviest loads the operating department liked to run. At this yard these engines were continuously in steam for a week at a time, and despite this high utilization they were remarkably free from running troubles. The 'Z' Class engines were built at Brighton works in 1929 and were numbered 950 to 959.

15. The 'Schools' Class

The origin of this famous and universally cherished class of locomotive lay in a request by the traffic department for an express passenger engine of a power class intermediate to the 'Lord Nelsons', but also having a route availability where the 'King Arthurs' could not go, for example the Hastings line. After some preliminary investigation the CME's department hit on the idea of making the proposed engine a 'three-quarter Nelson', using three cylinders instead of four and four coupled wheels instead of six. Cylinders, wheels, motion (other than length of rods) were to be the same on both 4-6-0 and 4-4-0, and the tractive effort a simple multiple of that of the 'Lord Nelson', three quarters of 33,500 lb—25,130 lb. Yet while the brilliance of the 4-6-0s in their original form came in 'fits and starts', as will be evident from a perusal of Chapter 13 of this book, their three-quarter size derivatives achieved a lustre that was sustained and ever-enhanced whatever duties they were put on to. It is perhaps an exaggeration that the outstanding position they attained in the locomotive world arose almost by accident, yet one can be fairly sure that when the detail design was on the drawing-boards those responsible hardly foresaw the eminence—nay, the pre-eminence—it would attain.

Drawing of a 'Schools' Class locomotive.

The 'Schools' Class, as introduced in 1930, was not quite as Clayton first conceived it. At first it was proposed to carry the interchangeability of parts between the 'Lord Nelsons' and the 'Schools' still further by use of a Belpaire firebox and the same flanged plates for the boiler. Fortunately the weight came out too heavy so instead they used a shortened version of the 'King Arthur' boiler, while using the same firebox, and the grate area of the later 'King Arthurs' and the 'S15' Class built from 1927 onwards. The use of this latter boiler on the 'Schools' was fortuitous beyond measure, because it was a grand steamer with all grades of coal. That of the 'Nelson' could be very touchy at times! An incidental advantage from the use of a round-topped boiler, like that of the 'King Arthur', was that the cab sides could be raked inwards to clear the restricted loading gauge of some of the tunnels of the Hastings line.

The basic dimensions of the design were therefore: three cylinders 16½-in diameter by 26-in stroke; four coupled wheels of 6-ft 7-in diameter; total heating surface 2,049 sq ft (against 2,215 sq ft) in the 'King Arthur') and grate area 28.3 sq ft. This latter was the same as on the later 'King Arthurs', and on the 'S15' mixed traffic 4-6-0s on which the water space round the firebox was increased as compared with that of the earlier 'King Arthurs', which had grates of 30 sq ft. On the 'Schools' however, the boiler pressure was

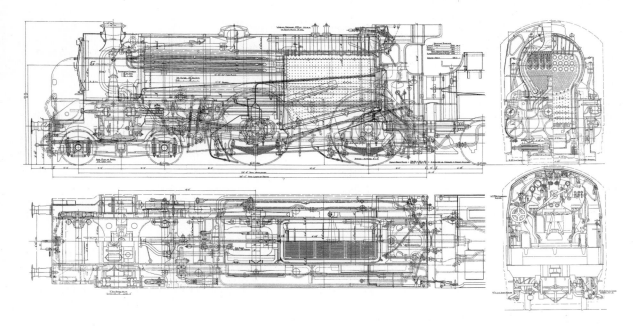

increased from the 200 psi of the 'King Arthurs' to 220 psi, and this gave a nominal tractive effort practically equal in the two classes. The adhesion weight of the 'Schools' was however no more than 42 tons, against 60 tons in the 4-6-0s, and the ratio of 598 lb of tractive effort per ton of adhesion weight on the 'Schools', against 422 lb per ton, made it necessary to use careful methods in starting the 'Schools' from rest. The actual nominal tractive efforts were 25,320 lb for the 'King Arthurs', and 25,120 for the 'Schools', both at 85 per cent working pressure. The 'Schools', named after well-known public schools of the south, were immediately accepted by the public as a handsome and powerful addition to the Southern locomotive stud, though at first few foresaw the potentialities that were eventually to be realized in these engines.

On the basis of nominal tractive effort the 'Schools' were the most powerful 4-4-0s ever built in Great Britain. As previously mentioned the total heating surface is 2,049 sq ft, this is made up as follows:

Large tubes	399
Small tubes	1,205
Firebox	162
Total evaporative	1,766
Superheater	283
Combined total	2,049

The small tubes were of 1¾-in outside diameter, with a length of 12 ft 3⅜ in between the tubeplates. This compares with 2-in diameter small tubes on the 'King Arthur' and a distance of 14 ft 2 in between tubeplates. Both boilers steamed very freely, even though very often fired with inferior fuel. The piston valves, as in the 'Lord Nelson', were 8-in diameter with a steam lap of 1½ in and a travel of 6½ in in full gear. As originally designed the lead was ¼ in. The 'Schools' ranked among the many modern engines with well-designed valve gear on which it seemed to make little difference in actual running whether they were driven with the gear linked up inside 20 per cent cut-off and the regulator opened wide, or whether they were driven with the first valve of the regulator only and cut-off 30 per cent or perhaps even more. With a relatively small tender carrying no more than five tons of coal and 4,000 gallons of water it might have been thought that their range of operation would have been limited on a line having no water troughs, in fact Mr C.S. Cocks in his paper 'A History of Southern Railway Locomotives in 1938' read before the Institution of Locomotive Engineers in 1948, definitely stated that this was so, and added: 'Had large tenders or water scoops been available there is not the slightest doubt that these locomotives would undertake work of a more exacting nature'. In view of what they actually did achieve on the Bournemouth route prior to the outbreak of war in 1939, one would be intrigued to discover what duties Mr Cocks had in mind.

The first engine of the class was completed in Eastleigh in mid-March 1930, and duly named *Eton* it was brought up to Waterloo for public exhibition on the 26th of that month. Not many days afterwards it was taken to Windsor for inspection by boys of the college. At first only ten engines of the class were built. They were named as follows:

E900	*Eton*	E905	*Tonbridge*
E901	*Winchester*	E906	*Sherborne*
E902	*Wellington*	E907	*Dulwich*
E903	*Charterhouse*	E908	*Westminster*
E904	*Lancing*	E909	*St Pauls*

For their initial trials the first engines of the class were temporarily stationed at Nine Elms where they could be under the eye of Eastleigh Works. They made a few runs from Waterloo to Salisbury and Bournemouth, and as no adjustments seemed to be needed they were handed over to the Eastern Section to take up regular duties. Although intended primarily for the Hastings line the civil engineering improvements then in progress were not completed, and it was not until the late summer of 1931 that engines of the class were

'Schools' Class No 902, Wellington, *as built without deflector shields, at Charing Cross. (The late W.J. Reynolds.)*

'Schools' Class No 909, St Pauls, *on Folkestone and Deal train at Charing Cross. (The late W.J. Reynolds.)*

stationed at St Leonards. Their first regular allocation was to Deal and Dover. At that time the former South Eastern passenger service to Folkestone and Dover, as distinct from the Continental trains, terminated at Deal and a number of express locomotives were stationed there. It was not until the train service was reorganized and extended to Ramsgate that the 'Schools' Class were transferred there from Deal. While in their preliminary running days, engine No 909, *St Pauls*, was fitted up for indicator testing with the usual shelter round the front end. Early in 1931 a full-dress trial was made between London Bridge and Eastbourne, with a gross trailing load of 345 tons.

In his book *Locomotive Adventure* Holcroft writes that although he was not on the train personally the results were passed to him for comment and analysis. No running times were included in the report, though the details of indicated horsepower and the coal con-

sumption suggest a very satisfactory performance. The coal was Kentish, from Chislet Colliery, and had a relatively high calorific value. Having regard to the power outputs revealed by the indicator card records shown in the following table, the overall consumption of 51 lb per train mile seems excellent. Judging from the speeds quoted in relation to the indicator card records it can be inferred that cards two, three and four were taken passing New Cross Gate, climbing Forest Hill bank and near Norwood Junction, that five was taken after a stop at East Croydon and six and seven were on the climb to Quarry Tunnel. After the fast running south of Earlswood card eleven would appear to have been made while speed was recovering from the regulation speed restriction at Keymer Junction, while thirteen was after the station stop at Lewes. Cards one and fifteen were found unsatisfactory and were rejected.

Indicator test run: London Bridge-Eastbourne

Engine No 909 *St Pauls*
Load 345 tons

Card	Regulator opening	Cut-off (per cent)	Speed (mph)	Boiler pressure (psi)	Indicated horsepower
1	—	—	—	—	—
2	Full	25	45.0	205	1,118
3	Full	31	31.5	210	1,016
4	Full	25	48.0	200	1,117
5	Full	Full gear	9.5	210	561
6	Full	28	39.5	215	1,133
7	Full	25	46.5	215	1,176
8	Full	Mid gear	53.5	210	475
9	¼	20	69.0	210	1,038
10	¼	20	76.0	180	1,009
11	Full	25	37.0	205	1,048
12	¾	20	62.5	200	1,098
13	Full	Full gear	10.0	215	585
14	⅓	20	63.5	195	1,061
15	—	—	—	—	—
16	Full	25	50.5	190	1,123

Top *'Schools' Class No 911* Dover *on Hastings train entering Crowhurst. (O.S. Nock.)*

Above *Waterloo-Portsmouth express approaching Haslemere, hauled by 'Schools' Class 4-4-0 No 930,* Radley. *(O.S. Nock.)*

Left *'Schools' Class No 931* Kings Wimbledon *on a Portsmouth express at Waterloo. (O.S. Nock.)*

Examination of these results led to the conclusion that in development of indicated horsepower the 'Schools' were equal to the 'King Arthurs' in justification of their nominal tractive effort. But there was more to it than that. As will be told later, when I come to describe some runs on the Bournemouth line, in actual power to pull a train the 'Schools' could surpass the 'King Arthurs'. That could be simply explained by the fact of the total weight of the 4-4-0 being nearly 30 tons less than its rival, and that difference meant adding another coach on the train. While in certain conditions of running the great adhesion weight of the 4-6-0 was an advantage, it is one that was gained at the expense of more internal friction. Nevertheless the 'Schools' undoubtedly required a great deal more finesse in handling than a 'King Arthur', particularly when starting away with a heavy load, or in difficult rail conditions. The lead of ¼ in on the valves occasionally caused difficulty through the engine stopping 'blind' and being unable to move in forward gear when the regulator was reopened. At London Bridge in particular this gave trouble with westbound trains, as owing to the proximity of points of rear setting back was not permitted. In his book Holcroft goes at great length into the experiments that were tried to get over this difficulty, and it was eventually solved by reducing the lead on the valves to ⅛ in.

By midsummer 1931 the civil engineering work on the Hastings line was finished and the four 'Schools' that had hitherto been stationed at Eastbourne, No 904 and No 907-No 909, were transferred to St Leonards. In the meantime the other six engines of the class which originally had been at Deal had been transferred to Ramsgate. In the late autumn I had occasion to make some journeys to Tunbridge Wells, and it was then that I experienced my first runs behind the new engines. These trips gave some interesting comparisons with the work of the existing power on the line. Hitherto all the express trains had been worked by the ex-SE&CR Class 'L' 4-4-0s, and my impression was they were doing the job very well, with loads up to 350 tons on that difficult road. With only four engines of the 'Schools' Class at first allocated to St Leonards the 'L' Class continued to do an important share of the work and, truth to tell, in the journeys I made over the line in 1931 I found little difference in the work, whichever class of engine was hauling the train. Of course the Hastings route of the former SE&CR was hardly a speedway; indeed when I next made some journeys over the line, six years later, when by many additions to the class the 'Schools' were in full possession, I found the running times and the loadings virtually the same as when the 'L' Class had the road to themselves. On the main line to Folkestone and Dover, of course, it was very different, as will be shown later.

Construction of further 'Schools' Class engines

began at the end of 1932, and the stud was made up to its final total of forty by March 1935. At first the names selected for them continued to be famous foundations in Southern Railway territory; but after the running numbers had reached 918 it seemed that those responsible for this particular nomenclature began to look further afield, or perhaps their own scholastic associations lay farther north. Nevertheless after excursions as far north as *Repton* and *Shrewsbury,* the last ten returned south, though it was a slightly sore point with me personally that the two Southern schools with which I have strong family connections, Reading and Monkton Combe, were not included! The full list, from No 910 onwards, was:

910	*Merchant Taylors*	925	*Cheltenham*
911	*Dover*	926	*Repton*
912	*Downside*	927	*Clifton*
913	*Christs Hospital*	928	*Stowe*
914	*Eastbourne*	929	*Malvern*
915	*Brighton*	930	*Radley*
916	*Whitgift*	931	*Kings Wimbledon*
917	*Ardingly*	932	*Blundells*
918	*Hurstpierpoint*	933	*Kings Canterbury*
919	*Harrow*	934	*St Lawrence*
920	*Rugby*	935	*Sevenoaks*
921	*Shrewsbury*	936	*Cranleigh*
922	*Marlborough*	937	*Epsom*
923	*Bradfield*	938	*St Olaves*
924	*Haileybury*	939	*Leatherhead*

I was able to witness, at first hand, a good deal of the day-to-day work of the 'Schools' on the Folkestone trains in 1934-36 and summary details of all my runs up to the end of 1936 are included in the two accompanying tables. On the down journeys, mostly made on the 12.55 pm Saturday train, there was no time to be booked against any engine, despite gross loads up to a maximum of 420 tons. In the up direction however, engine No 915 *Brighton* lost time on two occasions, once by as much as 3½ minutes. On two occasions I was privileged to ride on the footplate, and duly saw some contrasting styles in enginemanship. On No 921 *Shrewsbury*, Driver Hoskins of Ramsgate, with the 5.10 pm up from Folkestone, ran almost entirely on the first port of the regulator and used cut-offs varying between 25 and 31 per cent. He made the splendid run tabulated in the first column of my summary table. Engine 921 had the best of reputations, and many years later when I was discussing some details of this run with Mr T.E. Chrimes, the Motive Power Superintendent of later days he referred to her as 'the fastest thing on wheels'! In complete contrast to Driver Hoskin's methods, which were the most generally favoured

Top *Up Kent Coast express leaving Folkestone Central for Charing Cross hauled by 'Schools' Class 4-4-0 No 916,* Whitgift. *(O.S. Nock.)*

Above *'Schools' Class No 912* Downside *at Dover Priory on an express for Ramsgate. (O.S. Nock.)*

among the Ramsgate drivers of those days, Driver Keel, on the 12.55 pm down, worked No 916 *Whitgift* on short cut-off and used absolutely full regulator for the harder stretches, as from New Cross right up to Knockholt. This was another excellent engine and she responded to the driver's artistic use of the lever and regulator with a fast and economically-made run. His running cut-offs varied between 17 and 29 per cent and on the fast stretch east of Tonbridge he varied the regulator opening between the first port, full open and about two-fifths of the main valve.

Southern Railway: Charing Cross-Folkestone

Engine number Engine name	916 Whitgift	920 Rugby	912 Downside	919 Harrow	921 Shrewsbury	921 Shrewsbury	921 Shrewsbury	912 Downside	915 Brighton
Load Coaches	9	9	9	9	11	11	12	12	10
Tons (tare/full)	282/300	289/305	288/305	288/305	354/385	354/385	386/410	387/420	321/345
Schedule time (m s)									
Distance (miles)									
0.0 CHARING CROSS 0 00	0 00	0 00	0 00	0 00	0 00	0 00	0 00	0 00	0 00
0.7 Waterloo Junction —	—	—	—	—	—	—	—	—	2 43 / 3 30
4.9 New Cross 9 00	signal check 10 09	signal check 9 49	signal check 10 15	signal check 10 35	signal check 11 12	signal check 10 53 / signal check	signal check 11 52	signal check 11 40	10 44
16.6 Knockholt —	25 48	27 31 permanent way slack	26 40 permanent way slack	25 22	26 33 permanent way slack	27 09	28 10 permanent way slack	27 00	26 23
29.5 TONBRIDGE 38 30	38 02	41 04	46 03	38 32	41 20	39 52	45 53	39 55	39 11
34.8 Paddock Wood 44 30	43 15	47 09	51 42	44 00	48 30	45 40	51 57	46 02	44 35
56.1 ASHFORD 65 00	62 33	66 56	71 13	63 10	68 53	65 22	72 18	66 07	63 44

(Down trains — continued)

Distance (miles)	Location / Average	Schedule	Run 1 (p.w. slack)	Run 2	Run 3	Run 4	Run 5	Run 6 (p.w. slack)	Run 7	Run 8	Run 9 (p.w. slack)
65.4	Sandling Junction	75 00	75 10	76 33	80 25	72 02	78 26	77 21	81 52	75 57	75 09
69.9	FOLKESTONE	80 00	80 08	81 35	84 58	76 55	83 12	82 19	86 55	81 00	80 00
Averages											
11.7	New Cross–Knockholt	—	44.8	39.6 (checked)	42.7	47.4	45.6	43.1 (slightly checked)	42.9	45.6	44.8
21.3	Paddock Wood–Ashford	62.2 mph	66.2	64.7	65.3	66.7	62.8	64.8	62.9	63.4	66.8
35.9	Tonbridge–Sandling	59.0 mph	64.1 (net)	60.8	62.8	64.3	58.1	60.7 (net)	59.8	59.7	63.4 (net)
	Net time		75 30	78 00	77 30	75 30	78 30	77 30	79 00	78 15	76 95

Southern Railway: Folkestone–Charing Cross

Engine number / Engine name	Schedule time (m s)	921 Shrewsbury	910 Merchant Taylors	910 Merchant Taylors	919 Harrow	915 Brighton	915 Brighton	912 Downside	912 Downside	917 Ardingly
Load										
Coaches		9	9	9	9	9	10	10	11	11
Tons (tare/full)		282/300	288/305	288/305	287/305	287/305	324/345	323/345	354/390	356/390
Distance (miles)										
0.0 FOLKESTONE	0 00	0 00	0 00	0 00	0 00	0 00	0 00	0 00	0 00	0 00
			permanent way slack					permanent way slack			
13.8 ASHFORD	16 30	16 40	17 52	17 14	16 24	17 26	18 46	16 11	16 42	17 00
35.1 Paddock Wood	34 30	34 20	35 26	35 02	34 30	36 04	36 45	34 08	34 45	34 30
40.4 TONBRIDGE	39 30	39 07	40 45	40 10	39 31	41 20	41 41	39 16	39 47	39 09
			permanent way slack							
47.8 Sevenoaks	51 30	49 50	54 01	51 15	51 45	54 16	54 10	50 11	50 45	50 29
53.3 Knockholt		56 00	60 26	57 17	58 30	61 10	60 48	56 35	56 56	56 51
62.7 Hither Green	66 00	65 12	68 23	66 12	67 08	69 23	69 15	65 30	65 39	65 06
		permanent way slack	permanent way slack				signal check	signal check		
69.2 Waterloo Junction	76 00	76 20	78 55	75 55	76 35	79 28	80 26	76 35	75 30	74 49
69.9 CHARING CROSS	80 00	80 02	82 55	80 00	80 45	83 40	84 23	80 45	80 15	79 27
Averages										
21.3 Ashford–Paddock Wood	71.0	72.4	72.8	71.8	70.7	68.6	71.0	71.3	70.8	73.2
12.9 Tonbridge–Knockholt		45.8	39.3	45.2	40.8	39.0	40.5	44.7	45.1	43.8
Net time to Waterloo		74 00	75 30	76 00	76 30	79 30	77 00	75 30	75 30	74 45

Although a great deal of fine running was made on the Eastern Section lines the finest work done by the class was undoubtedly accomplished by the ten locomotives allocated first to Fratton Shed and afterwards transferred to Bournemouth Central after the electrification of the Portsmouth line. These engines were No 924-No 933. This route is extremely hilly, including severe ascents on 1 in 80 through both the North Downs and the South Downs. There were many regular service slacks, such as those at Woking Junction, Guildford and Havant, and yet the 73.6 miles

between Waterloo and Portsmouth were booked to be covered non-stop in 90 minutes. On this service the maximum tonnage handled by the 'Schools' was 350 tare, representing eleven heavy corridor coaches. Despite the difficulties of the route, engines of the 'Schools' Class kept excellent time, and usually had several minutes in hand. On two footplate journeys I made in 1936, engine No 924 with ten coaches, made a net time of 83 minutes, while No 925, with the maximum permitted load, achieved some still faster times, even though the train was so crowded with passengers as to represent a gross load of 395 tons behind the tender.

These two brilliant runs have been described previously but it is worthwhile recalling once more some of their salient points, and the logs are tabulated herewith:

Waterloo-Portsmouth

Train 11.50 am
Engine 4-4-0 No 924 Haileybury
Load 10 cars, 326 tons tare, 350 tons full

Distance (miles)		Schedule time (m s)	Actual time (m s)	Speed (mph)
0.0	WATERLOO	0 00	0 00	—
3.9	CLAPHAM JUNCTION	7 00	7 00	—
7.3	Wimbledon		11 15	57.0
—			permanent way slack	25.0
9.8	Malden		14 25	—
13.0	Hampton Court Junction	17 30	19 11	59.0
17.1	Walton		22 55	64.5
19.1	Weybridge		24 54	60.0/67.0
21.7	Byfleet		27 20	64.5
24.4	Woking	28 30	30 00	30.0*
26.8	Worplesdon		33 15	61.0
—			signal check	—
30.3	GUILDFORD	36 00	37 57	—
34.5	Godalming		43 14	59.0
36.3	Milford		45 08	56.0/58.0
38.5	Witley		47 52	43.0/58.0
43.0	Haslemere	54 30	54 55	26.0
46.9	Liphook		58 40	74.0
—			permanent way slack	15.0
51.5	Liss		64 40	60.0/68.0
54.9	Petersfield	67 00	67 55	59.0/63.5
58.0	Post 58		71 14	50.0
61.2	Idsworth Crossing		75 25	68.5
63.3	Rowlands Castle	77 30	77 25	45.0*
—			signal check	60.0/45.0
66.4	Havant	81 00	81 11	30.0*
			signal check	
69.5	Farlington Junction		84 53	
—			prolonged signal stop	
72.8	Fratton	88 00	109 05	
			signal check	
73.6	PORTSMOUTH	90 00	114 00	

Net time 83 minutes 30 seconds
*speed restriction

Portsmouth-Waterloo

Train 10.16 am Sundays
Engine 4-4-0 No 925 *Cheltenham*
Load 11 cars, 360 tons tare, 395 tons full

Distance (miles)		Schedule time (m s)	Actual time (m s)	Speed (mph)
0.0	PORTSMOUTH	0 00	0 00	
0.8	Fratton	2 00	1 56	
—			permanent way slack and signal check	
4.1	Farlington Junction		8 15	
—			signal check	
7.2	Havant	9 30	14 08	
10.3	Rowlands Castle		19 28	41.0
12.4	Idsworth Crossing		22 18	45.0
13.6	Milepost 60		23 58	40.0
15.6	Milepost 58		28 00	24.75
18.7	Petersfield	27 30	31 21	75.0
—	Stodham Crossing		—	83.5
22.1	Liss		33 59	74.0
24.6	Milepost 49		36 20	52.5/60.0
26.7	Liphook		38 32	56.0/64.5
30.6	Haslemere	41 00	42 33	48.5
—			—	74.0
35.1	Witley		46 56	permanent way slack 30.0
37.3	Milford		49 43	65.0
39.1	Godalming		51 26	eased
—			permanent way slack	15.0
43.3	GUILDFORD	55 00	57 10	30.0*
46.8	Worplesdon		62 22	66.0
49.2	Woking	63 00	65 06	30.0*
51.9	Byfleet		68 00	68.5/71.5
54.5	Weybridge		70 14	68.5
56.5	Walton		71 58	75.0
59.2	Esher		74 06	77.5
60.3	Hampton Court Junction	73 30	74 59	73.0
61.6	Surbiton		76 03	71.5
—			permanent way slack	20.0
63.8	Malden		78 05	—
66.3	Wimbledon		80 44	53.0
68.0	Earlsfield		83 29	61.5
69.7	Clapham Junction	83 00	85 09	—
—			signal stop	—
72.3	Vauxhall		90 43	—
—			signal stop	—
73.6	WATERLOO	90 00	93 58	—

Net time 82 minutes
Train packed. Many standing in corridors

'Schools' Class No 932, Blundells, *on a local train for Basingstoke near Reading West. (The late M. W. Earley.)*

I was not able to make the runs except at a weekend in the summer, and while this had the advantage of ensuring good rail conditions the line was apt to be congested, especially in the approaches to Portsmouth Harbour station. On the down run I travelled by the 11.50 am from Waterloo. Two relaying slacks were in operation, the second a very bad one on the fastest stretch of all, between Liphook and Liss. The driver had hoped to show off the paces of the engine after Haslemere but had to shut off steam after a speed of 74 mph had been attained just after Liphook. But so fine was the running elsewhere that Rowlands Castle was passed on time. From Bedhampton however we had to join in the queue and eventually reached Portsmouth 24 minutes late.

On the following morning, a Sunday, I came up with the 10.16 am train, another 90-minute service, and witnessed some running that was, if anything, more brilliant than ever. Our driver had the reputation of being a particularly hard-running man, but I hasten to add that while he ran very freely on the open stretches, as from Buriton Tunnel to Haslemere and from Woking to Hampton Court Junction, he was scrupulously careful in observation of speed restrictions. The long-sustained excitement of this journey arose from the loss of 4½ minutes out to Havant by adverse signals, and the recovery of time in the face of two severe permanent way checks at Shalford Junction and Malden. Another extraordinary feature of the run was that the driver set his lever in 29 per cent cut-off and never once changed it from start to finish.

The regulator was opened to the full extent of the first valve on the hardest stretches, but never on to the second valve. The speedworthiness of the engine in these circumstances was astounding not only in the swift dash through Petersfield, but in our glorious sprint on the main line east of Woking. It is now nearly fifty years since I made this journey on the footplate and I have an amusing personal memory of it. It was a hot sunny morning in late June and conditions were sweltering in the cab. When we arrived in Waterloo I stopped for some minutes leaning over the cab-side, talking to the driver, while watching the crowd of passengers we had brought surging to the barriers. Suddenly a lady passenger, evidently mistaking me for the fireman, and taking unjustified pity on my blackened and sweat-covered face, thrust an orange into my hand saying: 'Here eat this'!

It was however on the long steady gradients of the one-time London and Southampton Railway that the capacity of the 'Schools' was most clearly demonstrated. Here there is no opportunity of charging the gradients at high speed and relying to some extent upon impetus. Nothing can make up for sheer solid worth, in the form of high, continuous steaming capacity. The accompanying table gives summary details of eight runs with the Bournemouth expresses.

Waterloo-Southampton: 79.2 miles

Engine number	932	925	931	925	926	932	926	927
Engine number	*Blundells*	*Cheltenham*	*Kings Wimbledon*	*Cheltenham*	*Repton*	*Blundells*	*Repton*	*Clifton*
Number of coaches	12	13	14	14	14	15	15	15
Gross load behind tender (tons)	415	445	480	485	490	510	525	525
Actual time (m s)	82 30*	88 15	87 30	87 15	91 15	86 30	87 30	88 00
Net time (m s)	83 00	87 00	84 00	84 30	88 00	86 30	87 30	87 30
Net average speed (mph)	57.3	54.7	56.7	56.2	54.1	55.0	54.3	54.3

* passing time, equivalent time to stop

The schedule time for this run was then 87½ minutes, and it does seem incredible that 4-4-0 locomotives of no more than 67 tons total engine weight and 42 tons adhesion could have made such runs with fifteen-coach trains of 500 tons and more. These were no isolated efforts. Run after run in similar style was recorded by many different observers, and I shall not forget one in the late winter of 1938-39, against a furious south-westerly gale, when No 933 hauling a thirteen-coach train of 445 tons reached Southampton in 90¼ minutes, or 89 minutes net—a trifling loss of 1½ minutes.

When it comes to a more detailed analysis of the eight journeys tabulated the performance of the locomotives becomes even more striking. The journey may be sub-divided as follows:

On the eight runs previously mentioned the time over the 43 miles from Hampton Court Junction to Litchfield signal box ranged from 43 minutes 6 seconds to

One of the last 'Schools' Class engines to be built, No 935 Sevenoaks. (British Railways.)

Miles	Section	Road characteristics	Booked speed (mph)
13.3	Waterloo-Hampton Court Junction	Inner suburban area restrained speed	44.3
43.0	Hampton Court Junction -Litchfield Box	Steady climb on average speed of 1 in 675	56.1
5.6	Eastleigh-Southampton	Speed restrictions easy running to finish	42.0

48 minutes. The last named was the journey on which the net time to Southampton was the longest of all, 88 minutes. Some impression of the sustained power output involved can be gained from the further table herewith, on which the average speeds from Hampton Court Junction to Litchfield and the estimated drawbar horsepower are set out. Judging from post-war tests of locomotives in calculating figures for the accompanying table values have been taken of 10 lb per ton at 60 mph and 9 lb at 55 mph.

Run number	1	2	3	4	5	6	7	8
Engine number	932	925	931	925	926	932	926	927
Gross load behind tender (tons)	415	445	480	485	490	510	525	525
Average speed (mph)	59.8	55.0	57.1	58.3	53.7	58.6	54.8	55.8
Average estimated drawbar horsepower	935	885	985	1,040	895	1,095	1,000	1,034

From the graph of indicated horsepower, with full regulator and working in 25 per cent cut-off, the anticipated output at 55 mph is 1,230 ihp and at 60 mph 1,270 ihp. From the above table it would indeed seem that on the runs 4, 6 and 8 the locomotives were steaming up to, if not beyond this high standard. It is of interest to analyse still further the run of engine No 932 *Blundells,* in column 6 above, when the 43.0 miles from Hampton Court Junction to Litchfield were covered at an average speed of 58.6 mph.

Miles	Section	Average gradient	Average speed (mph)	Average estimated drawbar horsepower
5.8	Hampton Court Junction to Weybridge	1 in 1,800	63.9	1,040
11.9	Weybridge to Milepost 31	1 in 420 rising	57.4	1,250
11.2	Milepost 31 to Hook	1 in 1,950 rising	60.1	930
14.1	Hook to Litchfield	1 in 490	56.8	1,150

After this fine exhibition of sustained hard steaming on a long rising stretch the engine was taken at high speed down the 1 in 250 descent, covering the 15.5 miles from Micheldever to Eastleigh at an average speed of 77.5 mph and sustaining a maximum of 82 mph. Eastleigh 73.6 miles from Waterloo was passed nearly 2 minutes early, in 77 minutes 45 seconds and quite easy running followed into Southampton. Although this run was the most praiseworthy of all, the whole collection of eight forms a remarkable tribute to the efficacy of the 'Schools' as motive power units, units that in relation to their total engine weight of 67 tons must rank as among the most outstanding ever to run in Great Britain.

On the footplate, despite a rather attenuated cab, they were most comfortable to ride, easy on the track and kind to their privileged guests. Some of the fastest running I have personally recorded on them has been made while the engine was riding so steadily that I had no need to hold the cab-side for support and was able to make all my notes standing. After Maunsell retired some of these engines had multiple jet blastpipes and large diameter chimneys following the similar alterations made to the 'Nelsons'. While I have noted some very excellent performances with engines so modified, insufficient data is available by which to judge whether any substantial improvement has been made by this change, either in the maximum power output or in economy. At the time of this change the locomotives concerned were fitted with steam chest pressure gauges. In pre-war days observers on the footplate were often curious to know the effective regulator opening, when remarkable feats of running were achieved. Since the war, on engines fitted with multiple jet blast pipe I have seen the steam chest pressure gauge registering 195 psi with the regulator apparently no more than about half open.

An interesting high speed performance was made with one of the modified engines, when No 931 *Kings Wimbledon* worked the Saturday section of the 'Atlantic Coast Express' leaving Waterloo at 10.24 am in such style that Andover 66.4 miles from the start, was passed in 58¾ minutes with a load of 305 tons, the 38 uphill miles from Esher to Oakley, on a rising gradient averaging about 1 in 610, were covered in 30 minutes 45 seconds—74 mph average. This is roughly equivalent to an output of 1,000 dhp and reference to the curve of ihp shows that at 74 mph with full regulator and 25 per cent cut-off an output of about 1,270 to 1,280 might be expected. The difference of 270 to 280 horsepower, representing the frictional loss, seems rather on the low side for a speed of 74 mph and suggests that on this fast run No 931 may have been steamed rather heavier than the rate

The last built of the 'Schools', No 939 Leatherhead *on an up Kent Coast Express at Herne Bay. (The late W. J. Reynolds.)*

corresponding to 25 per cent. On a more recent run with No 930, *Radley,* the driver worked his engine in 32 per cent cut-off with almost full regulator on the climb from Tonbridge to Sevenoaks tunnel without any loss of pressure or falling of water level in the boiler. At the same time the low internal resistance of these engines, due to even turning movement, favours the development of a high drawbar horse-power, in relation to ihp. The success of the 'Schools' is due to high mechanical, as well as thermal efficiency. It only remains to add that the 'Schools' have always been universal favourites with the men, at whatever depots they have been stationed. The design will certainly go down in history as one of the masterpieces of British locomotive practice.

16. Maunsell—a retrospect

In the 1930s the avowed policy of the top management of the Southern Railway was to extend the electrified network as fast as funds permitted and restrict other capital investment on motive power to the absolute minimum. In comparison to what the other British railways were then doing with replacement of older locomotives, the LMS in particular, the Southern record of new engine building looks startling:

Engine class	1932	1933	1934	1935
'Schools'	5	10	6	9
'N' 2-6-0	6	7	2	—
'W' 2-6-4T	4	—	—	7

By that time Maunsell's health was giving cause for anxiety. While it would be wrong to say he was losing interest (indeed in his latter years in office he supervised the designing, in outline, of two notable, though stillborn, big engine projects) with the brilliant success of the 'Schools' it could be really said that his locomotive building work was virtually ended.

With main-line electrification completed to Brighton, to Eastbourne and to Hastings, by the LB&SC route, and work well advanced on those to Portsmouth, it might have been expected that a general slaughter would have been taking place among steam locomotives. This was far from the case however. When the time for Maunsell's retirement came in October 1937, the number of locomotives that had been built on the South Western, the Brighton and the SE&CR since 1900 and afterwards scrapped could be counted on two pairs of hands. On the Brighton line, despite the spread of electrification, one could still travel in express trains hauled by steam locomotives of pre-grouping vintage, and moreover showing no more signs of their age than their painting in Southern Railway colours. One summer weekend in the mid-1930s I paid a visit to Bognor and was rewarded by two excellent trips behind ex-LB&SC 'Atlantics' which by that time had been distinguished by the addition of names. I went down by the 6.20 pm express from Victoria and was surprised to find a load of not less than eleven corridor bogies, including a Pullman car, 347 tons tare, and headed by superheater 'Atlantic' No 2426 *St Albans Head.* With a weekend load and some passengers standing in the corridors the gross load was at least 370 tons.

On its non-stop run to Horsham that train which took the Brighton main line as far as Three Bridges had, in fact, the 'Southern Belle' timing to this point of divergence. Despite the heavy load the 'Atlantic' engine did excellently. A bad signal at East Croydon caused a loss of 2½ minutes, but a fine recovery followed up to Quarry Tunnel, making 44 mph to 47 mph all the way and then attaining 67 mph before slowing to take the junction at Three Bridges. On the undulating 8½ miles of cross-country line to Horsham we ran up to 60 mph, and arrived exactly on time, in 50 minutes for the 37.9 mile run from Victoria. Excellent running continued, passing Pulborough, 12.2 miles, in 14½ minutes with a top speed of 67 mph at Billinghurst, and reaching Arundel a minute early despite two permanent way checks, 20.6 miles in 25¼ minutes. On my return journey by the Sunday evening train, with one of the non-superheater 'Atlantics' No 2041 *Peveril Point,* we had an eight-coach train. We did very well from Arundel to Horsham and climbed in great style over the hilly road of the main Portsmouth line of the Brighton Railway to Ockley, topping the crest of the North Downs at 40 mph. But after touching 69 mph before Dorking and passing Leatherhead a minute early, we were checked repeatedly by signals all the way to Sutton.

I had another interesting run over this route just before it was electrified in 1938. I had been engaged on some signalling work and joined the 3.54 pm up at Arundel, a seven coach train of 250 tons hauled by one of the 'I3' 4-4-2 tanks, No 2030. We made good time to Horsham, roughly equalling the times of the 'Atlantic' No 2041 on the Sunday evening Bognor train. I was sorry however that more signalling business involved my leaving the train at Horsham, but neither electrification on that line, nor the intermission of the Second World War, could finally sever my personal acquaintance with the Brighton express tank locomotives. In 1947 some of the veteran 'I3s' were stationed at Tunbridge Wells, former LB&SC shed, and I was privileged to make some footplate trips on them. Working over the heavily-graded Oxted line I formed the impression that in their old age these engines were having to work harder than ever they had to in their prime! It was one thing to skate along over the sweeping ups and downs of the main line with the seven-car 'Southern Belle', and quite another pounding away between stops on the 1 in 100 gradients of the Oxted line, with an eight-coach train of 275 tons, which meant driving the engine literally 'flat-out' from each station stop. This merciless treatment continued for nearly half an hour after we had left East Croydon.

Perhaps the most remarkable example of the preservation of pre-grouping Southern locomotives, and the most gratifying from the historic viewpoint, was that of the two Earle-Marsh 4-6-2 tank engines No 2325 and No 2326, formerly named *Abergavenny*

Above *The 'Southern Belle', a flashback to steam days. The 3.10 pm down loaded to ten cars near Merstham and hauled by superheater Atlantic No 426. (Rail Archive Stephenson — F.R. Hebron.)*

Right *An 'I3' 4-4-2 tank, No 2076, on an up train from Lewes via Oxted line near Edenbridge (with the author on the footplate). (The late M.W. Earley.)*

Right *Lewes-Victoria stopping train near Woldingham hauled by ex-LB&SC 4-6-2 tank No 2325, formerly* Abergavenny. *(Author's collection.)*

and *Bessborough*. These two beautiful engines virtually became the 'odd men out' when Lawson Billinton discarded the 4-6-2 tank type in favour of the 4-6-4 in 1914. Of course the former were very good engines in themselves, and popular with the men, but that, by itself, could not be a reason for keeping two isolated non-standard units in an age when other administrations were busy scrapping whole classes of so-called non-standard engines. It was not enough for No 2325 and No 2326 to survive the Maunsell era. They remained, resplendent in malachite green, until entering national ownership. In the last year of the Southern Railway I enjoyed a footplate ride on No 2325 on one of these strenuous Tunbridge Wells jobs, via Oxted, and found the engine not only delightful to look upon but exhilarating to ride, and apparently good for many more years to come.

Their very powerful successors became redundant after the completion of the Brighton and Eastbourne electrification and it was proposed to use them on the Western Section. To enable them to be used in the

'King Arthur' link from Nine Elms shed it was decided to rebuild them as tender engines, and fit them with 5,000 gallon bogie tenders. In the process of conversion a shorter chimney was fitted to bring the engines within the standard Southern main-line loading gauge, and a new cab was fitted. Other changes in the interests of standardization were the substitution of the vacuum instead of the Westinghouse brake and a Davies and Metcalfe exhaust steam injector in place of the Weir feed pump. The rebuilt engines, which were designated Class 'N15X' had almost exactly the same nominal tractive effort as a 'King Arthur', but though at first an attempt was made at Nine Elms to use them on 'King Arthur' turns they did not have the speed and the generally free-running capacity of the Eastleigh engines. In their penultimate days on the Brighton line, before the first stage of main-line electrification led to their transfer to Eastbourne shed, I had two runs behind them on the 'City Express' from London Bridge. The 'King Arthurs' were well established on the Victoria line by that time

Left *Brighton 4-6-4 tank No 333,* Remembrance, *at Victoria prior to rebuilding as a tender engine. (The late W.J. Reynolds.)*

Left Remembrance *rebuilt as a 4-6-0 and classed 'N15X' at Waterloo. (The late W.J. Reynolds.)*

Above right *Rebuilt 4-6-0 No 2331* Beattie *(Class 'N15X') on a Bournemouth express south of Woking. (Rail Archive Stephenson — F.R. Hebron.)*

and worked 'The Southern Belle', but the turntable at London Bridge would not accommodate a 4-6-0 so the 4-6-4 tanks continued to be used.

The 1 pm Saturdays was a heavy train, always well patronized in those days of a 5½-day week in the City, of eleven corridor bogies, 360 tons tare and 385 tons gross. My recollection of the running of the celebrated 4-6-4 tank *Remembrance* was of her noisy exhaust in the acceleration across the initial level to New Cross Gate and in pounding up the Forest Hill bank. As was often the way we were checked by signals at East Croydon, and then made rather heavy weather of it up the bank to Quarry Tunnel, falling from 46½ mph at Coulsdon to 41½ mph, whereas the equally-loaded Brighton 'Atlantic' on the 6.20 pm Victoria to Bognor mentioned earlier in this chapter did not fall below 44½ mph. The 4-6-4s on the City Express were not given to hurrying up the banks despite their 22-in by 28-in cylinders. On my first trip on the 1 pm down, in February 1932, after the seemingly inevitable signal checks at East Croydon, speed had risen above 42 mph at Coulsdon and fell to 39 mph at the tunnel. By that time however timekeeping on the Brighton was much affected by preparations for electrification, and this run, on which we were hauled by engine No 327, formerly named *Charles C. Macrae,* finished into Brighton five minutes late. My earlier trip with the war memorial engine had been punctual.

The first of the 4-6-4 tanks to be converted was No 329, and the occasion was evidently important enough for the rebuilt engine, resplendent with her new number 2329 and restored name, *Stephenson,* to be put on exhibition at Waterloo on 8 January 1935. It was announced that the remaining members of the class, as they came to be rebuilt, would be named as follows, these were, of course, in addition to that of No 333 which had borne the name *Remembrance* ever since first built:

2327	*Trevithick*	2330	*Cudworth*
2328	*Hackworth*	2331	*Beattie*
2329	*Stephenson*	2332	*Stroudley*

Following No 2329, the next to be rebuilt and allocated to Nine Elms were No 2327 and No 2333. The last to leave Eastbourne, after electrification, were No 2328 and No 2331. The first time I travelled behind one of the rebuilt engines was when I joined the up 'Bournemouth Belle' at Southampton on an autumn evening in 1935. It was a poor run, much delayed by signal and permanent way checks and I did not copy the rough notes into my log book. In any case the 'N15X' Class did not prove very popular at Nine Elms and it seemed that they were soon relegated to the less prestigious tasks in the link.

For all that however, they enjoyed a brief, spectacular, and unprecedented blaze of public relations glory in the railway literary world in 1936. Its origin, though not connected with the 'N15X' engines in any way in the first place, lay in a complaint made by a shareholder at the 1936 Annual General Meeting of the Southern Railway as to the dull and unattractive livery in which the passenger engines were painted. He was not referring to their cleanliness, for at that time Southern engines generally were about the smartest and best kept in the country. It was that the dark myrtle green could do with a bit of livening up! The theme was naturally taken up in the railway press at the time, with many correspondents offering suggestions. Then, for a month or so all went quiet. Then in 1936, in its very first issue of the new year, *The Railway Gazette* not only featured an entertaining editorial article entitled 'The Railway Colour Question', but included a sumptious colour plate containing four suggestions for Southern Railway locomotives. Believe it or not, the class of locomotive depicted was the 'N15X' No 2327 *Trevithick*. The plate was also reproduced in the current issue of *The Railway Magazine,* tieing in with an article on 'Railway Liveries'.

One sensed there was not a little Brighton Railway nostalgia in both the origin and the execution of that composite colour plate. Before joining the Tothill Press, W.A. Willox, who was Associate Editor of *The Railway Gazette* and Editor of *The Railway Magazine,* had been in the Civil Engineer's department of the LB&SCR. O.J. Morris, who took the original photograph on which the colour plate of the Trevithick was based, was a professional photographer with strong railway leanings who specialized in superb 'portrait' studies of Brighton locomotives of all kinds. Their collaborator in the production of the colour plate that adorned both journals was an artist, M. Secretan, whose span of years in that activity was regrettably short. For his draughtsmanship, accuracy of line, tone and colour in portrait painting of locomotives has not been surpassed since. With O.J. Morris' photograph as a basis, he produced four versions of *Trevithick*. There was one in Stroudley's 'yellow', one in a handsome blue—mid-way between Caledonian and Great Eastern—and then there was a light brown, rather like that of the Midland and Great Northern Joint line. But to crown all there was a magnificent representation of the standard Southern style, in Maunsell days, in the myrtle green. Willox was not alone in his view that it was the most attractive style of all, if, he added, it was kept clean! Unfortunately the 'Remembrance' Class, as 'N15X' became known, deteriorated in quality of turnout as their duties grew less prestigious.

Turning now to the ex-L&SWR stock, although his four-cylinder 4-6-0s can be rated as the least successful of all Dugald Drummond's engine designs, it is nonetheless noteworthy that except for the ten 6-ft engines of the 'G14' and 'P14' series, which were replaced by the first Eastleigh series of 'King Arthurs', the remaining Drummond 4-6-0s—save for the unlucky 458 destroyed by a direct hit in the 'Blitz'—survived in some form or another to enter national ownership. Referring now to the earliest of them all, the '330', or 'F13' Class of 1905, those huge engines, even in Drummond's own day, spent most of their time on heavy goods working, at night, which explains why so few of them were ever photographed while at work. Then in 1924 they were called into the works for rebuilding as two-cylinder engines to bring them into line with Urie's 'H15' Class, some additions to which were then being completed at Eastleigh. With the '330' Class it must have been found that an unusually large part of the original engines was serviceable, for not only the frames and such items as the cabs, but also the boiler barrels and their mountings were used again. In the rebuilt engines one could tell at a glance the difference between them and the original Urie 'H15s' of 1913 and the new engines of 1924, by the truncated height of the boiler mountings, especially the dwarfed chimney. I shall always remember my first sight of one of the rebuilt '330' Class in the summer of 1925. I was at Exeter Queen Street Station waiting to photograph the arrival of the 11 am from Waterloo, in days before it was named the 'Atlantic Coast Express', and instead of the expected Urie 'N15' it was hauled by one of the rebuilt '330s'. I carried away the impression of what a top-heavy engine it looked.

It was also at Exeter that eleven years later I encountered one of those ponderous great engines, that time also in high summer heading the Sunday 'Atlantic Coast Express' to Salisbury. At that time the

Below left *No 334, a two-cylinder 4-6-0 rebuilt from a Drummond four-cylinder 4-6-0 '330' Class of 1905. (The late W.J. Reynolds.)*

Right *The Atlantic Coast Express approaching Honiton Tunnel, with 'King Arthur' Class No 768, Sir Balin. (O.S. Nock.)*

Right *Drummond 'D15' Class 4-4-0 No 463, rebuilt and superheated, leaving Waterloo on a Portsmouth express in 1935. (The late P. Ransome-Wallis.)*

Sunday train was timed as fast as during the week, stopping only at Sidmouth Junction to attach through coaches from the East Devon resorts. The resulting engine performance, which I logged in full detail, was in many ways the opposite to what I would have expected in comparison to what I was used to note with 'King Arthurs'. With the ex-L&SWR engines of the class, with the original valve gear, one was accustomed to record slightly slower uphill speeds on the steeply-graded line between Salisbury and Exeter, and very often higher speeds downhill, but with an engine having coupled wheels of 6-ft diameter and an equal tractive effort one would have expected to find faster climbing of the banks. This however was not so. From Sidmouth Junction the load was one of thirteen coaches, 450 tons with passengers and luggage, and the speeds made afforded an interesting comparison to those on a weekday run of the train with an almost identical load with a 'Scotch Arthur'. On the latter journey, made in the summer season, the train was made up to its full load when leaving Exeter and run

non-stop to Salisbury. The comparison of the speeds thus refers to the section east of Sidmouth Junction.

Location	Engine 333 (mph)	Engine 768 (mph)
Honiton Summit	22.5	25.5
Seaton Junction	83.5	82.0
Hewish Summit	37.5	42.0
Crewkerne	75.0	82.0
Milepost 126¼	52.0	61.5
Yeovil Junction	69.0	75.0
Milepost 115½	28.0	32.0
Below Templecombe	68.0	75.0
Semley	29.5	32.25
Dinton	74.0	75.0

The average speeds over the 68.7 miles between Honiton and Wilton were 53.5 mph by No 333 and 57.7 mph by No 768. The high speeds attained by engine No 333 were far in excess of any I noted on the Bournemouth route when the new batch of 'H15'

Class were introduced in 1924.

The introduction of the 'King Arthurs' on the Bournemouth line in 1925 led to the one-time L&SWR stalwarts of the 'D15' Class being transferred to Fratton after their large bogie tenders had been replaced by six-wheeled ones. While various modern six-coupled engines were subsequently drafted to the Portsmouth line, and then a batch of 'Schools', the 'D15s' were still being used on the London trains until the electrification of the route. I travelled behind No 465 on the 5.25 pm from Haslemere to Waterloo in May 1937, with a substantial load of nine of the latest corridor bogie coaches, and logged an excellent performance. It began with a spirited downhill dash down to Godalming reaching maximum speeds of 72 mph to 75 mph, and then after a signal delayed approach to Guildford we set out on the non-stop run to Waterloo to make times equal to those of the 90-minute non-stop Portsmouth 'fliers' over that section of the run. With a gross trailing load of 310 tons this was an exhilarating run behind a veteran locomotive. The log is tabulated herewith.

Haslemere-Waterloo

Train 5.25 pm
Engine Class 'D15' L&SWR 4-40 No 465
Load 9 coaches, 292 tons tare, 310 tons full

Distance (miles)		Time (m s)	Speed (mph)
0.0	HASLEMERE	0 00	—
0.5	Post 42½	2 27	—
—		—	72.0
4.6	Witley	6.47	57.0 (slack)
6.7	Milford	8 48	75.0
8.5	Godalming	10 50	—
1.0	Farncombe	3 02	—
—		signal checks	—
3.2	GUILDFORD	6 45	—
3.5	Worplesdon	6 49	58.0
5.9	WOKING	9 55	40.0 (slack)
8.6	Byfleet	13 04	61.0
11.2	Weybridge	15 37	66.0/61.0
13.2	Walton	17 31	64.5
15.9	Esher	19 57	68.0
17.0	Hampton Court Junction	20 55	66.0
	permanent way check		20.0
18.3	Surbiton	22 22	—
20.5	Malden	25 49	56.0
—		signal dead slow	5.0

Distance (miles)		Time (m s)	Speed (mph)
23.0	Wimbledon	30 02	—
24.7	Earlsfield	32 51	50.0
26.4	CLAPHAM JUNCTION	35 01	40.0 (slack)
29.0	Vauxhall	38 25	52.0
30.3	WATERLOO	40 45	—

Net time from Guildford 36 minutes 30 seconds

The Drummond 'T14' Class of four-cylinder 4-6-0s certainly did not measure up to the standards of reliability that had been established on the Southern by the year 1930, but they were fast engines capable of good work on the road and in 1930 Maunsell rebuilt engine No 460, removing the heavy splasher arrangement which had led to the engines being nicknamed the 'Paddleboats'. Mechanical lubricators were fitted to supply force-feed lubrication to the coupled-wheel bearings and a four-feed Wakefield sight-feed lubricator was provided for the cylinders. The smokebox was also redesigned and equipped with a Maunsell superheater in place of the Urie type fitted during the intermediate stage of the existence of these engines. The remaining nine engines of this class, 443 to 447, 458, 459, 461 and 462 were similarly treated, and with the exception of one that was destroyed in an air raid they all lasted until after the Second World War. While they never came back to first-class top link duties, the 'Paddleboats' in their third state did a great deal of very useful work. On Saturdays in the summer they came into their own, and in July 1939 I was fortunate enough to clock the excellent run tabulated herewith. They retained the short-lap, short-travel valves of the Drummond days, but the piston valve diameter of 9 in was large in relation to the size of the cylinders, and the large ports no doubt contributed to their freedom in running.

The 11.22 am was a through train to Swanage. We had immediately in front of us the 11.17 am to Bournemouth and the 11.20 am 'electric' to Portsmouth Harbour. In consequence our driver started rather slowly, so as to avoid signal checks. Speed only just exceeded 60 mph at Weybridge, but with the Portsmouth train out of the way from Woking onwards our driver began to open out. A minimum of 51 mph was noted on the long climb to Milepost 31, good, steady work was done over the easier stretch towards Basingstoke, but then adverse signals brought us down to 20 mph at that station. The recovery, up a continuous rise of 1 in 249 was vigorous with speed rising to 46 mph at Wootton, and then followed one of the fastest descents to Southampton I have ever personally clocked. At the peak of a long-sustained spell of high

Drummond four-cylinder 4-6-0 'Paddle-boat' No 443 rebuilt a second time, with Maunsell superheater. (Rail Archive Stephenson.)

speed running we reached a maximum of 82 mph and so reached Southampton in 92¾ minutes from Waterloo, in a net time of 88¾ minutes. With a normal start out to Woking we could easily have run from Waterloo to Southampton in 86 minutes on this excellent form.

Waterloo-Southampton

Train 11.22 am
Engine Rebuilt Class 'T14' 4-6-0 No 443
Load 10 coaches, 295 tons tare, 315 tons full

Distance (miles)		Actual time (m s)	Speeds (mph)
0.0	WATERLOO	0 00	—
3.9	CLAPHAM JUNCTION	8 05	—
7.3	Wimbledon	13 05	47.0
12.1	Surbiton	18 57	57.5
19.2	Weybridge	26 41	52.-0/61.0
24.4	WOKING	32 16	53.0
31.0	Milepost 31	39 51	51.0
33.3	Farnborough	42 26	58.5
36.5	Fleet	45 45	62.5
39.8	Winchfield	49 05	56.0
42.3	Hook	51 35	62.5
—		signal check	—
47.9	BASINGSTOKE	58 47	20.0
52.6	Wootton Box	66 32	46.0
56.2	Litchfield Box	70 45	56.0
58.2	Micheldever	72 40	65.0

Distance (miles)		Actual time (m s)	Speeds (mph)
61.9	Wallers Ash	75 46	74.5
64.6	Winchester Junction	77 55	77.0
66.7	WINCHESTER	79 32	79.5
69.9	Shawford	81 57	82.0
73.6	EASTLEIGH	84 45	76.5
75.8	Swaythling	—	74.0
77.2	St Denys	87 50	—
78.2	Northam Junction	89 17	—
79.3	SOUTHAMPTON	92 50	

Net time 88 minutes 45 seconds

At one time a four-cylinder 4-8-0 heavy mineral engine was proposed as an additional standard type. This was intended to have the 'Lord Nelson' boiler and the same cylinder and motion layout, but with 5-ft 1-in coupled wheels. It would have been one of the most powerful heavy freight engines in the country, with a nominal tractive effort, at 85 per cent boiler pressure, of 39,454 lb. The possible development of the Kent coal traffic, among other considerations, was in mind when this locomotive was schemed out. At the time, however, there was hardly the need for such an engine. The Southern was mainly a passenger line and on the main routes line occupation was high, with fast trains, and freights existed merely on sufferance during the day time. The length of such trains was governed by the ease with which they could be stowed quickly out of the way and long unwieldy trains were certainly not regarded with favour by the traffic department, even if the existing running loops and refuge sidings had been adequate for berthing

them. The proposal of the Chief Mechanical Engineer to build very large mineral engines met, therefore, with no response from the traffic side and the project was dropped.

Then in 1938, after Maunsell's retirement, there came the last of his designs to be actually constructed. This was the Class 'Q' inside-cylinder 0-6-0 goods, built as a modern replacement for the old Beattie and Stirling goods engines. Hitherto these engines had been maintained because they were the only ones permitted to run on certain lines. The 'Q' was not regarded as a standard, though it had many parts in common to the 'L1' 4-4-0 and the 'N' Class 2-6-0. The boiler was smaller than that of the 'L1' though generally similar in design. Stephenson's link motion, with long travel was used, but the valves had outside admission to give a short and direct passage for exhaust steam to the blast pipe. An Ashford feature retained was the Stirling steam reverser. These engines had a total weight of no more than 49 ½ tons in working order, while the nominal tractive effort at 85 per cent working pressure was 26,157 lb. With 5-ft 1-in coupled wheels they had a good turn of speed, and their duties included a certain amount of light passenger train workings. They have done good work on such branches as Wareham to Swanage and

Brockenhurst to Lymington with heavy holiday trains.

In concluding this account of Mr Maunsell's work it is appropriate to refer once again to the Salisbury-Exeter line, for nowhere else did his locomotives perform with more consistent brilliance than there. In the late 1930s the 'King Arthurs' had the course to themselves, and it was remarkable that while they seemed to have little margin in hand with 450-ton trains, on the more level stretches of line east of Salisbury on the Exeter road they would often pull off average speeds of nearly 60 mph, start to stop on the westbound run. I was amused to find in Sean Day-Lewis's book an assertion that over that road the 'King Arthurs' were 'extended' with loads of anything over eleven coaches, 355 tons—I wonder what he would have thought of *King Arthur* himself knocking six minutes off the 98-minute schedule from Salisbury to Exeter with a 450-ton train, of *Sir Balin* going two minutes quicker than that with 455 tons and of *Sir Colgrevance* pulling off an average only two decimal points short of a full 60 mph with 415 tons! The details of these three magnificent runs are set out in the adjoining table, together with a fourth in which the speed worthiness of the Urie predecessors of the 'King Arthurs' is well displayed.

Above *Maunsell Class 'Q' 0-6-0 goods engine built at Ashford just after he retired in 1937. (British Railways.)*

Left *'King Arthur' Class 4-6-0 No 771,* Sir Sagramore, *on an outward bound Continental express in the Warren. (The late W. J. Reynolds.)*

Southern Railway: Salisbury-Exeter

Run number	1	2	3	4
Engine number	744	779	453	768
Engine name	Maid of Astolat	Sir Colgrevance	King Arthur	Sir Balin
Load (tons tare)	361	388	420	421
Loads (tons full)	380	415	450	

Distance (Miles)		Run 1 Actual time (m s)	Run 1 Speed (mph)	Run 2 Actual time (m s)	Run 2 Speed (mph)	Run 3 Actual time (m s)	Run 3 Speed (mph)	Run 4 Actual time (m s)	Run 4 Speed (mph)
0.0	SALISBURY	0 00	—	0 00	—	0 00	—	0 00	—
2.5	Wilton	6 34	—	5 35	—	6 20	—	6 15	—
8.2	Dinton	13 43	58.5	11 40	63.0	13 15	57.0	13 05	59.0
12.5	Tisbury	18 30	54.0	15 55	—	17 55	—	17 50	53.0
17.5	Semley	24 21	45.5	21 05	52.0	23 35	45.0	23 50	42.0
21.6	Gillingham	27 57	83.5	24 25	82.0	27 10	79.0	27 30	82.0
23.9	Milepost 107½	29 46	66.0	26 18	63.0	29 05	60.0	29 19	64.0
28.4	TEMPLECOME	33 23	82.0	29 55	82.0	32 45	79.0	32 55	82.0
30.8	Milborne Port	36 06	48.5	32 30	51.0	35 25	49.0	35 30	50.0
34.5	Sherborne	39 27	82.0	35 37	85.0	38 40	82.0	38 45	85.0
39.1	YEOVIL JUNCTION	43 12	75.0	39 10	—	42 15	—	42 10	77.0
41.3	Sutton Bingham	45 20	48.0	41 05	56.0	44 15	50.0	44 05	54.0
47.9	Crewkerne	52 08	68.0	47 05	71.0	50 50	66.0	50 15	71.0
49.7	Milepost 133¼	54 49	32.5	49 15	42.0	53 23	36.0	52 45	37.0
55.9	Chard Junction	60 48	77.5	54 50	—	59 17	—	58 25	80.0
61.0	Axminster	64 42	82.0	58 40	79.0	63 08	80.0	62 00	86.5
64.2	Seaton Junction	67 21	65.0	61 20	—	65 45	—	64 30	71.0
69.0	Milepost 152½	76 10	19.0	68 50	25.0	73 40	23.0	71 30	26.5
70.0	Milepost 153½	78 43	26.0	71 01	29.0	75 50	27.0	73 31	32.0
71.2	Honiton	80 15	60.0	72 25	—	77 25	—	74 50	62.0
75.8	SIDMOUTH JUNCTION	84 03	83.5	76 10	80.0	81 05	82.0	78 35	82.0
—		—	69.5	—	68.0	—	71.5	—	65.0
79.5	Whimple	87 03	82.5	79 15	—	84 00	—	81 50	76.0
83.2	Broad Clyst	89 40	88.0	82 00	80.0	86 35	86.0	84 30	83.0
86.9	Exmouth Junction	92 45	62.5	85 35	—	89 25	—	87 45	—
—		—	—	signal stop	—	—	—	—	—
88.0	EXETER	94 51	—	88 10	—	92 00	—	90 00	—

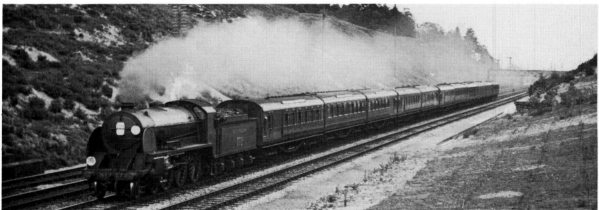

The first engine in this table, the *Maid of Astolat,* was consistently slower on the banks although her downhill speeds were some of the highest, including the maximum of 88 mph at Broad Clyst. Then engine No 779 *Sir Colgrevance* made an astonishing start out of Salisbury, so much so that Yeovil Junction was passed in 'even time'. After passing Crewkerne in the record breaking time of 47 minutes 5 seconds with a load of 415 tons, the effort was eased up—comparatively speaking—though even so passing Honiton summit, Milepost 153½, only a minute outside even time. On the third run *King Arthur* himself made another superb performance, while on the fourth, though dropping behind in the earlier stages, *Sir Balin* from Templecombe onward, developed a truly phenomenal effort. If one takes the time of *Sir Col-*

grevance to Yeovil Junction, that of *Sir Balin* to Honiton and of *King Arthur* to Exmouth Junction, the extraordinary aggregate of 83 minutes 15 seconds from Salisbury is attained. This can be improved by a further four seconds by substituting the times of *Maid of Astolat* from Gillingham to Templecombe. The summary time from Salisbury to Exeter thus becomes 85 minutes 17 seconds, an average of 61.8 mph, with an average gross trailing load of 425 tons.

17. Bulleid—the first phase

On 28 May 1937 there came an official announcement that the Southern Railway General Manager, Sir Herbert Walker, and their Chief Mechanical Engineer would be retiring within the present year. Maunsell, then in his 69th year, had not been in the best of health since 1934 and those closest to him had for some time been aware that with the rapid spread of electrification he had been inclined to let things slide so far as steam locomotives were concerned. The running department was in strong hands. Its superintendent, the veteran A.D. Jones had joined the South Eastern and Chatham Railway, from the Lancashire and Yorkshire in the same office in 1912, and when he retired in 1936 the succession was continued by the appointment of his chief assistant K. Cobb, another ex-SE&CR man whose railway career began with his pupilage at Ashford Works in 1900.

Maunsell's impending retirement had to some extent been anticipated before the announcement of 28 May, with the inevitable speculation as to his likely successor, naturally from his own staff. There was no particularly obvious choice. Pearson, his deputy almost from the time of joining the SE&CR, was nearly due for retirement himself, and the same applied to Clayton. Then there was Turbett, Works Manager at Eastleigh, and Maunsell's personal assistants, Holcroft and L. Lynes, the latter dealing with carriages and wagons. The choice had been made however before the May announcement, at any rate so far as the high management of the Southern Railway was concerned. Soon afterwards Sir Herbert Walker wrote to Bulleid asking him to come to Waterloo, and astonished him by inviting him to apply for the Chief Mechanical Engineer's job. Bulleid for his part was absolutely content with his berth on the LNER, as personal assistant to Sir Nigel Gresley, so Walker advised him to consult his own Chief General Manager, Sir Ralph Wedgwood. Back at Kings Cross he sought an interview with Sir Ralph, explaining that he had always been advised never to apply for any railway job. The reply he got was brief and to the point: 'I can assure you it is a mere formality, the job is yours'. And that was that!

Walker's successor in the General Managership of the Southern Railway was to be Gilbert Szlumper, son of the former Chief Engineer, and before that for many years that of the London and South Western. In later years it became generally known that Bulleid had, for some time prior to that momentous May of 1937, been Szlumper's choice for the new CME, and that he had been gently guiding Walker's thoughts towards that view. While among the highest management circles of the Southern it was felt that their new CME was 'a bit of a genius', as one director put it, when he took up office at Waterloo in the autumn of 1937 no one there imagined he was going to do much more than act as a kind of mechanical caretaker for the engineering department generally until the line was fully electrified. Under Walker's managership the Board had become used to little in the way of proposals for capital expenditure other than for electrification or other associated works like extension of colour light signalling. Bulleid, on the other hand, was equally well aware of the drifting position Maunsell's command had taken up during his last few years

The new livery — 'King Arthur' Class No 766, Sir Geraint, *in malachite green. (British Railways.)*

in office, and of the generally unsatisfactory situation in the working of the boat train services to Folkestone and Dover.

Maunsell, due to his personal friendship with Gresley, had been contemplating a 'Pacific' version of the 'Lord Nelson', and it was largely at the latter's suggestion that the 4-6-0 No 857 *Lord Howe* was rebuilt with the larger boiler as noted in Chapter 13. Encouraged by the results from this the 'Pacific' design was worked out sufficiently far for a weight diagram to be prepared, but the Chief Engineer would not accept his. Maunsell was not in the best of health even at that stage, and rather than face a confrontation with Ellson he let the project drop. Ever since the Sevenoaks disaster of 1927 the two chief engineers had never been on the best of terms. I remember an old friend, who had been on the management side of the Southern Railway, telling me that after the 'dressing down' both of them received from Walker, after the report was studied, both Ellson and Maunsell went in fear of losing their jobs and a row over any new engine was unthinkable. The CME's second try at an enlarged boat train engine, a 2-6-2, also foundered on the rock of Ellson.

On taking over his new command Bulleid immediately began a statistical assessment of the existing power, concentrating on age, as well as usefulness. It was a lengthy job and long before it was ready for submission to Gilbert Szlumper, the new General Manager, Bulleid was out and about, riding on the footplate of the principal express locomotive classes and making his own assessments. In the very first months the department quickly learned of his mercurial nature and of his determination to accept nothing on the basis of its being an old established Southern Railway tradition. His former colleagues

on the LNER were agog for news of what was going on. I was in the confidence of one or two of them at Kings Cross and some of the tales they told were diverting in the extreme. One came from a mutual friend in another branch of the service who had recently moved: 'How's the locomotive department' my friend asked, 'now that a new GOM (Grand Old Man) has arrived?' The reply was 'Base over apex, old boy', or words to that effect!

In those first months chief draughtsmen, works superintendents and running foremen tore their hair out with sheer frustration, but quickly enough the department as a whole realized that they had acquired a truly dynamic new leadership. As one of his senior assistants exclaimed 'If he had asked for square wheels we'd have given them to him'.

In his footplate riding Bulleid very soon became aware of the deficiencies of the 'Lord Nelsons', and the way he attacked the problem can be more readily appreciated by some reference to his previous experience on the LNER, in association with the work of Sir Nigel Gresley, on the improvement of locomotive front ends. He was frequently in France, on Sir Nigel Gresley's behalf, and was keenly aware of the prowess and development of the Chapelon principles. Bulleid had the task of taking the *Cock o' the North* to the SNCF stationary testing-plant at Vitry, and of witnessing some of the difficulties that famous engine got into during the trials. The *Cock o' the North* was probably the first British example of a really modern front end, with very large steam and exhaust passages and greatly-improved draughting arrangements. In favourable conditions the performance of that engine could be phenomenal, but certain lessons were also learnt both at Vitry and in regular working on the Edinburgh-Aberdeen line. The fruits of this expe-

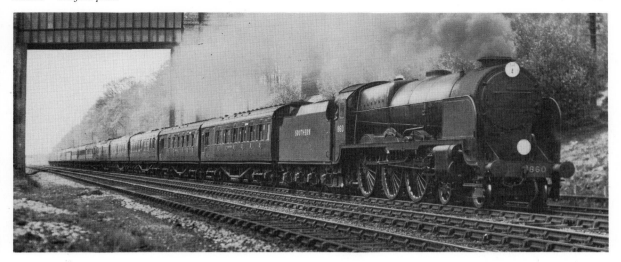

rience were embodied in the ever-famous 'A4' Class of 'Pacifics', not so much in the very skilful design of aerodynamic screening but in every feature of the steam circuit. I hardly need to remind readers that these engines proved to be the fastest steam locomotives ever to be constructed anywhere in the world.

When it came to considering improvement to the 'Lord Nelson' Class on the Southern Railway, Bulleid attacked the problem in exactly the same way that Chapelon had done on the Paris-Orleans Railway some dozen years earlier. Instead of the ordinary single blastpipe, Bulleid chose the Lemaitre arrangement, which consisted of a series of jets, in contrast to the double jet of the Kylchap used on the *Cock o' the North* and on some of the 'A4' 'Pacifics'. In passing, it may be mentioned that a double blastpipe had been tried by Maunsell on one of the 'Lord Nelsons', No 862 *Lord Collingwood,* but it did not appear to have made any difference to the steaming, in fact that engine in its modified condition contributed to the rather large collection of indifferent runs I personally experienced with the 'Lord Nelson' Class engines on the Southern Railway in the last years of the Maunsell regime.

The theory behind multiple, as distinct from single-jet blastpipes, is worth emphasizing at this stage because the multiple-jet blastpipe was to become a standard feature of all Bulleid locomotives on the Southern Railway. A locomotive designer has ordinarily to make a compromise between two opposing factors when it comes to designing a satisfactory draughting arrangement. One requires to have a strong draught in the smokebox in order to sustain a high rate of evaporation in the boiler; and in the past a regrettably easy way of doing this was to increase the speed of the jet from the tip of the blast-pipe to the chimney by keeping the blastpipe orifice small. This, in turn, created a relatively high back pressure in the cylinders and, of course, led to uneconomic working and a high rate of coal consumption. In certain circumstances good steaming would be more important than economic working. It is no use having a very economical locomotive if it will not do the job, and it was considered better to have an engine that would steam and get the train to its destination on time, albeit at the cost of higher coal consumption.

In earlier days, if an engine would not steam freely, it was a well-known trick on the part of individual drivers to fit a crude little device called a 'dart' over the blastpipe cap to sharpen up the blast and improve the draughting on the fire. Draughting on the fire is proportional, however, not only to the speed of the exhaust gases through the smokebox but to the surface area of the jet passing through; so that if one settles upon a certain cross-sectional area of the blastpipe to give economical working and low back-pressure, it is necessary to find some means by which the surface area of the cone can be increased without any alteration to the cross-sectional area. If this can be done the draught on the fire will be increased. The blastpipe of the Kylchap arrangement did this, and the multiple-jet of the Lemaitre achieved it in another way.

While it soon became evident that the Lemaitre multiple-jet blastpipe improved the performance of the 'Lord Nelsons' to a marked extent, Bulleid felt that the cylinders also needed complete redesigning. Accordingly engine No 851 *Sir Francis Drake* was fitted with new cylinders having internally-streamlined steam and exhaust passages of greater cross-sectional area, though on that engine the 8-in piston valves of the original design were retained. The finishing touch on this process of modernization was the substitution

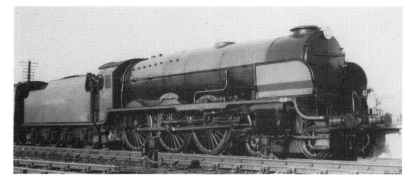

The 4-6-0 No 857, Lord Howe, with multiple jet blastpipe and in the new livery. (The late W. J. Reynolds.)

Two 'Lord Nelsons' with multiple jet blastpipes abreast of each other at Waterloo. On the left is No 856, Lord St Vincent, just leaving on the first part of the Atlantic Coast Express, while No 865, Sir John Hawkins, waits for the second part. (British Railways.)

of 10-in piston valves in association with the improved design of cylinders. By the outbreak of war in September 1939 almost the whole class had been modified, and Bulleid was certainly justified in claiming that 'a very nice improvement' had been made to the sixteen engines. Indeed, from units whose range of performance varied from the very good to the mediocre they stepped immediately into the front rank. I always felt it was a great pity that those engines, in their rebuilt form, were not subjected to some form of competitive trials against their contemporaries on other railways. In view of Bulleid's former association with the LNER, and particularly with dynamometer car testing on that railway, one felt sure something could have been arranged. In actual fact however Bulleid's work on the 'Lord Nelsons' could be regarded as no more than a preliminary exercise towards the larger engines he was already actively planning.

My own experience of the rebuilt engines prior to the outbreak of war in 1939 was confined to a single run from Bournemouth to Waterloo, but it was most impressive in the astonishing difference in the whole character of the running, as compared with what one had grown accustomed to with the 'Lord Nelsons' in

their original state. The engine in question, No 862 *Lord Collingwood,* seemed completely revitalized and where previous engines of this class, with loads of more than 400 tons, had seemingly scraped along with nothing in reserve—that is when they were not losing time—the modernized engine handled her load with ease and showed a positive contempt for the scheduled times. This was a very good run in itself, but when I came to ride on the footplate of engines of this class after the Second World War I was extremely pleased to find that their performance had not deteriorated at all during the emergency, although naturally they were not in the same immaculate external condition as they were when first rebuilt.

My run behind engine No 862, recorded in July 1937, is shown in the adjoining table. On the opening run through the New Forest, I found the running doubly exhilarating with memories of so many journeys on which time to Southampton, then 38 minutes, was barely kept. The way No 862 fairly sailed up Hinton Admiral bank, topping the last mile at 1 in 110 at 53 mph, where speed often used to drop to under 40 mph, was a novel experience for me, and to run the 'Forest' section without falling below 62 mph anywhere until the severe restriction through

Totton was equally good. The long climb from East-leigh to the Litchfield box was interrupted by signal checks costing at least 4 minutes past Winchester Junction; but the recovery was vigorous and Basing-stoke was passed practically on time. On the favour-able gradients eastwards it was easy work for so free running an engine, and despite a further signal check at Woking the driver was able to clock into Waterloo exactly on time.

Southern Railway: Bournemouth-Waterloo

Train 6.40 pm
Engine No 862 *Lord Collingwood* (multiple jet blastpipe)
Load 12 coaches, 387 tons tare, 410 tons full

Distance (miles)		Schedule time (m s)		Actual time (m s)		Speed (mph)
0.0	BOURNEMOUTH	0	00	0	00	—
1.2	Boscombe			3	43	—
3.7	Christchurch			6	33	64.5/58.5
6.9	Hinton Admiral			9	50	60.0/53.5
9.4	New Milton			12	35	66.0
12.4	Sway			15	28	62.0
15.2	Brockenhurst			18	01	71.5
19.9	Beauliea Road			22	18	62.0
22.5	Lyndhurst Road			24	50	67.0/63.0
—				—		68.0
25.4	Totton			27	38	(slack)
28.7	SOUTHAMPTON	37	00	33	18	—
1.1	Northam Junction	3	30	3	31	—
5.7	EASTLEIGH	10	00	9	45	58.0
12.6	Winchester			17	03	54.0
—				signal check		30.0
21.1	Micheldever			31	32	47.5
23.1	Litchfield Box			33	59	50.0
29.0	Worting Junction	39	30	40	08	62.5
31.4	BASINGSTOKE	42	00	42	20	77.5
37.0	HOOK			46	54	69.0
39.5	Winchfield			48	56	74.0
42.8	Fleet			51	43	72.0
46.0	Farnborough			54	33	68.5
48.3	Milepost 31			56	35	67.0
51.2	Brookwood			59	06	75.0
—				signal check		35.0
54.9	Woking	63	00	62	52	—
57.6	Byfleet			66	19	53.0
60.1	Weybridge			68	55	62.0/57.5
62.1	Walton			70	58	62.0
64.9	Esher			73	27	69.0
66.0	Hampton Court Junction	73	30	74	27	64.5
67.2	Surbiton			75	38	61.0
69.5	Malden			77	50	64.5
72.0	Wimbledon			80	13	63.0
75.4	CLAPHAM JUNCTION	83	00	83	50	—
77.9	Vauxhall			87	18	—
79.3	WATERLOO	90	00	90	00	—

Net time from Southampton 82 minutes 30 seconds

In 1945 when I had a footplate pass for the 8.40 am up from Bournemouth I was interested to find we had the same engine, with a similar twelve-coach load, except that as a sign of the times the coaches were packed to the limit of standing capacity and the gross load behind the tender was about 435 tons. Moreover the engine, in grubby unkempt black, looked so different from the spotless malachite green of 1939, and proved in a very much run down condition. From the very moment we started an appalling racket developed in the cab, with all the clanging, jolts and rattling of the sidesheets that usually mark an engine due for the shops. From other footplate experiences in 1945 I was quite used to that sort of thing and settled down to make the best of a rough trip, but we ran magnificently to Southampton, beating by a few seconds the time I had recorded in 1937. The driver linked the engine right up from the start, and by Boscombe the cut-off was inside 15 per cent and the regulator wide, if not quite fully, open. From the summit point one mile east of Hinton Admiral, where we were doing 52 mph, the driver changed over to the first valve of the regulator, and there it remained till the Totton speed restriction. From Southampton we ran at the moderate speeds required by the timetable of 1945. The maximum speed through Brockenhurst was 72 mph.

Although Bulleid's interest extended to every facet of mechanical engineering work on the railway, he was above all a locomotive man with an intense interest in every detail of locomotive working and manufacture and in the first months after he took over from Maunsell he spent a considerable time riding on Southern Railway locomotives and forming his own opinions of them. The rebuilding of the 'Lord Nelsons' was one of the first fruits of this activity of the new Chief. Apparently his impressions of the 'King

Arthurs' were not particularly favourable, and I shall always remember with amusement an experience in connection with an earlier book on locomotive working, in which I had a chapter entitled 'Modern 4-6-0 locomotives of the Southern Railway'. It dealt with the 'King Arthurs' and the 'S15' mixed traffic 4-6-0, as well as the 'Lord Nelsons'. Mr Bulleid had been kind enough to help me in many ways towards collecting the data for this book and I sent the draft of the chapter to him for his scrutiny. It came back with an alteration in the title, because he felt that the engines about which I had been writing could not be considered as modern!

On the other hand, he was delighted with the 'Schools' Class, and was full of praise for the ease with which these relatively small locomotives handled very heavy trains on the Bournemouth service. He fitted one or two of them with multiple-jet blastpipes to improve their performances further. By way of an experiment, a test was made with engine No 931, *Epsom*, fitted with multiple-jet blastpipe, on the winter run of the 'Atlantic Coast Express' between Waterloo and Salisbury and the resulting performance was certainly a record for the run up to that time. The full log of this most exciting affair is shown in the accompanying table. Some of the multiple-jet blastpipe engines were put on to the Hastings line and did very good work, and two runs in particular that I made on the footplate just after the war showed a high standard of performance. Nevertheless the change at the front end did not make so much difference to the 'Schools' as it had done to the 'Lord Nelsons'. In the former case Bulleid, of course, was dealing with inherently good engines, whereas the original 'Lord Nelsons' had been, on the whole, disappointing.

Just before the war there was a proposal to stream-

Below left *Post-war 'Lord Nelson' Class 4-6-0 No 865, Sir John Hawkins, on an up Ocean Liner boat train, Southampton Docks to Waterloo, approaching Clapham Junction. (The late Derek Cross.)*

Right *'Schools' Class 4-4-0 No 930, Radley, with multiple jet blastpipe and in wartime plain black livery with cab side window blacked out. (British Railways.)*

Southern Railway: Waterloo-Salisbury

Engine 'Schools' Class 4-4-0 No 931
Load 288 tons tare, 305 tons full

Distance (miles)		Schedule time (m s)	Actual time (m s)	Average speed (mph)
0.0	WATERLOO	0 00	0 00	—
3.9	CLAPHAM JUNCTION	7 00	7 10	32.6
7.3	Wimbledon	—	10 55	54.4
12.0	Surbiton	—	15 20	63.8
14.4	Esher	—	17 15	75.2
19.1	Weybridge	—	21 15	70.6
21.7	Byfleet	—	23 20	74.8
24.4	WOKING	30 00	25 30	74.8
28.0	Brookwood	—	28 30	72.0
33.2	Farnborough	—	32 45	73.5
36.5	Fleet	—	35 15	79.2
42.2	Hook	—	39 35	78.9
47.8	BASINGSTOKE	53 00	43 50	79.1
52.4	Oakley	—	48 00	66.4
55.6	Overton	—	50 45	69.8
61.1	Hurstbourne	—	55 00	77.6
66.4	ANDOVER	70 00	58 45	84.7
72.8	Grateley	—	64 00	73.2
—		—	signal check	—
78.3	Porton	—	71 20	—
—	—	—	74 30	—
83.8	SALISBURY	88 00	81 50	—

line at least some of the class, a feature on which Bulleid had become an expert with Gresley, and which in 1939 was still the height of fashion. It was felt that as a high-speed, limited, streamlined train was essentially lightweight, these distinguished 4-4-0s might be just the engine for the job. No 935 *Sevenoaks* was in fact fitted at Eastleigh with a mock-up in wood of the proposed design. The boiler was covered with a curious kind of inverse scalloping. The cab and windows were tipped forward at the slope and the appearance was improved by carrying the casing to the front of the buffer stocks. The first mock-up was without deflector plates but these were later added and the engine was numbered 999, perhaps to show that murder had been done. *Sevenoaks* was never steamed in her streamlining and was returned to traffic in her origi-

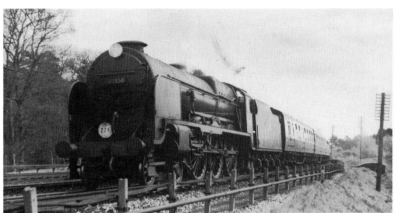

From top to bottom

A Ramsgate and Folkestone to Charing Cross express passing Paddock Wood, hauled by No 30931, Kings Wimbledon, *with multiple jet blastpipe. (The late Derek Cross.)*

A Bournemouth to Waterloo express approaching the Battledown flyover, with 'Lord Nelson' Class 4-6-0 No 30861, Lord Anson. *(The late Derek Cross.)*

A Waterloo to Bournemouth express near Pirbright Junction, hauled by engine No 30850, Lord Nelson. *(R. W. Beaton.)*

Outward bound Continental boat express near Hildenborough hauled by 'Lord Nelson' Class 4-6-0 No 859, Lord Hood, *with 6-ft 3-in wheels and multiple jet blastpipe. (Author's collection.)*

nal state. One can well imagine something of Bulleid's enthusiasm for a Southern counterpart of 'The Silver Jubilee', hauled by a streamlined 'Schools' Class 4-4-0 and running, perhaps, between Waterloo and Bournemouth in 1 ¾ hours.

In the years leading up to the Second World War Bulleid had shown that he had little regard for the traditional, either in the detail of locomotive design, in administration, or in anything else. He was a natural publicist, and it was characteristic of him to persuade the management of the Southern Railway to change the locomotive and carriage livery from a rather sombre olive green to an intensely vivid malachite green. A Maunsell train with engine and carriages in the old colours was quite unobtrusive either in the open country, or in an area of intense railway activity, among many other trains; but a Bulleid train with both engine and carriages in malachite green was a startling apparition that simply compelled attention, and that was just what Bulleid wanted.

It goes without saying that he completely changed the organization of the Chief Mechanical Engineer's department. Whereas Maunsell had set great store upon team work and had played the part of a fatherly but very shrewd administrator, Bulleid was himself the initiator of all new activity. He required intelligent executive assistants, not to advise him or to put forward ideas, but simply to carry out his commands. Maunsell's two personal assistants, James Clayton and Harold Holcroft, stayed on for a time, but with every vestige of their previous power gone.

Bulleid's ideas were worked out by his chief draughtsman, Clifford Cocks. It was a difficult and unsettling time for a staff which had been so long used to Maunsell's ways, but Bulleid, by sheer force of personality, carried his new department along with him and he was to achieve some remarkable feats of productivity, not only in locomotive design, but in carriage and wagon production. Shortly after the outbreak of war, Gilbert Szlumper was succeeded as general manager of the Southern Railway by E.J. Missenden and Bulleid was fortunate in enlisting his sympathy and backing for his entire programme. It is very important that the development of this pleasant relationship at Waterloo should be fully appreciated, because otherwise it is very difficult to appreciate how Bulleid obtained authority for large-scale construction of new steam locomotives after the end of the war, while Maunsell, in his time, had been forced to exist on a shoe-string for so many years.

Although Bulleid had a slight figure and a rather shy demeanour he had the heart of a lion. He had served in France in the Railway Operating Division during the First World War, and he let it be known to all around him that he regarded the Second World War not so much a tragedy as a challenge to his ingenuity and resource, and to his department as a whole. Far from being overawed or disheartened by the restrictions placed upon him by war conditions, he actively sought out means of furthering the plans he had for development on the Southern Railway, despite the circumstances imposed by the war. Wartime austerity was made the excuse—if one may express it so—for the production of one of the most extraordinary-looking locomotives that has ever taken the road in Great Britain, but before I come to describe this weird creation reference must be made to the last Maunsell new design for the Southern Railway, the 'Q' Class 0-6-0 goods engine of 1938.

The design was wholly traditional, using a great number of existing patterns and tools, and the engine's economical performance was ensured by the incorporation of long-lap, long-travel valves. Bulleid, however, was quite disgusted that such a nondescript, pedestrian type of engine should have been built in the year of 1938 and in referring to them he was once heard to remark that he arrived on the Southern Railway too late to prevent them being built. What he would have done as an alternative in those pre-war years we do not know, but when the need arose in the early days of the war for new general-purpose engines he himself produced the rather fantastic 'Q1' Class.

While Bulleid was giving close attention to ways of improving the existing locomotive stock his main object in his first years of office was directed towards the design of a super-express passenger engine to supply the power in which the 'Nelsons' were deficient. Some years later he said that his remit was to produce a locomotive capable of averaging 60 mph between Victoria and Dover Marine with a 600-ton load, and his first proposal was for an enormous 4-8-2. It is probable that this idea stemmed from a Gresley proposal that was on Bert Spencer's drawing board at Kings Cross even before Bulleid left for Waterloo. This latter was for a non-streamlined 4-8-2 version of the 'A3' 'Pacific'. The Southern proposal was turned down flat by Ellson, and Bulleid next turned to the 2-8-2 type of which he has a particular affection from his close association with the *Cock o' the North,* in France, on Gresley's behalf. The 2-8-2 type would facilitate use of the very large firebox, about 50 sq ft, that he felt was essential to raise the steam he needed for the 600-ton boat train. But Ellson would not hear of it. No express engines would ever again be permitted to run on the Southern having leading pony trucks. Bulleid did give some consideration to a 4-8-0, having regard to the great success of the Chapelon rebuilds on the Paris-Orleans Railway; but the project was not put forward formally. Thus he had to fall back on the 4-6-2 type.

18. 'Merchant Navy' and 'West Country' Classes

Constrained to use of the 'Pacific' type, and mindful of their eventful use on fast freight as well as express passenger trains, Bulleid settled on a coupled-wheel diameter of 6 ft 2 in, as on the *Cock o' the North*. In France, as well as on the LNER main line south of Doncaster, that engine had shown itself capable of attaining 85 mph with the greatest of ease. Moreover, one of the design features Bulleid was aiming at was making his new engines capable of a far higher standard of utilization, for example, having run to Exeter and back with an express passenger train the same engine would set out from Nine Elms with a night freight to Exeter. Then after shed duties at Exmouth Junction the 500-mile roster would be run in the reverse direction, finishing up at Nine Elms in the early hours of the third day. The precept of greatly increased utilization per day was furthered by incorporation of novel design features like the totally enclosed casing for the motion and the chain driven valve gear, but one of the prime objects of the entire locomotive design was the achieving of maximum power potential for minimum weight. While Ellson's strictures always hung like 'the sword of Damocles' over the whole project, Bulleid himself treated the attitude of the Chief Civil Engineer as a challenge.

In view of the loading and average speed requirements set out in the previous chapter the nominal tractive effort of the new engines, no more than 37,000 lb, seemed on the small side; but Southern Railway history had already provided, in the Maunsell superheated rebuilds of the SE&CR 'E' Class 4-4-0s an example of the way a brilliantly conceived design can make nonsense of the normal predictions of power output based on the tractive effort formula. The designed adhesion weight of the first class of Bulleid Pacifics was 63.5 tons. One

wonders what Ellson would have said if he had seen the figure as printed in Sean Day-Lewis' fine book *Bulleid: Last Giant of Steam* where the adhesion weight was inadvertently printed as 635 tons! It was characteristic of that 'last giant' of wanting to outdo his fellow CME's in some qualifying factor in the tractive effort formula, and the boiler pressure gave him the opportunity. The highest boiler pressure that had then been used on the other three main line railways of Great Britain was 250 psi. While in North America there were by that time several cases of 300 psi, 280 psi would give Bulleid a British 'first', though it will be shown later that it was rare for the steam chest pressure much to exceed 150 to 175 psi: even when the engines were working really hard.

Going back to fundamentals, the vital task in designing these large engines was to keep the weight down. In this respect Bulleid was fortunate in having to draw on a valuable experience in electric arc-welding dating back to his military service in World War 1, when welded construction was called for in building barges for a strategic assignment. Back on the LNER, in association with Gresley, he applied this wartime experience to the construction of welded underframes for coaches. In his 'Pacific' locomotives for the Southern Railway however he progressed further than any British railway engineer had ever done towards an all-welded locomotive. The boiler and firebox was entirely fabricated, and although the main frames were cast steel all the cross-stays, brackets and so on were welded. In the boiler and

An up West of England express near Hook, with new 4-6-2 locomotive No 21C8, Orient Line, with the author on the footplate. (The late M.W. Earley.)

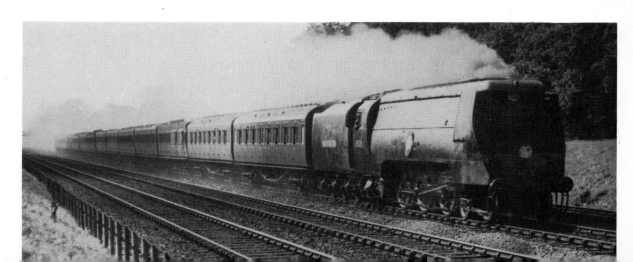

firebox particularly there were no lap joints, the adjoining plates were all edge-welded and the fact that no rivets were used in the construction further lessened the weight. The main frames, as received from the steel foundry, came out rather too thick and had to be planed down. The boilers and fireboxes for ten locomotives were contracted out to the North British Locomotive Company, but the remainder of the highly specialized work was done at Eastleigh. A team of welders was assembled for the job, but even with skilled men it was sometimes difficult to restrain the operators from applying too much weld metal. The techniques had in many cases to be subjected to 'trial and error' methods before proceeding with regular production routines and the incidence of increasingly heavy pre-occupation with purely wartime tasks in the works did not make the job any easier.

The production of a new super-power main-line locomotive in wartime, and moreover one which involved so much work that was of a novel kind, might well have received the Governmental veto, as was suffered by another notable project later in the war, but for Bulleid's own invaluable 'public relations' activities in emphasizing that the new engines were to be used in freight as well as passenger work and that by hauling sixteen coach trains they would make possible wartime economies in working. So far as general proportions were concerned, the firebox of the Belpaire type had a grate area of 48½ sq ft and it was noteworthy that this was the only dimension quoted in Bulleid's original specification of the locomotive that related to the steam raising capacity other than the boiler pressure of 280 psi. Actually the boiler barrel had an inside diameter of 6 ft 2¼ in, the length between the tube plates was 17 ft and the heating surfaces were; tubes 1241.6 sq ft, flues 934.3 sq ft, firebox 275 sq ft and superheater 822 sq ft—a mighty big

boiler, and a mighty big steam raiser it proved! The cylinders were small, 18-in diameter by 24-in stroke, but this was in full accord with Bulleid's aim to keep the weights down, using small cylinder volume in conjunction with high boiler pressure. At this stage it is interesting to compare the basic dimensions with those of three other British 'Pacifics'. The extent Bulleid succeeded in keeping the weight down will be apparent from the last line in the table, wherein the ratio of the tractive effort is related to the total engine weight (see page 201).

In order to ensure improved boiler circulation and give added security against overheating of the crown plate, two Nicholson thermic syphons were fitted in the firebox. Their inclusion accounts to some extent for the increased firebox heating surface over those of the other Pacifics in the accompanying table. The shortness of the barrel, in combination with the large diameter of the ordinary flue tubes would, in themselves, assist in producing a very free-steaming boiler; but the inclusion of thermic syphons in the firebox and the benefits of the multiple-jet blastpipe combined to produce a boiler of such vast steam-raising capacity that its limit proved to be beyond anything that could be determined on test. We shall never know what the maximum rate of evaporation of a 'Merchant Navy' boiler was! The boiler barrel was designed to give maximum steam space by tapering underneath and being horizontal on top. The taper allowed the smokebox floor to be above and clear of the inside cylinder and valve, as well as assisting the gravitational flow of water to the firebox from the clackboxes on the front ring of the barrel. Three 'pop' safety valves were also fitted on the front ring of the barrel, an unusual position dictated by the possibility that water as well as steam might be lifted from the turbulent area over the firebox fitted with syphons.

Thus far, in developing the design for his super-locomotive, Bulleid had worked on more or less conventional lines, although using the technique of electric arc welding to avoid lap joints in the boiler and firebox plates and so to notably reduce weight. But the

The 'Devon Belle' climbing Honiton bank, with engine No 21C8 Orient Line. It was a fourteen Pullman train. (W.N. Lockett.)

Up West of England express near Hook, in August 1945, with 'Merchant Navy' Class 4-6-2 No 21C19 before that engine was named French Line CGT. *(The late M. W. Earley.)*

outer clothing of the boiler was another matter. Having been associated with Gresley in the design of the *Cock o' the North* and in the adaptation of the Bugatti front end to the streamlining of the famous 'A4' 'Pacifics' one could be sure Bulleid would have wished to impose a style of his own on the new Southern 'Pacifics', particularly as the LMS had blazed streamlined fashion still further in their 'Coronation' Class of 1937. But Bulleid's new engines were being built in wartime, ostensibly as much for freight service as for passenger, and pure streamlining, as an outward facade, would not then have been in the patriotic interest of the day. Bulleid achieved novelty, and a great deal of publicity, by declaring that his new engines had a smooth exterior and could be cleaned merely by passing them through a carriage washing plant. The outer casing was described as 'air-smoothed' and quickly earned the engines their nickname of 'spam cans'. Nickname or not, the casing, consisting of light channel section ribs covered with light plating, was attached to the main frames. The boiler was free to expand within it and the whole casing was easily detachable, with a smooth exterior which could be cleaned with ease.

Another novel feature was the wheels. The conventional wheel consisted of a cast-steel spoked centre on which a rolled steel tyre was shrunk. When such wheels were retyred it was often seen that flexing between the spokes had occurred, causing fretting corrosion between the centre and the tyre. The stresses set up in a wheel centre were investigated by polarized light on celluloid models in the laboratory at Ashford and showed great variation in a conventional centre and between the spokes. To ensure greater strength against both the vertical load and the lateral thrust of flange against rail, Bulleid decided to adapt the American Boxpok method. With the collaboration of the Sheffield steelmakers Messrs Thomas Firth and John Brown, he evolved the BFB (Bulleid Firth-Brown) type of cast-steel wheel centre. It was shown with models that stresses in the wheel rim and the tyre had been equalized round the circumference. Almost as

important was a weight reduction of ten per cent.

In working out the rest of the design Bulleid introduced a number of somewhat revolutionary features which unhappily were not so successful in service as the boiler. With the idea of reducing the day-to-day maintenance work at sheds to a minimum, the whole of the valve motion was completely enclosed, as were the centre connecting rod and crank axle. The idea was that these parts, running completely enclosed in an oil bath, would need no attention during the entire span of service of the locomotive from one works overhaul to the next. This feature, which was novel so far as steam locomotives were concerned, brought a number of problems, not the least of which was that of keeping the oil in the oil-bath. Unless the engines were exceptionally well maintained it seemed to get everywhere else—on to the track, into the boiler lagging and, worst of all, on to the wheel treads.

Even so, it was not the oil bath and what escaped from it that proved the 'Achilles' heel' of the Bulleid 'Pacifics', though it was certainly the decision to have it that led to still greater troubles. The space inside was relatively small. No ordinary valve gear could be got in, so Bulleid designed a special gear to meet the circumstances—one set for each of the three cylinders. The principal feature of this new valve gear was that it was chain driven, and that no valve spindles of the conventional kind were used at all. All three sets of valve gear were inside the frames. If connection had been required to ordinary valve spindles it would have had to be made at some point through the casing of the oil bath, thus introducing a further source of leakage.

When new or newly-shopped after general repair this special radial valve gear gave excellent results and contributed to a very free-running engine; but it seemed to lose its adjustment very quickly and the valve timing then became erratic. It was very difficult to keep engines running at a constant cut-off. The steam distribution would appear to vary, and when one of the 'Merchant Navy' Class engines was on the stationary testing point at Rugby it was impossible,

even in such carefully-controlled conditions, to keep the distribution from wandering about, cut-off wise. Even when the bridle rod was bolted there was still variation in cut-off. On the majority of engines the steam-operated reversing gear was difficult to set, and certainly difficult if any fine adjustment to cut-off was desired by the driver. In consequence, drivers found some position of the reverser in which the engine ran freely, and then drove almost entirely on the throttle. When one of these engines was on test at Rugby two different series of trials were run, on the first of which the engine was worked in the theoretically-correct way, with wide-open regulator and cut-off adjusted to produce the power required, and on the second with a much longer cut-off and power output varied by means of the regulator. There was actually very little difference in thermal efficiency between these two methods of working, and on the engine in question full-regulator working and short

cut-offs tended to produce severe vibration.

In riding on these engines I found that the steam reverser was a rather fiddling thing to adjust, and one felt sympathetic to the driver who found some position of good compromise and left it there. It has often been said that on any locomotive the pointer scale of the reverser is 'the biggest liar on the engine', and in certain of the Bulleid 'Pacifics' on which I rode even this would be an understatement. I shall always remember a trip on one of the 'West Country' Class engines, when we were storming up the bank from New Cross towards Elmstead tunnel in terrific style I crossed over momentarily to the driver's side to see what the cut-off was. If the pointer was to be believed the engine was in backward gear!

At first a number of attempts were made to demonstrate their high haulage capacity, and fast trial runs were made over the Bournemouth, West of England and Continental boat-train routes. But neither in the

fast trial runs made just after the war, nor in any subsequent task set, did the requirements approach the specification which Bulleid had been set at the time the engines were first designed. The Southern operating authorities always set great store on accurate timekeeping, and there is no doubt that they favoured schedules which gave a considerable margin in reverse to the locomotives employed. It would have been grandly heroic to try and run a train of fourteen Pullmans non-stop from Waterloo to Salisbury at an average speed of 70 mph, as Bulleid stated he had legislated for when the engines were first designed; but in actual practice, and in fairness to Bulleid, I feel that there were very few engines in the links at Nine Elms, Salisbury, or Exmouth Junction which could have run regularly up to that standard.

The story of 'Merchant Navy' performance over the years was punctuated all too frequently by engines becoming complete failures on the road. There is no doubt that the totally-enclosed valve gear and inside connecting rod was one of the main causes of trouble. Running men have explained it very vividly to me by saying that, with the centre big-end totally enclosed, one could not smell it when it was getting hot, nor hear it when it was knocking; consequently the first thing one knew about any problem was when the connecting rod came clean through the bottom of the oil bath.

Bulleid set great store by having the connecting rod totally enclosed, and when the engines were rebuilt with conventional valve gear, and there was trouble at first with the middle big-end, he took a certain amount of impish delight in this difficulty. But the fact remains that the middle big-ends did fail, oil bath or no oil bath, and they had a way of doing so in the most inconvenient places. Many are the stories told—some of them exaggerated and others perhaps apocryphal—but one failure I recall, which caused a gargantuan hold-up of road as well as rail traffic, took place one summer Saturday, when an engine transfixed itself right in the centre of the level-crossing at Brockenhurst. Both road and rail traffic were blocked until a breakdown gang from Eastleigh could cut away the damaged parts and remove the engine. I have already mentioned the leakage of oil and this not only caused slipping and other difficulties, but sometimes led to fires, though, fortunately, none were of a very serious character. At their best the 'Merchant Navy' Class engines were as strong and fast as any engine in the country, at their worst they were a nightmare.

On the West of England road, in 1945, I made one trip on a really dreadful engine. It was not long after the end of the war and the engine seemed well overdue for shopping. She was very weak on the banks and the vibration was indescribable, especially when the

driver let her go full tilt down Seaton bank to try to make up some lost time and we reached a maximum speed of 85 mph at the bottom. Generally, however, I found the 'Merchant Navy' Class very steady-riding engines, if they were not always smooth. They never glided along like the 'Pacifics' of the Northern lines, one never got that 'Rolls-Royce' feeling that so often came on a Stanier 'Duchess' or a Gresley 'Pacific'. The vibration was nearly always there and I shall not soon forget an occasion on the outward-bound 'Golden Arrow' when the driver really opened out after Ashford and took a 425-ton train over Westenhanger summit at 72 mph. The vibration in the cab was so terrific that it danced the driver's tea-can off the shelf just above the fire door.

Generally speaking, I never experienced from the footplate those incessant bouts of slipping that were indulged in all too frequently by the 'Merchant Navy' Class engines, though on one occasion, when the rails were bad, I did see one slip itself to a standstill backing 'light engine' out of Waterloo. One of the worst cases I had with slipping was on the inward-bound night ferry train, when we had a bad rail out of Dover and the engine was slipping incessantly most of the way to Folkestone. Slipping was most alarming when it occurred at high speed, and I had one hair-raising occasion on the up 'Golden Arrow' when the engine suddenly went into a violent slip when travelling at 75 mph. It was not nice! The crack drivers became very expert at checking the slipping of these engines, but there were times when it could not be avoided and there were some very difficult moments in later years when one of them was being tested on the controlled road testing principle, with a dynamometer-car, on the Settle and Carlisle line.

There is no doubt that the unconventional appearance of these engines captured public imagination to a remarkable degree. After the drab years of endurance and austerity during the war, and the necessity to make do with existing tools, there was, all over the country, a yearning for new things, whether they happened to be locomotives, household goods, or even one's own personal wardrobe. Anything with a 'new look' was welcomed, and however much locomotive enthusiasts with a love of the conventional deplored the strange apperance of Bulleid's creations, to the public they were something 'new' and as such they were widely acclaimed.

I shall never forget an incident that occurred one day in the late summer of 1945 when I travelled down to Exeter to make my first footplate journeys on 'West Country' 'Pacifics' operating between there and Ilfracombe. I had come down from London on a 'Merchant Navy' and at Exeter Central we duly changed engines. The 'Merchant Navy' was still in wartime black but the 'West Country' which backed

'Merchant Navy' Class 4-6-2 No 35017, Belgian Marine, *on Interchange Trial. It is shown near Potters Bar on a run from Kings Cross to Leeds. (The late M.W. Earley.)*

The 'Devon Belle' passing Raynes Park, hauled by 'Merchant Navy' Class engine No 35016, Elders Fyffes. (Author's collection.)

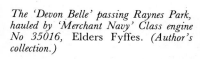

Engine No 35005, Canadian Pacific, *at Clapham Junction before a constant speed dynamometer car trial to Salisbury. (The late W.J. Reynolds.)*

Left *'Merchant Navy' Class engine No 35029 at Nine Elms, with cover plates over its nameplates prior to ceremonial naming as* Ellerman Lines. *(E.D. Bruton.)*

Left *The 'Golden Arrow' arriving at Dover Marine hauled by 'West Country' 4-6-2 No 34039 then unnamed but later called* Boscastle. *(Author's collection.)*

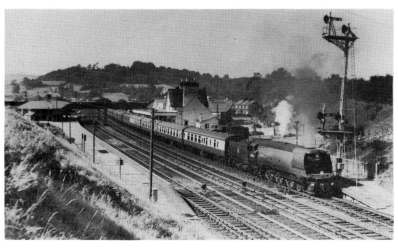

Left *Plymouth to Brighton express at Seaton Junction hauled by an unnamed 'West Country' 4-6-2 No 34106, afterwards christened* Lydford. *(The late Derek Cross.)*

Above right *The 'Golden Arrow' passing Chelsfield hauled by 'West Country' Class 4-6-2 No 34092,* City of Wells. *(The late Derek Cross.)*

on in its place was brand-new, positively glittering in the pre-war livery of garish malachite green and yellow, and as this apparition came backing down on to the train one could sense the hush that came over the group of onlookers. When I went forward and climbed up on to the footplate several people, thinking I was a railway official, came forward to bombard me with questions about the new engine. I remember one man in particular who remarked in an awestruck voice: 'Don't they look powerful?'. How a rather shapeless steel casing could give the impression of power, I do not know. But for good or ill, Bulleid had accurately interpreted popular sentiment of the day and in the public view the Southern was the only rail-

way in the country that seemed to be breaking fresh ground.

The 'West Country' 'Pacifics' reproduced faithfully all the strength and all the weakness of their larger contemporaries, but there can be no doubt that the management of the Southern were satisfied with their record. The first order was for seventy of them, and the type was eventually multiplied until there were no fewer than 110 of them at work. At the time of nationalization all the first batch of 'West Country' engines had been completed, with numbers ranging from 21C101 to 21C170. The remainder were built between April 1948 and January 1951.

British 'Pacifics'

Railway	LNER	LNER	LMSR	Southern Railway
Class	'A3'	'A4'	Duchess	Merchant Navy
First introduced	1928	1935	1937	1941
Designer	Gresley	Gresley	Stanier	Bulleid
Cylinders				
Number	3	3	4	3
Diameter (in)	19	18½	16½	18
Stroke (in)	26	26	28	24
Coupled wheel diameter (ft in)	6 8	6 8	6 9	6 2
Heating surfaces (sq ft)				
Evaporative	2,477.0	2,345.1	2,577.0	2,175.9
Firebox	215.0	231.2	230.0	275.0
Superheater	703.0	749.0	856.0	822.0
Grate area (sq ft)	41.25	41.25	50.0	48.5
Boiler pressure (psi)	220	250	250	280
Total engine weight (tons)	96.25	103.0	108.0	94.75
Nominal Tractive Effort (lb)	32,909	35,455	40,000	37,500
Tractive effort per ton of engine weight (lb)	343	344	370	396

19. Postscript

The end of the war in 1945 was followed by the General Election and the return of a Labour Government with a huge majority in the House of Commons made certain the nationalization of the railways at an early stage in the life of the elected Parliament. Once the Bill had been introduced, and the two-tier form of administration propounded—the British Transport Commission and beneath it, for railways, the Railways Executive—it was inevitable that there would be much unobtrusive jockeying for position among the senior officers of the former railway companies. Among the Chief Mechanical Engineers, Bulleid was by many years the most senior, and, by his 'Pacific' engines had shown himself the most forward looking of the four; but he was an outspoken opponent of Socialism in general and railway nationalization in particular, and that probably counted against him when the choice of the Member for Mechanical and Electrical Engineering was being made. His former chief on the Southern Railway, Sir Eustace Missenden, was only the second choice for the Chairmanship of the Railway Executive, after Sir James Milne, the former General Manager of the Great Western Railway had turned it down. So for twenty months after vesting date Bulleid continued as Chief Mechanical Engineer of Southern Region and although he came to disagree with many of the policies put forward, as one of his new found colleagues said to me some years later, 'he never once attempted to rock the boat'. He even remained calm after he was refused entry to the dynamometer car when one of his own engines was being tested in the Interchange Trials of 1948—he had omitted to ask previously for a permit!

But at New Year 1946 the Southern Railway had two more years of independence before being merged in 'BR', and Bulleid had the same time under the kindly chieftainship of Eustace Missenden. Ever since his appointment to succeed Gilbert Szlumper as General Manager in the early months of the war, Missenden had backed Bulleid up to the hilt in all his novel development projects and it was his advocacy, no doubt, that persuaded the Southern Railway Board in 1945 to authorize the construction of no fewer than seventy of the new 'West Country' Class of 'air-smoothed' 'Pacifics'. It was not that the teething troubles of the first batch of 'Merchant Navy' Class had been ironed out—far from it. When newly out of the shops they were magnificent, but Bulleid's entire philosophy regarding the introduction of those engines was that they would maintain their quality and standard of performance from one general overhaul to the next. That, in his view, meant at least 100,000 miles of running. One of my earliest footplate runs on one of these engines, on 21-C-5 *Canadian Pacific* was in the late summer of 1945. In contrast to others I made at about the same time on engines 21-C-4 and 21-C-8 the former engine was somewhat run down, and in addition to giving us a very rough and uncomfortable ride she was very weak on the banks.

When I read the passage in Sean Day-Lewis' book about the superiority of the 'Merchant Navy' Class over the 'King Arthur' Class on the Salisbury-Exeter line I turned up my log of the *Canadian Pacific* run of 1945 and compared it with one I recorded in 1931 behind No 768 *Sir Balin*, on the up 'Atlantic Coast Express', with an almost identical load—455 tons and 445 tons. The 'Pacific' took 67 minutes for the start-to-stop run of 48.9 miles from Exeter to Yeovil Junction, whereas the 'King Arthur' with only 10 tons less load took 58¼ minutes to pass through at speed. This

was equivalent to making a stop in about 59½ minutes from Exeter. The Bulleid engine was consistently slower on the banks and to keep the slower schedule of 1945 the driver had to let go up to 85 mph downhill! The pandemonium on the footplate as we approached Seaton Junction was indescribable! On the contrary the engine that took over at Salisbury was a pleasure to ride. In those days however it was not a novelty, in a single express journey in Great Britain, to alight from one engine that was like a bag of nails and to step on to another of the same class and the same vintage that was as sweet as silk. The difference in the case of the 'Merchant Navy' Class was that in the short life of the ten original engines of the class they had shown themselves susceptible to failures of unpredictable character, even when on show for the highest officers and directors of the Southern Railway. Riding on an engine like the *Canadian Pacific* as it was in the summer of 1945, and at such a speed as 85 mph, one could have been pardoned for wondering what was going to happen next!

Of course the 'nigger in the wood pile' was Bulleid's special chain-driven valve gear, snugly ensconced in a totally enclosed oil bath. The principle was so absolutely *right* that one can only wonder that locomotive engineers had not developed the idea many years previously. Of course there were practioners like Maunsell whose philosophy was 'make everything get-at-able', but the giants at the opposite ends of the field of automobile engineering, Sir Henry Royce and Henry Ford, and indeed all those intermediately between them, never subscribed to those precepts. Bulleid was merely applying to steam railway locomotive engineering what the road motor men had been doing for upwards of fifty years. The difference began to be appreciated when the Board of the Southern Railway, in 1945, was induced to

authorize construction of seventy engines of the 'West Country' Class. It was a time on all the British railways for making up arrears in locomotive construction occasioned by six years of wartime constraints. But on the Southern, as related in earlier chapters of this book, steam locomotive building had necessarily been at a low level because of the rapid expansion of the electrified network, and the retention in good order, for other duties, of the steam locomotives that would have been made redundant otherwise. Nevertheless an order for seventy mixed traffic locomotives for general use over a high proportion of Southern Railway mileage would have seemed a reasonable proposition, even in anticipation of the early resumption of the electrification programme.

The big problem was the type of 'mixed traffic' locomotive. A scaled-down version of the 'Merchant Navy' Class, with its magnificent boiler and its freedom in running would have been widely acceptable. I shall always remember the remark one Southern man made during tea prior to a meeting at the Institution of Locomotive Engineers about that time, concerning the Bulleid 'Pacifics' generally. He said: 'They'll steam on anything—egg shells, garden refuse, anything you like to chuck in!' But apart from the boiler there was the largely unsolved imponderable question of the valve gear and its oil bath. It would have been easy enough to state categorically that these novel features should have been tried on a limited number of engines and these subjected to exhaustive testing to iron the 'bugs' out before they were incorporated in a large standard class like the 'West Countrys', but that was not to know the personality of Bulleid himself. He had supreme confidence in what he was doing, and the idea of his building five smaller 'Pacifics' with totally enclosed chain-driven valve gear, and 65 with ordinary Walschaert's gear, was unthinkable. Whether 'Pacifics' were suitable or

Left *The outward bound 'Golden Arrow' leaving Martello Tunnel with 'Battle of Britain' Class 4-6-2 No 34089, 602 Squadron. (The late Derek Cross.)*

Right *Inward bound relief Continental boat train passing Bromley with engine No 30469* Sir Balan *with the author on the footplate. (John G. Click.)*

Left *Inward bound Continental boat train leaving Abbots Cliff Tunnel hauled by 'Battle of Britain' Class 4-6-2 No 34067, Tangmere. (The late Derek Cross.)*

Below *The boiler of the 'Q1' Class ('Austerity') 0-6-0 locomotives.*

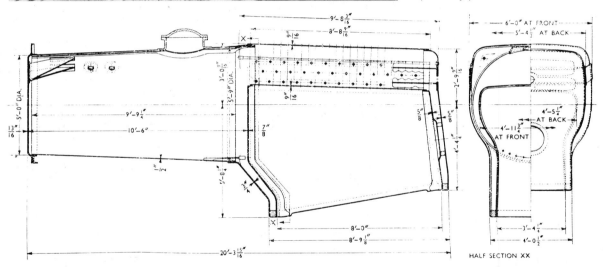

HALF SECTION XX

necessary for some of the mundane duties they were given down in the West Country is another matter. Where Bulleid engines were concerned, the uncharitable thought occurs that it would have been better, and cheaper, to have had a further batch of fifty 'Q1' 0-6-0s, for all their unorthodox appearance, and less 'West Country' 'Pacifics'.

The 'Q1' Class had a nominal tractive effort almost equal to the 'West Countrys', 30,000 lb against 31,000 lb, and with long-travel valves and an excellent valve gear they had a good turn of speed, despite having wheels of no larger diameter than 5 ft 1 in. As in his original specification for the 'Merchant Navy' Class, Bulleid based everything upon the firebox. In a talk to the locomotive men at Feltham in 1942, follow-

ing the introduction of Class 'Q1', he emphasized that the evaporative capacity of a boiler was dependent on the grate area and the firebox heating surface and volume. The largest firebox, as regards width at the top and allowing proper vision from the cab, which could be fitted within the Southern loading gauge was that of the 'Lord Nelsons', and this Bulleid copied in a slightly shortened form, with a grate area of 27 sq ft. This represented a notable advance on that of the 'Q' Class, which was only 21.9 sq ft. The latter engines had a total weight, in working order, of 49.1 tons, and for the new engines Ellson advised that he was prepared to accept a weight of 54 tons, which could run over 93 per cent of the total track mileage of the railway. The wheelbase was to be the same as for

'Q' Class and the cylinders, as previously, 19-in diameter by 26-in stroke; these factors determined the
length of the boiler, and with the grate area already
settled at 27 sq ft and the working pressure at 230 psi,
the weight came out at 21¼ tons in working order.
This left only 32¾ tons for the rest of the engine.

How it was done was by a masterpiece of engine
designing, discarding everything that was deemed
unnecessary, with Bulleid himself delighted by the
chorus of disapproval from the traditionalists. Never
had there been such a stark and seemingly unfinished
engine on the railways of Britain, but the plain fact
was that in the middle of a desperate war forty new
very powerful freight engines and tenders had been
produced at a reduced weight of 14 tons each, or a
saving of 560 tons on the total order. The actual
engine weight had come out at 51½ tons, 2½ tons less
than Ellson's target figure. The 'Q1' proved an
excellent and generally reliable motive power unit.
With the Stephenson link motion and long-lap, long-
travel valves they were free running, although Bulleid
himself confessed that he had not tried to see if they
would do more than 75 mph! Even so, a six-coupled
goods engine having a tractive effort of 30,000 lb and
capable on occasions of running up to 75 mph was a
pretty useful tool at anytime, even if not very

decorative to look at. Some years later, when some of
'West Country' 'Pacifics' were introduced on to the
Somerset and Dorset line and proved that by their
liability to slip that they could not take more than
eight of the latest LMS bogie coaches up the severe
gradients between Evercreech Junction and Bath, no
more than a Stanier 'Black Five' 4-6-0, I sometimes
wondered if a 'Q1' would have been more sure-
footed. Experience on the 1 in 50 banks of the
Somerset and Dorset certainly prompted my view
that for general mixed traffic duties more 'Q1s' would
have been better than at least some of the 'West
Countrys'.

However much some of the running men may have
torn their hair out over the idiosyncrasies of 'West
Country' and 'Merchant Navy' performance both
classes proved a gold mine for the publicity department at Waterloo in staging special occasions for the
naming of individual engines by prominent directors
or senior officers of shipping lines, and by civic
dignatories of West Country localities. On the
'Merchant Navy' Class the handsomely-styled
nameplates included the flags of the shipping lines
concerned. Twenty of these locomotives had been put
into service by the end of 1945. The remaining ten followed four years later, actually after nationalization.
The three successive batches were named thus:

Right *The cylinders of the 'Q1' Class
('Austerity') 0-6-0 locomotives.*

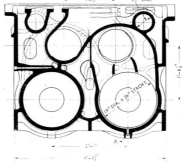

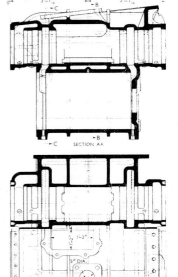

Below *On the Somerset and Dorset Line —
an express from Liverpool and Manchester to
Bournemouth leaving Combe Down tunnel,
south of Bath, with an unidentified 'West
Country' 4-6-2 piloted by an LMR 0-6-0.
(Kenneth Leech.)*

1941 built

21C1	*Channel Packet*	21C6	*Peninsular & Oriental SN Co*
21C2	*Union Castle*	21C7	*Aberdeen Commonwealth*
21C3	*Royal Mail*	21C8	*Orient Line*
21C4	*Cunard White Star*	21C9	*Shaw Savill*
21C5	*Canadian Pacific*	21C10	*Blue Star*

1945 built

21C11	*General Steam Navigation*	21C16	*Elders Fyffes*
21C12	*United States Line*	21C17	*Belgian Marine*
21C13	*Blue Funnel*	21C18	*British India Line*
21C14	*Rotterdam Lloyd*	21C19	*French Line CGT*
21C15	*Nederland Line*	21C20	*Bibby Line*

1949 built and numbered in the British Railways series

35021	*New Zealand Line*	35026	*Lamport & Holt Line*
35022	*Holland-America Line*	35027	*Port Line*
35023	*Holland-Afrika Line*	35028	*Clan Line*
35024	*East Asiatic Company*	35029	*Ellerman Lines*
35025	*Brocklebank Line*	35030	*Elder Dempster Lines*

The new system of numbering, initiated by Bulleid on these engines in 1941 was discarded on nationalization. It was used only on the 'Q1' Class and on the earlier batches of the 'West Country' Class.

The naming of the 'West Countrys' recalled the Stroudley days on the Brighton, though in the sophisticated years from 1945 onwards one could not have expected that passengers would be confused by the engine's name into boarding the wrong train. Certainly the first few of the new engines were named after major main-line stations in ex-London and South Western territory, but by the time the numbers had reached no further than 34021, from the initial 34001, reckoning by the BR equivalents of the Bulleid 21C101 etc, they represented places where there was not any station. Some of those West Country names were certainly delightful like *Blackmore Vale, Yes Tor, Eddystone, Clovelly, Boscastle,* and above all *Lundy.* Then as many more engines were built and further West Country names were inappropriate, a series from Nos 34049 to 34089 were titled after personalities, events and RAF units connected with the Battle of Britain which was fought in the skies covering the areas in which the newer engines of the class were to be employed. The batch stationed at Ramsgate, particularly, came to do some fine work on the Kent Coast expresses.

With eventually 110 of these engines on the books, and a considerable proportion of them on humdrum duties, they did not receive the attention really needed for top link work. Moreover, the common-user nature of much of the work allotted to them all too often resulted in units which were in run-down condition being allocated to important trains, and it was then that some of the spectacular failures that occasionally 'hit the headlines' took place. The trouble

was that though Bulleid evolved a design intended to need the very minimum of day-to-day attention, it never finally reached that stage of reliability, and it was the more neglected members of the class that let the party down. From all accounts, in the early days at any rate, failures did not unduly worry Bulleid himself. He took the view that every failure provided a lesson further to be learned about his engines. They did him proud in the Locomotive Interchange Trials organized by the Railway Executive after nationalization in 1948; and in this respect he was magnificently backed up by Pelham Maitland, the shed superintendent at Nine Elms, from which all the competing engines came. The 'Merchant Navy' Class engines used were 35017 on the E and LM regions, 35018 on its home ground, 35019 on the Western; 34004 on the E and Scottish, 34005 on the LM, and 34006 on the Western.

Thanks to the enthusiasm of their 'boss', who briefed all the Nine Elms drivers and firemen personally and individually before they set out on each 'foreign' run, some superb performances were made with not a suspicion of the heating troubles that were known to haunt the engines, particularly when heavy work was involved. But it was the 'West Countrys' that notably excelled themselves. They ran the Great Central and the Midland routes from London to Manchester and the Great Western from Bristol to Plymouth, but most of all they covered themselves in glory on the Highland line between Perth and Inverness. Moreover the crew of No 34004 *Yeovil* worked their way over the entire 450 miles from Euston and Perth on passenger trains before taking on the test runs proper on the Highland main line. In the course of these runs they achieved some of the highest outputs of power in the complete series of Interchange

Right *A Birkenhead to Dover express leaving Reading hauled by Maunsell Class 'U' 2-6-0 No 31804. (The late M.W. Earley.)*

Below *A Bournemouth to Brighton express leaving Christchurch hauled by ex-LB&SCR 4-4-2 No 32421,* South Foreland. *(Rail Archive Stephenson — D.M.C. Hepburne-Scott.)*

Bottom *An unusual scene at Basingstoke — 'Schools' Class 4-4-0 No 30901,* Winchester, *with multiple jet blastpipe alongside ex-Great Central 4-4-0 No 62663* Prince Albert, *arrived from an excursion from the Eastern Region. (Ivo Peters.)*

Trials anywhere on British Railways, though it had been left to the sister engine No 34004 *Bude* to cap the ʼentire record with an equivalent drawbar horsepower of 2,010 when climbing the Whetstone bank, south of Leicester, on the Great Central line. On the Highland the maximum efforts were 1,912 and 1,950 dhp.

The fact that the maximum drawbar horsepower records in all the trials of 1948 were made by locomotives of a design having a nominal tractive effort of no more than 31,000 lb, while others were engaged having up to 40,000 lb, seems to have escaped comment in the official report. It seemed evident that the astounding power potential of both classes of Bulleid 'Pacific' was largely ignored by the Railway Executive because of incidental troubles in their working. Certainly the weather was generally fair-to-fine during the time when the Interchange Trials of the express passenger and mixed-traffic engines were in progress, and the Bulleid types do not appear to have been affected by slipping to any appreciable extent, even on the formidable gradients of the Highland line. Far otherwise was their all-the-year round record of heavy-grade pulling on the Somerset and Dorset joint line. If any one of the locomotive designs engaged in the Interchange Trials can be distinguished by having emerged with uniformly flying colours that class was undoubtedly that of the 'West Country' 'Pacific'. All the others 'blotted their copy books' in various ways, a few in their mere mediocrity. The 'West Countrys' certainly burnt a lot of coal, but as Bulleid more than once expressed it, the fact the engines were burning a lot of coal meant they were doing a lot of work!

It always seemed strange to me, in view of their performance in the Interchange Trials and the fact that they were a very numerous mixed traffic type, that the 'Merchant Navy' and not the 'West Country' should have been chosen for scientific testing on the Rugby stationary plant, under the auspices of the Railway Executive. It was not until the beginning of the year 1952, more than three years after Bulleid himself had resigned from British railway service and taken a post in Eire, that one of the 'Merchant Navy' Class engines was sent to Rugby. Much to his mortification he was not advised of this, nor of any progress or incidental happenings, either on the stationary plant trials nor of the subsequent road trials on the Settle and Carlisle line. In view of Bulleid's eminence as the most senior of the railway Chief Mechanical Engineers in 1947, not to mention his Presidency of the Institution of Mechanical Engineers in 1946, it could be regarded as a slight of no mean order. Nor did the ensuing report published by the Railway Executive escape criticism, not because of its actual technical content but in its virtual ignoring of certain shortcomings in the design, and of the 'West

Country' Class which many locomotive engineers considered were fundamental. Bulleid himself was nothing if not a realist, and it is interesting to speculate how he might have proceeded had he had the uninterrupted use of one of the dynamometer cars and its staff, and the back-up facilities of one of the stationary testing plants without the Railway Executive breathing down his neck all the time!

Anyone who had ridden on the footplate on either of these classes of 'Pacific' locomotive would be made aware that the 'text book' style of driving, with wide opening of the regulator and the valve gear linked up to use the maximum expansive qualities of the high pressure steam in the boiler was not on—to use a colloquialism. The vibration in the cab would be insufferable. And yet this is just how the boffins of the Railway Executive demanded that engine No 35022 *Holland-America Line* should be driven at Rugby Testing Plant. The report of the tests includes the following passage:

'The valve gear is a special feature of the design which gave rise to some difficulty in testing. It was found that the actual cut-off bore no definite or consistent relationship to the setting of the reversing gear, not only for the locomotive as a whole but especially for the individual cylinder ends. In the shorter cut-offs particularly, there was a general tendency for the actual mean cut-off to lengthen with increasing speed but not in a smooth or regular manner. The power output in the short nominal cut-offs in the upper part of the speed range was found to be greater than that of other locomotives, size for size, and was in some cases more than would theoretically be possible at an actual cut-off equal to the nominal cut-off, even assuming that the cylinders were completely filled up to the point of cut-off with steam at full steam chest pressure and that no early release occurred. The true cut-off must have been longer than the nominal. At times quite random changes occurred that appeared to be caused by minute changes of speed or boiler pressure. Some of these random changes were relatively small, though enough to upset the test conditions, but others were of a relatively large amount. Whilst changes that occurred over a period of weeks or months might be ascribed to wear of the motion, however small, this could hardly be the case with changes from one day to the next or which occurred, sometimes more than once, in a single test period'.

The distinguished Editor-in-Chief of *The Engineer*, Loughnan Pendred, had entrusted me with writing a commentary on each successive bulletin as they were issued by the Railway Executive on the testing of various types of locomotive. After he had retired and been succeeded in the editorial chair by his son, Benjamin, this arrangement was continued, with the honour, on certain occasions, of drafting leading articles for him. One such occasion came in November 1955, when it was evident that the bulletin covering the testing of the 'Merchant Navy' Class called forth criticism at editorial level: After having commented that the bulletin was of more than usual interest, in that Bulleid clearly foresaw the difficult conditions likely to develop towards the end of the Second World War and embarked on several novel features as a basis of a design for mixed traffic, the leading article that I then wrote continued thus:

'That the locomotive proved erratic and difficult to test is obvious from the merest glance at the bulletin; but these characteristics should not be allowed to divert attention from the central feature underlying the design—that to reduce daily servicing and periodic maintenance to a minimum the whole of the valve gear, together with the inside connecting rod, should be totally enclosed, and run in an oil bath. That there would be teething troubles, necessitating modifications in detailed design, was to be expected; but the ideal aimed at was one worth prolonged perseverance. Between the measured phraseology of the bulletin, in recounting some of the difficulties experienced, one can read that a high time was had by all; but while experiments were made to try and improve the combustion, by altering the draughting arrangements, and trials were made with and without

The preserved 'West Country' 4-6-2 No 34092, City of Wells, *on the northbound 'Cumbrian Mountain Pullman' crossing Arten Gill viaduct on the Settle and Carlisle line in May 1982. (David Eatwell.)*

thermic syphons in the firebox, there is no report in the bulletin of any research towards the real causes of erratic performance, which undoubtedly lay in the special valve gear fitted to these engines. An engine of the ''Merchant Navy'' Class was in the hands of the Locomotive Testing Committee for more than two years, and it would have seemed an ideal opportunity to subject the valve gear, detail by detail, to full examination on the Rugby testing plant. But this, apparently, was not done, and instead we have merely an account of the odd fluctuations in power that arise from internal antics, at the nature of which one can only guess. No doubt the brief given to those in authority at Rugby was limited in scope. Certain characteristics of performance were to be investigated, and no more. But the principles that gave rise to the ''Merchant Navy'' valve gear seem so worthwhile that one is a little surprised that no sustained attempt has been made to eradicate the weaknesses in detail. This group of tests does tend to bring to the fore the objects to be aimed at in quantitative analytical tests on locomotives. With a new design, like the ''Britannia'', every facet of performance has to be determined; but with the ''Merchant Navy'' it was surely different. Here was a type well established as one of the fastest and most powerful anywhere in the country, but one obviously having a serious weakness in the unreliable working of the valve gear. With an engine set aside for extensive testing it would seem obvious to us to concentrate efforts, at first, at any rate, upon the weak spot, the valve gear. The steaming and the effects of different grades of coal appear as

so many academic studies, compared with the primary need for setting the valve gear to rights and enabling the engines to be worked more economically, with a wide regulator opening and short cut-offs.

'Of course, the locomotive policy pursued since nationalization has followed along very different lines, towards extreme simplicity, and all running gear outside and readily accessible. On this account it may not have been felt worthwhile attempting to develop the ''Merchant Navy'' gear in any way. But, on the other hand, the capital value represented by the 140 first-line ''Pacific'' engines to which it is fitted is considerable, and conversion to a more conventional form of valve gear would be costly. Unless there is some inherent and ineradicable fault in the valve gear (of which there is no proof at all) there is nothing to suggest that its modification might not make ''Merchant Navy'' Class locomotives more economical than they are at present in service, in addition to having the remarkable ''power to pull''. Surely the object of testing existing types should be to improve performance as well as to provide reliable information for those handling day-to-day traffic on the line. Certainly that seems to have been the policy with other classes tested. Why, then, was no attempt, apparently, made to discover where lay the faults in the valve gear, nor to discover whether or not they promised to be eradicable? Two Bulleid innovations, the multiple blastpipe and thermic siphons, of which the beneficial effects were doubtful, came in for experimental modification. A third innovation,

known from the beginning to be faulty, was left alone! No doubt the reasons lay, as we have already suggested, in the limited brief given to those in authority at Rugby. But the unfortunate result is a series of tests having the appearance of being unfair to the locomotive's designer. This bulletin, therefore, leaves an uneasy feeling in the mind. With the urgent need to arm the steam locomotive to the teeth for its final and most difficult years of campaigning we do hope that the testing policy will prove to be one of tackling first things first, and not of conducting lengthy trials which, though interesting enough in themselves, are not of primary concern to those handling day-to-day traffic on the line, whose real desire, we feel, is to see faults eradicated and reliability and performance improved'.

It is now thirty years ago since I drafted that 'leader', and with all the experience of advancing years I see no reason to recant upon anything I wrote about the Bulleid 'Pacifics' in 1955. I suppose in a postscript about Southern Railway locomotives I might be expected to write something of the way those engines were rebuilt, but I prefer to end my references to them in Bulleid's own words, uttered in a slightly different context, when he heard the opening of a long playing record covering the sounds of these engines: 'Take it off, take it off', he cried. 'They aren't my engines'.

What of the ill-starred 'Leader' Class? The fact that this remarkable conception originated some little time before the railways were nationalized, and con-

Left *'King Arthur' Class 4-6-0 No 30768,* Sir Balin, *on a Ramsgate express at Bromley with the author on the footplate. (John G. Glick.)*

Top right *Preserved 'S15' 4-6-0 No 841 heading a train on the Nene Valley Railway near Peterborough. (Laurie Manns.)*

Above right *The preserved Southern 4-6-0 No 850,* Lord Nelson, *on the down Cumberland Coast Express near Seascale in August 1980. (John Titlow.)*

struction of the first five of a projected batch of 35 had been authorized as early as 1946, could lay the claim that the 'Leader' was a Southern Railway loco-motive. But the first of the new engines was not completed at Brighton Works until June 1949, not many months before Bulleid himself left for Dublin, and while a certain amount of experimental running was made, punctuated by failures of various kinds, an edict was issued in November 1950 by the Railway Executive that all further tests must cease. The first engine, disabled after a run from Eastleigh to Basing-stoke, was left to rust in the open and the two further engines, under construction at Brighton, were abandoned and towed to a breaker's yard at New Cross Gate. As the pioneer engine never turned a wheel in revenue earning service I feel justified in dropping the veil over the entire episode.

As a peroration to the long, fascinating story of Southern Railway locomotive development I have many happier memories of the last years even after the death knell of steam traction had been sounded. Despite the spread of electrification in Southern Region, and the introduction of new British standard steam locomotives in certain districts, in the height of the summer traffic the old favourites had a way of coming up again. The shades of Dugald Drummond must surely have been stirred when the Western Section called upon two of the 'D15' 4-4-0s of 1912, his last design, in the mid-1950s, to work the Saturdays-only boat trains from Waterloo to Lymington. The express engine went as far as Brockenhurst, and because the turntable there could only accommodate an eight-wheeled engine 'King Arthurs' could not be used. These trains were made up to ten of the latest stock, 332 tons tare, a far heavier load than was worked on the crack Bournemouth trains in the pre-1914 prime of these engines. More than this, when I saw them they were packed with passengers, with many standing, lining the corridors and making a gross load of about 370 tons behind the tender. These trains stopped intermediately at Basingstoke, Winchester and Southampton, and it was on the homeward run that I had two excellent trips behind 4-4-0 engine No 30464.

On the first occasion I was on the footplate, and after signals delayed both stages of the uphill run from Southampton we made some fine running from Basingstoke, passing Hampton Court Junction 34.5 miles in 35½ minutes. On a later occasion during the same summer engine No 30464, with the same load, put up some really magnificent running, covering the 24.5 miles from Fleet to Surbiton in 20¾ minutes, an average of 71 mph with a well-sustained maximum of 79 mph on the moderate descending gradient from Woking towards Weybridge. Before the wartime decelerations of 1916 the fastest start-to-stop run on the London and South Western Railway was that of the 5.03 pm up from Basingstoke which covered the 46.5 miles to its stop at Vauxhall in 49 minutes, an average speed of 57 mph. The passing time through Clapham Junction, 43.9 miles, was 45 minutes and the load was about 250 tons. Yet on this run of 1955, with a load nearly fifty per cent heavier, and the engine itself more than forty years older, the train passed Clapham Junction in 42¾ minutes.

In the late 1950s a group of family friends, including several expert photographers, used to picnic at selected spots in the West Country on summer Saturdays, and watch the trains and record engine workings. One of our locations was near Semley, where the up West of England expresses were going hard. The Southern Region had been little affected by nationalization at that time, and while one could see the occasional 'BR5' 4-6-0 on the Kent Coast, for week-end extras west of Salisbury the 'King Arthurs' still reigned supreme. One day we had not been at Semley for long before *Sir Torre* came up the bank, going strong with a twelve-coach train. The only change from the original condition, apart from the BR number was the substitution of a Urie double-bogied tender for the original Drummond inside-framed pattern. Then, after several rebuilt 'Merchant Navy' Class engines, came the star-turn of the day. The second portion of the up 'Atlantic Coast Express' was signalled and when it came into sight round the curve every camera in our party was ready to record it—what a 'cop' too, for at the head of a gleaming roof-boarded twelve-coach train was none other than No 30453 *King Arthur*.

Bibliography

Books
British Locomotives of the 20th Century, O.S. Nock, Vol 1 1900-1930, Patrick Stephens 1983, Vol 2 1930-1960, Patrick Stephens 1984.
British Railways in Action, O.S. Nock, Nelsons 1956.
British Railways in Transition, O.S. Nock, Nelsons 1963.
British Steam Railway Locomotive, Vol 1 1825-1925, E.L. Ahrons, Ian Allan, 1960, Vol 2 1925-1965, O.S. Nock, Ian Allan 1966.
Bulleid—Last Giant of Steam, Sean Day-Lewis, George Allen & Unwin 1964.
Lectures on the Locomotive, Dugald Drummond, Locomotive Publishing Co 1921.
Locomotive Adventure H. Holcroft, Ian Allan 1965.
Locomotives of R.E.L. Maunsell, O.S. Nock, Edward Everard 1954,
Manual of Locomotive Engineering, Pettigrew & Ravenshear, Charles Griffin & Co 1899.

Southern King Arthur Family, O.S. Nock, David & Charles, 1976.
Southern Steam, O.S. Nock, David & Charles, 1966.
William Stroudley—Craftsman of Steam, H.J. Campbell-Cornwell, David & Charles 1968.
Locomotive and Train Working in the Latter Part of the 19th Century, Vol 5, E.L. Ahrons, Heffer, Cambridge 1953.

Technical papers
Institution of Civil Engineers:
1885 'Brighton Railway Locomotives', W. Stroudley.
1895 'Trials of an Express Locomotive (L&SWR)', W.F. Pettigrew.
Institution of Mechanical Engineers:
1946 'Notes of the "Merchant Navy" Class Locomotives of the Southern Railway', O.V.S. Bulleid.
1947 Presidential Address, O.V.S. Bulleid.

Engine No A791, formerly River Adur, after conversion to the 2-6-0 type. (The late W. J. Reynolds.)